"This book will save lives! Seeing people at the point of their need is what we should be aiming for in mental health services across the world. The contributors to this seminal book, superbly edited by Drs. Bobele and Slive, show how this can be done. So, 'come in, sit down, no appointment needed'."

Windy Dryden, PhD, *emeritus professor of Psychotherapeutic Studies, Goldsmiths University of London*

"As often happens in human history, a great challenge, in this case, the COVID-19 pandemic, forced a better solution. The open-access (OA) service delivery model developed by Bobele, Slive, and others expands their earlier Walk-In No-Appointment-Necessary SST model to a much wider and breakthrough service model. This is a groundbreaking and must-read book for all mental health providers, clients, managers, and policymakers."

Moshe Talmon, PhD, *founder of the International Center for Single-Session Therapy. Author of* Single Session Therapy: Maximizing the Effect of the First (and Often Only) Therapeutic Encounter

"*Implementing Single-Session Psychotherapy: When No Appointment Is Necessary* is a major development in improving mental health services around the planet. Kudos to Bobele, Slive, and their colleagues for this important contribution!"

Michael F. Hoyt, PhD, *independent practice, author of* Single Session Therapy: A Clinical Introduction to Principles and Practices *and* Brief Therapy and Beyond

"*Implementing Single-Session Psychotherapy: When No Appointment Is Necessary* is a critical read for those committed to transformative changes in access to mental healthcare. Bobele and Slive, renowned experts in the field, skillfully demonstrate the capacity of single-session therapy to effectively and sustainably address the needs of diverse populations. Scaling single-session therapy within the context of whole-system transformation has the potential to address many existing shortcomings in mental healthcare worldwide."

Peter Cornish, PhD, *University of California, Berkeley, founder of* Stepped Care 2.0

"*Implementing Single-Session Psychotherapy: When No Appointment Is Necessary* is essential when we aim to be useful and creative in highly complex scenarios: violence, lack of resources, and inequalities. OA/ SST provides socially just and effective meaningful conversations at the right time, addresses clients' specific concerns, and maximizes everyone's resources. This book provides a unique mindset for the current and future Mexican therapists' toolboxes."

Nora Rentería-Cobos, *Marriage and Family Therapist, Psychology Department, Universidad Nacional Autónoma de México, Mexico City*

"The editors and contributors are among the world's most respected of single-session therapy (SST) practitioners. Discover how SST adapts to the digital age offering virtual, phone, and text-based services in addition to the more familiar in-person format. A timely and culturally responsive volume that empowers therapists of all theoretical orientations to enhance accessibility."

John J. Murphy, PhD, *professor emeritus and author of* Solution-Focused Therapy *(2024, American Psychological Association)*

"*Implementing Single-Session Psychotherapy: When No Appointment Is Necessary* is an excellent practice guide for psychotherapists offering immediate psychological support. Readers will find the most relevant strategies for working in culturally diverse client treatment settings and addressing complex themes. The authors emphasize cultural sensitivity as a key factor, making this book appealing to us in Mexico. This text is undoubtedly an essential everyday tool for therapists."

Clara Haydee Solis Ponce, PhD, *Profesora del Área de Psicología Clínica y de la Salud, Carrera de Psicología, FES Zaragoza, Universidad Nacional Autónoma de México*

Implementing Single-Session Psychotherapy

This book provides the theoretical underpinnings, research, support, and techniques, to implement open-access/single-session therapy.

Open-access services have moved beyond walk-in or drop-in services and expanded to on-demand teletherapy, virtual, or same-day scheduling. This book explains how best to implement single-session therapy in all such services, highlighting how this kind of therapy can reduce barriers to care. It includes chapters on training single-session therapists, global applications, and major obstacles. A team of expert contributors provide clinical examples and applications from around the world.

This book is essential for clinicians and professionals offering or thinking about offering single-session therapy in open-access services.

Monte Bobele, PhD, is a psychologist, family therapist, and professor emeritus at Our Lady of the Lake University in San Antonio, Texas. He is the author and co-editor of numerous publications including *When One Hour Is All You Have: Effective Therapy for Walk-In Clients, Single-Session Therapy by Walk-In or Appointment,* and *Creative Therapy in Challenging Situations.*

Arnold Slive, PhD, is a psychologist and family therapist in independent practice in Austin, Texas. He is the author and co-editor of numerous publications including *When One Hour Is All You Have: Effective Therapy for Walk-In Clients* and *Single-Session Therapy by Walk-In or Appointment.*

Implementing Single-Session Psychotherapy

When No Appointment Is Necessary

Edited by
Monte Bobele and Arnold Slive

Routledge
Taylor & Francis Group

NEW YORK AND LONDON

Designed cover images: © Getty Images

First published 2026
by Routledge
605 Third Avenue, New York, NY 10158

and by Routledge
4 Park Square, Milton Park, Abingdon, Oxon, OX14 4RN

Routledge is an imprint of the Taylor & Francis Group, an informa business

ISBN: 978-1-032-39787-0 (hbk)
ISBN: 978-1-032-39786-3 (pbk)
ISBN: 978-1-003-35137-5 (ebk)

DOI: 10.4324/9781003351375

Typeset in Sabon
by codeMantra

Contents

About the Contributors

Nick Barrington is a psychiatric nurse, family therapist, and practice consultant with the Bouverie Centre.

Cheri Bilitz is a PhD candidate in Social Work at Wilfrid Laurier University. In addition to her interest in single-session therapy and walk-in, Cheri's research centered on examining leaders' education, training, and experiences of leadership.

Katie Burke is a change management consultant based in Nova Scotia, Canada. She is accomplished in guiding and supporting teams through complex initiatives with a people-centered approach for lasting positive change.

Cheryl-Anne Cait, PhD, is an associate professor in the Faculty of Social Work at Wilfrid Laurier University in Kitchener, Ontario. Her research looks at (1) death, dying, and adolescent grief and identity and (2) single-session therapy in the walk-in counseling model.

Flavio Cannistrà is the co-director of the Italian Center for Single-Session Therapy that directed the IV International Symposium on SST in Rome, Italy. His books include *Single-Session Therapy: Principles and Practices* (w/ F. Piccirilli) and *Brief Therapy Conversations* (w/ M. F. Hoyt).

Alesya Courtnage received a Master of Arts degree from Drexel University in Philadelphia, PA, in 2001. She is currently completing her PhD at Wilfrid Laurier University in Kitchener, Ontario.

Elizabeth George is a family therapist and teaching-focused academic at La Trobe University in Melbourne, Australia. She enjoys working collaboratively with families across all life stages, especially those impacted by mental health and trauma.

Bernard Goguen is a psychologist with over 30 years of experience in helping individuals experiencing substance use and mental health issues. He has worked as a clinician, a manager, and a director in mental health services. He recently worked with Stepped Care Solutions, focusing on improving and expanding mental health systems in New Brunswick Canada.

Marina González founded Casa Tonalà in December 2012 to support community work through narrative practices in Mexico City. She designs therapeutic models, teaches, and has written and translated publications on narrative practices while promoting justice and ethical care.

Eliza Hartley is a clinical psychologist, specializing in the mental health and well-being of children, parents, and families. Her research centered on infant and perinatal mental health, attachment, and family stress. She is a Research Fellow at The Bouverie Centre in Melbourne, Australia.

Montana M. Holmes, PsyD, MS, LMFT, is a doctoral fellow at Presence in Austin, Texas. She co-founded Mind Unwind PLLC, a telehealth practice that offers single-session therapy to individuals and couples in Texas. Currently, she is grounding herself in exposure response prevention for the treatment of obsessive-compulsive disorder.

Aaron Knuckey (MClinFamTher) is a family therapist, teacher, and trainer. In collaboration with his dear friend and colleague Lynda Moore, he developed The Bouverie Centre's Walk-in Together Clinic in Melbourne, Australia.

Mikko Mäkelä is a theologian and a teacher. He has a master's degree in theology. He is the Director of the Finnish Association for Children and Youth and a Reverend of the Evangelical Church of Finland. He has worked at the YMCA and the Church Council of Finland. His aim is to prevent exclusion and to see a miracle in every person.

Nancy McElheran RNMN RMFT (supervisor), one of the leaders in developing the single-session approach in Canada, currently offers consultation, supervision, and training specific to single-session/one-at-a-time counseling at the Eastside Community Mental Health Service in Calgary, Alberta, Canada.

Jennifer McIntosh is a family therapist, researcher, and clinical psychologist. She is the Director of The Bouverie Centre in Melbourne, Australia. She is committed to making theory relevant and interventions accessible to vulnerable family populations.

John K. Miller (PhD) is a former professor at Fudan University in Shanghai and an adjunct professor in the Psychology Department at the Royal University of Phnom Penh (RUPP) in Cambodia. He is the Director of the Sino-American Family Therapy Institute (SAFTI).

Lynda Moore (BSW, MClinFamTher) is a social worker, family therapist, trainer, and consultant. Her career highlight is working alongside Aaron Knuckey to propose and establish Walk-in Together at The Bouverie Centre in Melbourne, Australia.

Dan Neuls (MA. Counselling), R. Psych (Registered Psychologist in Alberta, Canada), and the clinical coordinator of Wood's Homes Eastside Community Mental Health Services (ECMHS) therapy team. He oversees the day-to-day at ECMHS and also plays a key role in the recruitment, training, and supervision of clinical staff, volunteers.

Jason J. Platt, PhD is an AAMFT Professional Member and approved supervisor in Mexico City. His research includes internationalizing mental health services binational couples, and facilitating productive and constructive political dialogues.

Vanessa Pergher is a member of the Italian Center for Single Session Therapy. She manages the ICNOS Institute's walk-in center, One Session in Rome.

Tuomas Perkiö holds a Bachelor of Social Studies degree with a special emphasis on solution-focused brief therapy. He is a therapist in Finland and primarily a youth worker. He works with young first-time offenders, aggressively behaving youth, and early-stage mental well-being support.

Sean Ruby currently works as a data analyst at Campus Wellness, University of Waterloo in Ontario and was involved in this research during his time as a research assistant for Campus Wellness' Counseling Department while he completed his Bachelor of Science.

Marn Sokhon is a Cambodian social worker with degrees in Psychology and Education from the Royal University of Phnom Penh. He served from 2010 to 2012 at the Cambodian Acid Survivors Charity, where he provided psychological counseling, coordinated support groups, and facilitated comprehensive rehabilitation services—including medical care, legal advocacy, and vocational training—for acid burn survivors and their families.

Janet Stewart, MEd, RPsych, is the associate director of the Eastside Community Mental Health Services in Calgary, Alberta, Canada and led the development of the Mental Health Hub service framework.

Karen Story is a qualified social worker, teacher, child and adolescent psychotherapist, and family therapist in Melbourne, Australia. She teaches and facilitates training and workforce development in family-inclusive practice and single-session work. She was important in the development of the The Bouverie Centre's Walk-in Together project.

Kelly Tsorlinis is a Social Worker and Clinical Family Therapist. She works at the Bouverie Centre in Melbourne, Australia and is a clinical member of the Walk-in Together Team.

Jeff Young, PhD, is an emeritus professor of family therapy at Latrobe University, Melbourne, Australia. He is the author of *No Bullshit Therapy* and was the director of The Bouverie Centre (2009-2022).

Saúl Cruz Valdivieso earned his MA in clinical psychology from the Universidad de las Américas in Mexico City. He is a psychotherapist in private practice and serves as the assistant director for Organización Armonía, making education available to the indigenous communities of Mexico.

Acknowledgments

Monte and Arnie's joint acknowledgments:

- Our Lady of the Lake's Community Counseling Service has been a laboratory for developing open-access/single-session therapy for over 30 years. Its Director, Dr Bernadette Solorzano, has supported us in this development for a long time, and we appreciate her collaboration with us. Ms. Gayla Murr, the CCS administrator, has been the face of the walk-in service at the CCS for years, and without her, the service would never have been successful.
- We want to thank Routledge/Taylor Francis for its enthusiastic support of our single-session work. Special thanks to our editors Sarah Rae, Ellie Broadhurst, and Pragati Sharma.
- We want to acknowledge the support of our many single-session colleagues whose publications have spread the word about these approaches.
- We thank our families and friends for their encouragement and love.
- We thank one another for our long-term collaboration.

Arnie's acknowledgments:

- I am very grateful to Wood's Homes, Calgary, Alberta for supporting the development of the first open-access single-session service in Canada and for creating the opportunity to learn how to do it and how to train/supervise others and to my colleagues there for continuing to "grow these ideas" and developing new and creative open-access options.
- I am also thankful to my colleagues for their continuing support for the dissemination and development of these forms of services across Canada.
- I would like to appreciate the *Journal of Systemic Therapies* for encouraging and supporting the dissemination of these new ideas to the professional mental health community.

- My special thanks go to Susan for her unending love, support, and encouragement.

Monte's acknowledgments:

- I am grateful to the hundreds of graduate students, workshop participants, and colleagues I have worked with for helping me formulate many of the ideas and examples in this book. There are too many to name. Their questions, challenges, and doubts have been invaluable.
- Stepped Care Solutions provided me with an opportunity to participate in a large research project that led to a preliminary formulation of the SST ingredients described in this book. Our Lady of the Lake doctoral students Montana Holmes, Emily Tran, Leo Scaletta, and Andrea Nava Quintero were the pillars of that project.
- Other recent students who helped develop these ideas were Joe Cox, Olivia Hinojosa Galvan, Alyssa Arredondo, Kelsey Tovar, Zumal Zeebair, and Cristina Alejandra López Delgado.
- I want to thank the Our Lady of the Lake University Library and its staff for their tremendous research assistance in providing research assistance for this book.
- My hat's off to the hundreds of workshop participants who have helped me refine my thinking and teaching over the years. Every workshop has taught me something new and valuable about the theory and practice of SST.
- Finally, the support of the OLLUSA Psychology Department, especially Dr Joan Biever and Dr Deborah Healy, whose support and encouragement made my work over the last three decades possible.

Foreword

Open-Access/Single-Session Psychotherapy: When No Appointment Is Necessary

We were honored to be invited to provide the foreword for this book. The rich history of the ideas for this book spans the past 30 plus years; 1990 marked a breakthrough year with the publication of Moshe Talmon's seminal book *Single-Session Therapy: Maximizing the Effect of the First (and Often Only) Therapeutic Encounter* as well as Arnie Slive's opening of the Eastside Family Centre's Walk-in Clinic in Calgary, Alberta. In the late 1990s, Monte Bobele introduced an SST model to Our Lady of the Lake University's Community Counseling Service and helped to develop a walk-in service at a university clinic in Mexico. In this book, Monte Bobele and Arnie Slive propose the latest development in SST, which is open-access/single-session therapy (OA/SST).

We have a strong resonance with Monte and Arnie's work and have a long history of working both together and separately in the areas of brief and single-session therapy. We were both practicing in mental health organizations in Ontario, Canada, that were challenged with the traditional, clogged service pathways that are addressed in this book. The "more is better," deficit-focused, ways of thinking resulted in daunting wait lists and multiple barriers to people seeking the help they needed. We felt strongly that the pathways to services were in desperate need of revisioning, and we reshaped our focus to "give people the help they need when they needed it." Karen opened a walk-in clinic at her organization. Jim operated a brief therapy training program that included clinical services, research, and training. Early on we appreciated our shared worldview that included the ideas and practices of brief and single-session therapy and our therapeutic approach, i.e., narrative practices. Most single-session environments engage in therapeutic conversations that are based on postmodern, social constructionist, and/or systemic perspectives.

Over many years, we both provided extensive training to organizations throughout the Province of Ontario. In 2012, we were commissioned to write a policy-ready paper for the government introducing the ideas of

collaborative, non-pathologizing, brief, and single-session therapy as via-
ble alternatives to traditional services. After conducting a province-wide
study, we recommended that brief (single-session, walk-in services) be
made available to families in every community in the Province of Ontario.
That recommendation was accepted and implemented by the Ontario
Government.

Since that time, a groundswell of walk-in/SST clinics have opened in
Ontario. There has been an increasingly steady interest in training therapists and a significant proliferation in the literature on the subject (e.g.,
upsurge in papers submitted to the *Journal of Systemic Therapies (JST)*
of which Jim is the editor). We are now witnessing more timely access
to mental health services based on the assumption that one session may
be enough—practical and ethical service delivery. Monte and Arnie have
significantly contributed to the knowledge development of single-session
therapy leading up to this present moment.

We initially met Monte and Arnie in Toronto many years ago at a brief
therapy conference that Jim's organization produced. We met again in 2013
in Texas at the Conversation Fest/Winds of Change 6 conference that Jim's
Institute produced in collaboration with the Houston/Galveston Institute.
Karen presented a workshop with Monte and Arnie at that conference.
Over the years that followed, Karen contributed a chapter to one of Monte
and Arnie's previous books, both Monte and Arnie served as reviewers
for *JST*, Jim was on a panel with them at an annual Texas Association for
Marriage and Family Therapy (TAMFT) conference, and Monte invited
Jim to teach a workshop at Our Lady of the Lake University.

This innovative book calls into question taken-for-granted beliefs "that
therapy is supposed to be a long-term, multi-session enterprise." Conversely, OA/SST offers a therapeutic encounter rather than an assessment
at the first session. Monte and Arnie have yet again produced a book that
supports the continuance of the revolution in the field of psychotherapy
toward one-session-at-a-time open-access therapy. They have consistently
delivered steadfast rigor in the field for giving people the help they need
when they need it.

Despite the many publications in the field regarding single-session ther-
apy/walk-in clinics/quick and open-access services, several of these publications being books edited by Monte and Arnie, there continues to be a
debate about the place of single-session therapy within the scope of psychotherapy. There has been controversy about whether single sessions of
therapy can indeed be considered psychotherapy at all. In Ontario, Canada, a provincial regulating body for psychotherapists proposed that single
sessions are not psychotherapy and began to refuse clinical hours toward
accreditation as a psychotherapist for therapists working in SST settings. A
legal challenge was brought forward in one of these cases, and Karen was

approached by the lawyer involved to write a brief and testify at a hearing. The result of that hearing was an independent appeal board decision that SST should be considered psychotherapy and that the regulating body should accept the hours of psychotherapy provided to clients in single-session service contexts. Throughout the process, as Karen prepared for the hearing and wrote the brief, Monte and Arnie, along with Jim, Michael Hoyt, and Moshe Talmon, provided ideas, references, and support.

This bold new book edited by Monte and Arnie provides an important contribution to a growing body of literature that makes visible, validates, and encourages the continuing development of OA/SST in a variety of contexts. Contemporary research supports that SST is feasible, reliable, and valid. As psychotherapists, whether you work in a brief service context or not, we believe that it benefits us all to work in ways that assume that the first session may be the last session and to think in terms of one-session-at-a-time therapy instead of making assumptions about therapy taking a long time. The concept of "open access psychotherapy" gives people the help they need when they need it, reduces the burden of wait lists on both clients and therapists, is emotionally and financially cost-efficient, and, most of all, is ethical. OA/SST is a humanizing approach that transforms the way we think about how people change and what we do together. It can be considered an act of social justice.

Readers will benefit from the rich stock of OA/SST examples present in this book that represent this strongly emerging shift in thinking and a fresh new attitude about change. Many years ago, Steve de Shazer told me (Jim), "it's easy to get complicated, it's hard to keep things simple." It requires restraint and intentionality to avoid dipping into well-established and complicated traditions of thinking and talking about persons as disordered. Instead, a competency-oriented OA/SST approach foregrounds people's abilities rather than their deficits, possibilities rather than their limitations, and what is strong in people rather than what is wrong in people.

When people can avoid complicated and cumbersome intake protocols and gain open access to the help they need, it is abundantly meaningful for them. When their first contact with a mental health professional includes a collaborative therapeutic encounter, there is the potential within that fertile moment for a sense of connection and rapid engagement. The collaborative nature is critical to the process and facilitates a mutuality between the mental health professional and people who consult them that prepares them to take on challenges together. There is potential for an optimistic spirit that lifts people up and introduces a heightened sense of energy that inspires hope and a sense of purpose, for both the people seeking consultation and the mental health professional.

Kudos to Monte and Arnie for producing this book that invites readers to join this energizing and inspiring movement toward giving people clear access to the help they need when they need it through OA/SST.

Jim Duvall
Co-Director & Editor
JST Institute (*Journal of Systemic Therapies*)
Karen Young
Windz Centre

Chapter 1

Welcome to Open-Access/ Single-Session Therapies

Arnold Slive and Monte Bobele

In this book, we're tackling some of the biggest hurdles people face when trying to get mental health services. You know what we're talking about. The endless paperwork, intrusive questions, and those time-consuming intake interviews that seem to go on forever. Not to mention the long waiting lists and limited resources that leave many folks without the help they want when they need it, and once they finally get to talk to a therapist, they find that they may need to make an expensive, time-consuming commitment to weekly meetings. But there's another way. As Milton Erickson said: "Therapy is often a way of tipping the first domino" (Rossi, 2021). That's exactly what we're exploring here. We're talking about Open-Access/Single-Session Therapies – a way of thinking we wrote about several years ago called walk-in/single-session therapy (Slive & Bobele, 2011). The landscape of SSTs has changed a lot in the last decade. Open-Access is a more inclusive term we have adopted in our work that includes many of the service delivery modes in addition to walk-in, that were exacerbated by the COVID-19 pandemic. It's a service delivery model that's already innovating some medical practices (Huff, 2017) and mental health settings (Bloom & Tam, 2015; Harper-Jaques & Leahey, 2011; Sarmiento & Reid, 2022; Shaffer et al., 2017). It's all about making it easier for clients to get the help they need when they need it, improving efficiency, reducing overtreatment, leading to fewer emergency service calls, and potentially lowering costs. Sounds pretty good, right?

For several decades, single-session therapies (SSTs) have been provided by appointment and open-access forms. We have defined SST this way: "SST is therapy that the therapist expects, from the beginning, to potentially comprise a single visit. The therapist acts as if the first session will be the last" (Hoyt et al., 2018, p. 4). This definition fits the Open-Access forms of SSTs described in this text and the traditional by-appointment forms. Now, we know that some think therapy should be a long-term, multi-session enterprise where a client meets with a therapist weekly for an indeterminate number of sessions, sometimes weeks, months, or even years. Well, while

DOI: 10.4324/9781003351375-1

traditional multi-session therapy has its place and has been proven effective (Wampold, 2013), researchers have found that single sessions often can be helpful (Harris-Lane et al., 2023; Hymmen et al., 2013; Lamsal et al. 2018; Riemer et al., 2018). In fact, no specific service delivery model, therapy theory, psychotherapeutic technique, or number of sessions is superior to any others (Wampold, 2013; Wampold, et al., 2006).

So, the real question is, how can we make mental health services more accessible and affordable? How can we help the 50% or more of people who, according to researchers (Center for Collegiate Mental Health, 2024; Hoyt et al., 1992; Talmon, 1990; Young, 2018), only give mental health providers one opportunity to be helpful? Imagine a person contemplating suicide able to have a caring conversation right away without filling out extensive paperwork and assessments. Or someone who's just experienced trauma having a mental health intervention at that crucial moment. How about a worried parent being able to discuss problem-solving options with a family therapist for their kid without being put on a two-month waiting list while the problem may worsen? Picture even those skeptical about therapy dipping their toes in the therapy waters without signing up for a long-term commitment to weekly sessions.

This book explores exactly that. Get ready to discover how Open-Access/Single-Session Therapies in mental health can expand the options available when delivering psychotherapy services. You will encounter applications of OA/SSTs around the world. Let's get started by orienting you to single-session therapy.

Planned Single Sessions

Moshe Talmon and his colleagues, Michael Hoyt and Robert Rosenbaum (Talmon,1990), pioneered a new possibility in the 1980s at Hayward, California's Kaiser Permanente Clinic. Talmon was curious why clients who attended a first session of planned ongoing psychotherapy did not return for further sessions, even when a second appointment had been scheduled. He was concerned that this was a sign of failure. He decided to telephone them and ask about their decision not to return for another session. He was surprised to learn from these clients that 78% of 200 that he contacted did not return because they were satisfied with their single sessions (p. 9). This led Talmon and his research project colleagues to develop a model for planned single-session therapy that offered clients an appointment they knew beforehand was scheduled for a single session.

Walk-In/Unplanned SSTs

While Talmon, Hoyt, and Rosenbaum were refining their planned single-session model, Arnie and his colleagues (Slive et al., 1995; Stewart et al.,

2018; McElheran, 2021) in Calgary grew concerned about the increasing waiting lists for young people at Woods' Homes, a treatment center focusing on adolescents and families offering services including residential and by-appointment outpatient psychotherapy services. They did not yet know about Talmon's work. At Wood's Homes' Eastside Family Centre (EFC), they developed an innovative form of walk-in single sessions that did not require an appointment. Clients could walk-in when convenient for them and receive a therapy session provided by a qualified clinician. The waiting list disappeared and was no longer necessary. Clients could walk into the EFC six days a week and receive needed mental health care without making an appointment or being assigned to a waiting list. It wasn't long before the EFC learned about their colleagues' innovative work in California. The planned single-session ideas in Talmon's seminal book (Talmon, 1990) were rapidly adapted to Arnie's no-appointment necessary model.

In both of these forms of service delivery, planned single sessions with or without an appointment, therapists and clients are both aware from the start further sessions may not be needed. And, from the beginning, clients are always informed that further sessions may be arranged. The clinicians providing these planned single sessions operated from what Talmon (1990) called a "single-session mindset," where clinicians have confidence in the idea that *this* session could, and often will, be the last. That positive change can, and frequently does, occur in one session.

Much has been written and researched about the by-appointment and no-appointment forms of service delivery (Budman et al., 1992, Hoyt et al., 2014, 2018, 2021; Hoyt & Cannistrà, 2015). Both are referred to as Single-Session Therapy (SST). Our previous book (Slive & Bobele, 2011) focused on the no-appointment, walk-in form of SST. For reasons you will find in Chapter 2, that term no longer fits well, and we are now using the term Open-Access/Single-Session Therapy (OA/SST). Our own experience has focused on the OA form of SST: developing this service delivery model, teaching and training SST clinicians, and researching the effectiveness of OA/SST. We see OA's key role as increasing accessibility to mental health services by reducing or eliminating wait lists. OA makes it simpler and more accessible for clients to avoid the hurdles of cumbersome intake procedures.

About This Book

This book describes many recent developments in OA/SST services, which are increasing in number and geographic location. Since the onset of the COVID-19 pandemic in 2020, services have emerged in various formats that do not require in-person contact, including virtual, telephone, and text-based. Despite the return of the in-person opportunity and because COVID-19 infection has become less worrisome, these new OA services remain available to clients, thereby broadening choices.

In the following chapters, you will find descriptions of OA/SST services in many locations around the globe, including North America, Europe, Australia, and Asia. The impact of COVID-19's effect on many of our contributors' service delivery models is evident. There are also creative examples where OA/SST services ease client access, such as public libraries and churches. You will encounter several descriptions of actual Open-Access sessions in the coming chapters. We believe that OA/SST effectively responds to the increasing public health concerns about challenges to accessing mental health services (https://www.npr.org/sections/health-shots/2023/12/13/1218953789/most-americans-with-mental-health-needs-dont-get-treatment-report-finds). As well, in Chapter 2, readers will see that OA/SST can make accessing mental health services less challenging for those who are reluctant or skeptical about mental health services. We hope readers not currently offering Open-Access/SST consider adding it to your practice.

Introducing a new OA/SST service is not for the faint of heart. Single-session therapy is not taught in most graduate programs. We regularly ask participants in workshops whether they encountered SST in their training programs. Rarely is the answer "Yes!" Our suggestions about handling challenges you are likely to face are in Chapter 2. Some of your colleagues are likely to be skeptical and even critical of these ideas. SST challenges the common idea that multiple sessions are almost always the preferred treatment plan. Some might object that OA is questionable because lengthy and costly pre-assessment and screening intake processes are standard procedures. We wrote this book for those already providing OA/SST and looking for new and different ways to continue being creative. We wrote this book for those of you who are curious about or considering adding OA/SST services to your current ways of working. We wrote this book for those of you who are program planners, administrators, qualified clinicians, clinicians-in-training, clinical supervisors, and clinic managers. We hope that the many examples of OA/SST services described in this book will inspire and give confidence to those considering this step.

The Chapters that Follow[1]

Chapter 2: What is Open-Access/Single-Session Therapies? Presents a brief case example, defines Open-Access, summarizes its history, proposes its benefits, addresses its challenges, and speculates where this form of service delivery might be headed.

Chapter 3: Single-Session Therapies in Three Acts: In this chapter, we describe our current model of conducting SST; we review the current thinking on the SST mindset, introduce the 3 Act play structure for SST, and the active ingredients for successful SST. The chapter contains many detailed examples of conducting a successful SST with or without an appointment.

Chapter 4: SST in Action: In this chapter, we present two detailed examples of our work providing SST. These sessions involve cases that provoke common questions from those new to SST work, such as, "How can you be helpful to a trauma survivor?" "How can you assess for risk, provide effective therapy, and develop a safety plan in SST?"

Chapter 5: Implementing Open-Access Therapy in the Province of New Brunswick: Katie Burke and Bernard Goguen were involved from the beginning in developing and implementing a successful OA/SST service in the Canadian Province of New Brunswick, Canada. They describe the administrative challenges and how their Addictions and Mental Health service trains and supports clinicians providing the service.

Chapter 6: Eastside Community Mental Health Services: The evolution of a walk-in single-session service to a mental health hub: Arnie, along with Nancy McElheran, one of this chapter's authors, were instrumental in the founding of the original Eastside Family Services that influenced the subsequent development of OA/SST services across Canada. Stewart, McElheran, and Neuls describe how the ECMHS evolved during and since the COVID-19 pandemic. What began as in-person OA/SST, which was referred to "walk-in," is now also offering virtual, telephone, and text-based OA/SST services at their center as well as at the public library.

Chapter 7: Walk-in Together: Online Therapy for Families, When and Where They Want It: Australia is a world leader and innovator in developing and providing SST by appointment. Jeff Young and his team at The Bouverie Center in Melbourne recently piloted an online, walk-in single-session family therapy service called *Walk-in Together* (WIT) that emphasizes OA/SST with families. Lynda Moore and others on the Bouverie team describe WIT's introduction to the community and the operation of its virtual platform.

Chapter 8: Applying Open-Access/Single-Session Therapy to clients from Mexican Indigenous Communities: Saúl Cruz and his humanitarian organization have been providing education and mental health services to the indigenous communities for decades in the Mexican state of Oaxaca. Recently, he adapted OA/SST for those communities. Saúl and Montana Holmes describe this adaptation, emphasizing the importance of building the community's trust through strong working alliances. They illustrate immersing Western service providers into the Oaxcan cultures to adapt their Eurocentric ideas to be compatible with those ancient cultures that evolved over millennia.

Chapter 9: A Visit to Our Home: A Brief Journey through the History of the Community Care Center at Casa Tonalá: Marina González directs the Narrative Therapy training and services at Mexico City's Casa Tonalá. She and her colleagues found OA/SST a crucial addition to their clinical training and services during the pandemic. Her chapter explains how implementing OA/SST supports Casa Tonalá's focus on Narrative Therapy. It details the session structure and the use of Reflecting Teams in an OA/SST format. The chapter also includes personal and professional reflections from Tonalá's therapists and a moving case example of their work.

Chapter 10: Single-session Therapy for Survivors of Acid Attack Violence in Cambodia: Miller, Platt, and Marn provide a vivid example of OA/SST with the indigenous Khmer peoples of Cambodia. Miller and Platt have long been working with Cambodian therapists like their co-author Marn to develop innovative mental health services. Their chapter tells us how they created an innovative community service project in Phnom Penh to train Cambodians and Westerners to provide an innovative OA/SST to the survivors of acid burn attacks.

Chapter 11: Everyone Matters. The Single-Session Center in Italy: Pergher and Cannistrà, two Roman psychologists at the pioneering Italian Single-Session Center (ICSST), had long been training, teaching, and providing SST by appointment in their communities. When Italy was severely affected by the COVID pandemic, face-to-face appointments became nearly impossible for those in need. The ICSST found that virtual OS/SST was an ideal extension of their training and service missions. The authors describe the ICSST's efforts in training providers in OA/SST and present a case example.

Chapter 12: Miracle on Ice and Snow: How Walk-in Therapy Caught on in Finland: In late 2020, Mäkelä attended a virtual training in OA/SST. Inspired by this, he and his colleague Perkiö, both solution-focused therapists, decided to address the declining mental health of Finland's young people. They partnered with the Evangelical Lutheran Church to offer free OA/SST services in local churches. This service has expanded to churches across Finland with government support, increasing access to mental health support for young Finns.

Chapter 13: Walk-In Single-Session Therapy at a University Counselling Clinic and Clinician Experience: University counseling centers in Canada and the United States have been increasingly interested in OA/SST services to mitigate long waiting lists and students' increased desire for counseling services. Cait, Bilitz, and Courtnage offer their experiences at the University of Waterloo in Ontario. They tell their implementation story, report the effectiveness of the service, and provide an interesting qualitative perspective on clinicians' experiences with the OA/SST model of service delivery.

Chapter 14: Epilogue: Looking Forward: The final chapter is a speculative look into a future that includes increasing OA/SST services. In this closing, we revisit our list of benefits to implementing Open-Access/SSTs and what effects more widespread adoption might have on communities, mental health systems, and the education and training of therapists.

Note

1 Chapters 1–4 and 14 were collaboratively co-authored by the editors.

References

Bloom, K., & Tam, J. A. (2015). Walk-in services for child and family mental health. *Journal of Systemic Therapies*, *34*(1), 61–77.

Budman, M., Hoyt, M. F., & Friedman, S. (Eds.), (1992), *The first session in brief therapy*. Guilford Press.

Center for Collegiate Mental Health. (2024). *2023 Annual Report*. https://ccmh.psu.edu/assets/docs/2023_Annual%20Report.pdf

Harris-Lane, L. M., Keeler-Villa, N. R., Bol, A., Burke, K., Churchill, A., Cornish, P., Fitzgerald, S. F., Goguen, B., Gordon, K., Jaouich, A., Lang, R., Michaud, M., Mahon, K. N., & Rash, J. A. (2023). Implementing one-at-a-time therapy in community addiction and mental health centres: A retrospective exploration of the implementation process and initial outcomes. *BMC Health Services Research*, *23*(1), 1–13. https://doi.org/10.1186/s12913-023-09923-5

Harper-Jaques, S., & Leahey, M. (2011). From imagination to reality: Mental health walk-in at South Calgary Health Centre. In A. Slive & M. Bobele (Eds.), *When one hour is all you have: Effective therapy for walk-in clients*. (pp. 167–183). Zeig, Tucker & Theisen.

Hoyt, M., Bobele, M., Slive, A., Young, J., & Talmon, M. (Eds.). (2018). *Single-session therapy by walk-in or appointment: Administrative, clinical, and supervisory aspects of one-at-a-time services*. Routledge.

Hoyt, M. & Cannistrà, F. (2015). *Single session therapies: Why and how one-at-a-time mindsets are effective*. Routledge.

Hoyt, M. & Talmon, M. (2014). *Capturing the moment: Single session therapy and walk-in services*. Crown House.

Hoyt, M., Rosenbaum, R., & Talmon, M. (1992). Planned single session therapy. In S. H. Budman, M. Hoyt, & S. Friedman (Eds.), *The first session in brief therapy* (pp. 59–86). Guilford Press.

Hoyt, M., Young, J. & Rycroft, P. (2021). *Single session thinking and practice in global, cultural, and familial contexts*. Routledge.

Huff, C. (2017). To keep patients, some physicians get creative. *Health Affairs*, *36*(12), 2040–2043. https://doi.org/10.1377/hlthaff.2017.1341

Hymmen, P., Stalker, C. A., & Cait, C. A. (2013). The case for single-session therapy: Does the empirical evidence support the increased prevalence of this service delivery model? *Journal of Mental Health*, *22*(1), 60–71. https://doi.org/10.3109/09638237.2012.670880

Lamsal, R., Stalker, C. A., Cait, C.-A., Riemer, M., & Horton, S. (2018). Cost-effectiveness analysis of single-session walk-in counselling. *Journal of Mental Health*, *27*(6), 560–566. https://doi.org/10.1080/09638237.2017.1340619

McElheran, N. (2021). The story of the Eastside Family Centre: 30 years of walk-in single session therapy. In M. Hoyt, J. Young, & P. Rycroft (Eds.), *Single Session Thinking and Practice in Global, Cultural, and Familial Contexts.* (pp. 125–132) Routledge.

Riemer, M., Stalker, C. A., Dittmer, L., Cait, C.-A., Horton, S., Kermani, N., & Booton, J. (2018). The walk-in counselling model of service delivery: Who bene-fits most? *Canadian Journal of Community Mental Health, 37*(2), 29–47. https://doi.org/10.7870/cjcmh-2018-019

Rossi, E. L. (2021). Psychological shocks and creative moments in psychother-apy. *American Journal of Clinical Hypnosis, 64*(2), 171–184. https://doi.org/10.1080/00029157.2021.1999146

Sarmiento, C., & Reid, G. J. (2022). Mental health walk- in clinics for children and families: A provincial survey. *Advances in Mental Health, 21*(1), 43–54. https://doi.org/10.1080/18387357.2022.2032777

Shaffer, K. S., Love, M. M., Chapman, K. M., Horn, A. J., Haak, P. P., & Shen, C. Y. W. (2017). Walk-in triage systems in university counseling centers. *Journal of College Student Psychotherapy, 31*(1), 71–89. https://doi.org/10.1080/87568225.2016.1254005

Slive A., & Bobele, M. (2011). *When one hour is all you have: Effective therapy for walk-in clients.* Zeig-Tucker.

Slive, A., Maclauren, B. J., Oaklander, M., & Amundson, J. (1995). Walk-in single sessions: A new paradigm in clinical service delivery. *Journal of Systemic Thera-pies, 14*, 3–11.

Stewart, J., McElheran, N., Park, H., Oakander, M., MacLaurin, B., Fang, C. J., & Robinson, A. (2018). Twenty-five years of walk-in single-sessions at the East-side Family Centre: Clinical and research dimensions. In M. F. Hoyt, M. Bobele, A. Slive, J. Young, & M. Talmon (Eds.), *Single-session therapy by walk-in or appointment: Administrative, clinical, and supervisory aspects of one-at-a-time services* (pp. 72–90). Routledge/Taylor & Francis Group. https://doi.org/10.4324/9781351112437-5

Talmon, M. (1990). *Single-session therapy: Maximizing the effect of the first (and often only) therapeutic encounter.* Jossey-Bass Publishers.

Wampold, B. E. (2013). The good, the bad, and the ugly: A 50-year perspective on the outcome problem. *Psychotherapy, 50*(1), 16–24. https://doi.org/10.1037/a0030570 (Psychotherapy Outcome).

Wampold, B. E., Ollendick, T. H., & King, N. J. (2006). Do therapies designated as empirically supported treatments for specific disorders produce outcomes supe-rior to non-empirically supported treatment therapies? In J. C. Norcross, L. E. Beutler, & R. F. Levant (Eds.), *Evidence-based practices in mental health: Debate and dialogue on the fundamental questions.* (pp. 299–328). American Psycho-logical Association. https://doi.org/10.1037/11265-007

Young, J. (2018). Single-session therapy: The misunderstood gift that keeps on giving. In M. F. Hoyt, M. Bobele, A. Slive, J. Young, & M. Talmon (Eds.), *Single-session therapy by walk-in or appointment: Administrative, clinical, and supervisory aspects of one-at-a-time services.* (pp. 40–58). Routledge/Taylor & Francis Group. https://doi.org/10.4324/9781351112437-3

Chapter 2

The Journey from Walk-in to Open-Access/Single-Session Therapies

Arnold Slive and Monte Bobele

A Case Example

One afternoon, Joe and Sally,[1] a married couple, walked into Our Lady of the Lake University's Community Counseling Service (CCS) in San Antonio, Texas, which provides training to its doctoral counseling psychology and marriage and family therapy graduate students. The CCS offers the option, at certain times of the week, for clients to be seen that same day without an appointment. Usually, when prospective clients call the CCS, or walk in, they are provided information about the walk-in service, including the available days and times. When they called earlier, the CCS staff reviewed the CCS's policies, including the possibility that they would have graduate student co-therapists. Despite the one-at-a-time nature of the walk-in service, they were reassured that, if needed, additional sessions could be arranged at the end of their walk-in session. The couple completed a brief two-page intake form when they arrived, and after a short wait, they met their co-therapists, Rachel and Simon.

When Simon asked about the purpose of their visit, Joe explained that earlier that morning, they had met with a lawyer from the district attorney's office to prepare for testimony in an upcoming trial. He told the therapists that two years earlier, he had been assaulted during a robbery and was severely injured. Joe told the therapists that he became highly anxious during the meeting with the prosecutor. He said he could not answer the DA's preparation questions clearly. The DA suggested that a visit with a psychotherapist might help Joe get a handle on his anxiety before further testimony preparation was done. Sally and Joe left the DA's office and immediately began looking online for a place where Joe might get some help quickly. They eventually phoned the CCS and learned they could walk in without an appointment that day. They drove directly to the CCS.

Sally told the therapists that after the assault, Joe was lying unconscious in the street, and paramedics were called. At one point, he was pronounced dead. He spent several weeks in the hospital. Joe said he thought he had

DOI: 10.4324/9781003351375-2

since fully recovered physically. Following the assault and his recovery in the hospital, he had not talked about what happened in any detail to anyone other than Sally. Joe told the therapists that when he met with the prosecutor earlier in the morning to prepare for his testimony that required recounting the assault, he experienced panic and, at one point, almost fainted.

Simon reflected that the experience during the robbery and the panic earlier in the day were apparently emotionally painful for Joe and Sally. Rachel agreed and invited them into the single-session mindset by telling them, "Many people find that one session often helps them to take a beginning step in dealing with an issue like the anxiety and panic you experienced this morning." Sally and Joe looked reassured to know that they might get help that day. Simon asked how Joe and Sally would know that the session had been helpful. "When you decided to walk in to the clinic this morning, what were you hoping would be a good outcome?" Joe said that he would feel a little more confident about talking about what happened to him and be better prepared for his upcoming testimony. He went on to say that he would be able to respond clearly and on point to the lawyer instead of being anxious or panicky. So, the therapists had a fairly clear goal established early in the session and the clients were feeling more hopeful already than they had when they came in.

Rachel asked Joe if he thought using the session as practice telling the story would be helpful. Looking at Sally (they had been holding hands), he said, "Yes!" For the rest of the session, he detailed what had happened while the therapists and Sally listened carefully and asked some clarifying questions. In other words, the session became a "dress rehearsal" for his court testimony.

As the session progressed, it became plain that Joe felt shamed and embarrassed for not handling himself better when confronted by the robber because he was a retired law enforcement officer. Joe said, for that reason, he felt responsible, somewhat, for the seriousness of his injuries. As the session proceeded, he recalled how he had dealt with those feelings by avoiding discussing the particulars with anyone but Sally. So, it became apparent to the therapists how his earlier meeting with the prosecutor had been so frightening to him. He was inexperienced in talking about the assault and his feelings about it with anyone, especially an intimidating figure such as the DA. During the session, though, he shared many of those details. The therapists commended him and Sally for their trust in them and Joe's courage in taking the risk of talking about the assault with them during the session. By the session's end, Joe said he felt much more confident about telling his story in court. He said he was relieved and felt much less overwhelmed with his emotions that morning in the prosecutor's office. He added that he was glad that Sally had been in the session with him this morning and planned to look at her if he started feeling anxious in court for a reassuring reminder of the practice session.

When Rachel asked about any further small steps, he said that during the drive to their session, he had decided to join a men's group at his church where he would get more practice in sharing the story. This was an example of pre-session change, which we will elaborate on in Chapter 3. The simple awareness of the possibility of help from an upcoming session often leads clients to develop creative ideas about addressing a problem.

He and Sally then thanked the therapists for meeting with them on that very difficult day. They were invited to return for a follow-up visit if he needed more practice if they thought it would be helpful, or if something new came up. As of this writing, they have not returned to the CCS.

What Do We Mean by Open Access?

In this example, the couple arranged a much-needed therapeutic conversation with mental health professionals (in this case, professionals in training) at the moment that was highly meaningful to them and when the motivation for the change was high. This form of service delivery makes accessing mental health services easier, avoiding the usual hurdles of waits for appointments, wait lists before an appointment can be made, lengthy intake processes, completing pre-assessment forms, or meeting with an intake coordinator. This process is also rewarding for therapists because they find themselves with clients who are ready to work hard and collaborate with the therapist to arrive at positive endings to the session.

What Are Open-Access Single-Session Therapies (OA/SSTs)?

The primary distinguishing feature of the planned OA/SST model emphasized in this book is that OA/SST sessions don't necessarily require an appointment ahead of time. More broadly speaking, Open Access includes the idea of immediate or same-day appointments, which reduce the time between when a person decides that a mental health consultation would be helpful and when help is provided. The option of such open-access ("no appointment necessary") services has long been available in general healthcare settings (e.g., hospital emergency rooms and walk-in medical clinics) and is becoming more common in mental health settings around the world. The chapters in this book provide examples of the variety of these practices.

When Arnie started a traditional outpatient family and adolescent service at Wood's Homes in Calgary, Alberta, Canada, in the 1980s, it operated in the conventional appointment-making way (Slive et al., 1995). An intake coordinator interviewed prospective clients who asked for an appointment. They were then placed on a waiting list. Often, several months later, when a clinician had an opening, they contacted the client to make an appointment. Frequently, the clients were no longer interested or had found another place to get help. Of the ones who accepted an appointment at that time, only about half who made a first appointment arrived for a therapy session.

As a result of these frequent cancellations and no-shows, Wood's Homes had a series of discussions within the organization and with stakeholders in the community. Everyone wanted to find a way to be more immediately helpful to those who wanted a therapeutic conversation. These discussions and subsequent planning led to the formation of the Eastside Family Centre's walk-in SST service that opened in 1990 (coincidentally the same year Talmon's seminal book, Talmon, 1990, was published) and has continued to this day. Now called Eastside Community Mental Services, it is described in detail in Chapter 6. The Eastside walk-in/SST model was the first in Canada. A multitude of walk-in/open-access clinics have spread across Canada in the last 34 years (Duvall et al., 2012; Harper-Jaques & Leahey, 2011; McElheran et al., 2020; Josling & Cait, 2018; Young, 2018).

In Canada, to this day, single-session therapy is primarily delivered in walk-in or virtual environments. Bobele brought Eastside's walk-In/open-access model to Our Lady of the Lake University in San Antonio, Texas, in the late 1990s. Today, the Open-Access form of SST has spread beyond Canada and Texas (Bobele & Slive, 2025; Piccirilli, 2023; Söderquist, 2018, 2023; Söderquist et al., 2021). Open-access/single-session therapy services are now available throughout North America and worldwide, including South America, Asia, Europe, and Australia.

Those "no-appointment necessary" (Open-Access) services were developed to meet the need for rapidly available mental health services. In the broader healthcare industry, alternatives to by-appointment scheduling of patients and professionals have been explored for quite some time (Huff, 2017; Kaplan, 2015). In community mental health clinics, a significant factor leading to the development of an Open-Access option has been aimed at reducing ever-lengthening waiting lists (Lamsal et al., 2018; Shaffer et al., 2017; Stalker et al., 2012; Young, 2018). For many mental health providers, Open-Access scheduling may present some implementation challenges (Young et al., 2014). In this chapter, we will address the most frequent ones we have encountered and provide some examples of implementing Open-Access services.

Our Current Use of the Term Open-Access/SSTs

When we began this work, we used the terms "walk-in counseling" or "Walk In/SST." This was an easy choice because "walk in" is a commonly used term in English-speaking countries. In the United States and Canada, it is common to see "Walk-ins Welcome" signs for various services (e.g., hair stylists or barber shops, oil change kiosks, mall optometry clinics, etc.). However, recently, concerns have been raised about the term "walk in" because it might be offensive or disrespectful to persons with mobility issues. So, we now recommend using more neutral terms instead, such as "drop-in," "no appointment necessary," "one-at-a-time," or "open access."

Synonyms for "open access" may also be unavailable in other languages. In Spanish-speaking countries, *sin cita previa* or *sin cita* (without an appointment) is commonly used to describe such services. One colleague in Mexico (Rodriguez, 2018, 2022) collaborated with her local community to find a suitable name for their service. It was initially called *Terapia Sesión Sola, Sin Cita* (Single session, no appointment needed), but few clients showed up. An employee of the sponsoring school overheard a conversation where a resident declined the offer of a "single session without an appointment," saying that one session would not be enough and preferring to make an appointment instead. The team realized "single session without an appointment" was confusing and unfamiliar. They changed the name to *Terapia Breve, Sin Cita* (Brief Therapy, No Appointment), conveying three key ideas: short-term therapy, walk in without an appointment on designated days, and the option to attend one session at a time. The new name successfully clarified the service for clients and staff. Similarly, in Canada, French speakers use the expression *sans rendez-vous* (without an appointment). We agree that Open Access may be better understood when implying no appointment, same-day services, or immediate virtual access.

Recent Developments

The onset of the COVID-19 pandemic accelerated the development of Open-Access services to meet the increased demand for accessible mental health services. In many countries, in-person therapy sessions were discouraged for public health safety. Newer ways of offering counseling were initiated. Those in need could make immediate or same-day appointments in many clinics that had previously required appointments. Instead of going to a mental health provider's office, clients could have a session with their therapist over Zoom or on a regular telephone call. The ubiquity of cell phones naturally led to text-based services, especially for youngsters. In the coming chapters, we will see the rise of Open Access/SST in novel settings in many places worldwide.

Virtual Mental Health

At the pandemic's start, the Canadian government funded Wellness Together Canada, a nationwide initiative to provide free Open-Access/

Single-Session Therapy[2] to all Canadian citizens (Basnet & Chaiton, 2024; Cornish et al., 2020). Notably, these services were available seven days a week, 24 hours a day, providing immediate flexible support. The Wellness Together Canada web portal provided information about the services and telephone numbers so that children and adults could access services by telephone or chat. Clients could call a phone number and be immediately connected with a qualified counselor. Callers were invited to call again as needed and were provided additional resources if desired. Now that the pandemic has ended, WTC has closed, and Canadian provinces have been receiving federal and provincial funding to continue providing similar Open-Access services. Strides Toronto (2023) is one such agency that began implementing these new Open-Access services just as the pandemic was winding down. One Stop Talk is available throughout the province of Ontario to any person 17 years old and younger. A youngster calls a number or sends an email, answers some brief questions, and is immediately connected virtually with a qualified clinician in Ontario. One innovative feature of this service is that when requested by the clinician and client, a "navigator," located in a part of Ontario near the caller, can be brought into the virtual conversation to assist the youngster in connecting to additional mental health resources. In northern Ontario, Hands the Family Health Network began a provincially funded program that offers online and in-person single-session services through Hands Counselling Clinics.

Geographic

New instances of OA/SST are springing up in many countries outside the United States. We have already alluded to those in Canada, Africa, and Finland. Miller and his colleagues (Miller et al., 2018, 2021) have described their extensive work adapting Open-Access SST ideas in China and Cambodia. They have worked to understand and utilize the natural healing methods of the Khmer people and adapt these OA/SST ideas, where therapy often occurs outside of offices and is rarely by appointment (Chapter 10).

And again, in Mexico, Monte and Jason Platt adapted Boal's Theater of the Oppressed (Boal, 1979) to street venues in México City (Platt, 2016). Recognizing that ToO shared many characteristics of OA/SST, they merged ToO and OA/SST (Platt & Bobele, 2022; Platt & Mondellini, 2014). This innovative approach aimed to move psychotherapy into public spaces, creating a more culturally relevant and meaningful client experience. This led to a model of service delivery where participants in the ToO could be invited to visit the walk-in clinic right around the corner (Bobele & Ceja, 2020; Bobele et al., 2018). The reader will encounter an example of another such innovation in Mexico in Chapter 8, where Cruz and Holmes illustrate a novel application in rural Oaxaca.

Settings

Service providers have become increasingly creative in considering new and novel places to make mental health services more accessible to their communities. In Calgary, Eastside Community Mental Health (see Chapter 6) expanded its OA/SST services to in-person walk ins, same-day virtual appointments, telephone, text, and live chats with mental health professionals. Their truly innovative development is the Wellness Desk, which is not in a traditional mental health setting but is available in several Calgary Public Libraries. The Wellness Desk offers immediate mental health and addiction support, health information, and service referrals.

In Finland, OA/SST services are offered for young people in several churches through a cooperative arrangement with the national church (see Chapter 12). An initiative in West Africa to train hairdressers in mental health counseling has provided relief to hundreds of clients in a region with the world's least access to therapy. To meet those needs, mental health professionals are now providing hairdressers three days of training in which they learn basic counseling skills to talk with their customers, who can walk in and receive a counseling session from a trained paraprofessional while getting their hair done (Peltier, 2023).

Starting in 2016, Sidewalk Talk (https://www.sidewalk-talk.org/) was established in the San Francisco Bay area and has since spread to other communities. Pairs of chairs facing each other are set up in a busy pedestrian area, allowing one to sit down and share personal difficulties with a trained listener. The listeners, who are volunteers trained in the listening process, wear t-shirts that say "You Talk. We Listen." We should emphasize that Sidewalk Talk and the hairdressers are not professional mental health providers but serve as another example of providing easy access to meaningful, community-building conversations.

Two other unusual settings for OA/SST are in Mexico. Dr. Vagon (literally, Dr. Train Car), begun over ten years ago in Mexico, is a train that travels throughout Mexico, providing first-come, first-served medical services to people who are in rural areas of the country. A few years ago, a former student of Monte's, Ana Dejar, initiated an OA/SST service on Dr Vagon. Another former student, Erika Valtierra, spent several years in the Sierra Madre Mountains of Chiapas training Indigenous women in the SST mindset who volunteered to become mental health first aid providers in remote regions where professional health care is practically non-existent.

University Counseling Centers

Many university counseling centers (UCCs) in the United States and Canada had already begun by the beginning of the pandemic to explore the use of Single-Session Therapy as a way of making services more accessible and reducing wait times. Even before the pandemic, UCCs were one of the largest adopters of SST in the United States and this has since expanded (Cornish et al., 2017; Shaffer et al., 2017; Finch et al., 2023; Robinson et al., 2021). The pandemic accelerated UCCs' adoption of Open Access/ SST. Clinicians in many of these settings have received training in Open Access/SST and offer students both by-appointment and open-access single sessions. See Cait (Chapter 13) and Zhu et al. (2023) for analyses of research support for Open Access/SST at UCCs.

Single-Session Interventions

Schleider and her colleagues have been at the forefront of Single-Session interventions (SSIs), which they define as "structured programs that intentionally involve only one visit or encounter with a clinic, provider, or program; they may serve as stand-alone or adjunctive clinical services" (Schleider et al., 2020, p. 265). This definition includes SSTs, but SSIs refer more broadly to immediate access online, self help, and single-session interventions that Schleider and others have developed. Many SSIs do not require face-to-face sessions with a professional therapist. SSIs focus on a variety of mental health concerns, including adolescent depression, eating disorders, and clients on wait lists (Ahuvia et al., 2023; Schleider et al., 2020; Schleider et al., 2023; Sung et al., 2023). A user can log onto an "intervention" and access a 30-minute video that provides ideas for addressing an issue of concern. SSIs significantly contribute to Open-Access services, mainly because they are offered with or without an appointment and with or without a therapist. This is an area of significant promise, and more of these online single-session interventions are currently being developed.

Telehealth

Telehealth refers to remote healthcare delivery for physical and mental health. Telehealth has been used for many years over telephones, video calls and other means that have the healthcare provider and the patient or client in different locations. Before the COVID-19 pandemic, only about 17% of US mental health providers routinely used telehealth services. Due to a number of factors, including significant government funding, by the middle of 2020, over 40% of US mental health providers were using telehealth on a daily basis (Rosenthal et al., 2022). So, while a large number of mental health providers have added telehealth to their practices, a number of commercial mental health-focused telehealth services have emerged as people have become less reluctant to seek mental health services. BetterHelp, Humanest, TalkSpace, and Sondermind are just four of the more recent entries into this field. Specialized telehealth services have arisen to respond to the needs of University Counseling Centers in the wake of the pandemic. Humanest, VirtualCare, and Together are three of the largest providers that offer open-access single sessions primarily to UCCs as an additional service to their students.

So far, no evidence exists that any format (in-person, virtual, telephone, or text) is superior to another. Therefore, giving clients a choice of format is a positive development because what will likely work best for a given client is what the client thinks is the best fit. As the increase in access to mental health has led to increased opportunities, insurance providers and licensing boards have been challenged to redefine how reimbursable services are defined and how those services may be delivered outside of a professional licensee's jurisdiction. So, you can see that "walk in" no longer captures the range of services we call Open-Access/Single-Session-Therapy. This term can be applied to walk in/SST, virtual online SST, over-the-phone SST, on-demand text-based SST, and same-day appointments for SST.

Advantages of Open-Access/Single-Session Mental Health Services

In our previous work (Slive & Bobele, 2011, 2012, 2018, 2019; Bobele & Slive, 2021, 2025), we used the term "walk in" in the title and throughout the text. We now refer to our work as Open Access/SST for the reasons described earlier. We prefer retaining the SST term because it seems to be the most straightforward and consistent with the existing literature. Here are the three advantages that were previously offered to mental health professionals for providing OA/SST services (Slive & Bobele, 2018), and we have since added a fourth.

Open Access/SSTs Seize the Moment

When clients like Joe and Sally arrive for a session at a moment of their choosing without jumping over intake hurdles and waiting for an appointment, they will likely be motivated to address their issues with a mental health clinician. In fact, in our work, clients frequently report that improvement has already begun once they have decided to contact our clinic. We can start the session by encouraging and planning for continued progress. This increases the likelihood that the session will be productive, lead to positive outcomes, and address the client's important reasons for the visit. Also, as an essential byproduct, highly motivated and satisfied clients lead to happy and satisfied therapists.

Open Access/SSTs Work

An increasing number of researchers find that clients report satisfaction with their OA/SST sessions in community mental health centers (Boyhan, 1996; Harris-Lane et al., 2023; Harper-Jaques & Foucault, 2014; O'Neill, 2015) and in university counseling centers (Finch et al., 2023; Shaffer, et al., 2017). Clients reported a reduction in levels of distress by the end of their session and positive outcomes immediately after the session and at follow-ups several months later (Barwick et al., 2013; Harper-Jaques & Foucault, 2014; Riemer et al., 2018). A growing body of research in primary care settings confirms that people seeking health care are more satisfied with their care when some version of open-access scheduling is available to them (Huff, 2017; Richter et al., 2017).

Open Access/SSTs Are Efficient

OA/SST services lower administrative costs associated with cumbersome intake processes, managing waitlists, and expensive emergency services utilization. They eliminate "no-shows" and cancellations. They also minimize overtreatment by inviting the client to focus on taking one small step to manage an immediate concern (Beyer, 2024; Horton et al., 2012).

Open Doors Are Easier to Enter

We had found from early on in our own Open-Access services that we were seeing a number of clients who had never had counseling, a higher number identifying as male, and more cultural diversity in our clients. Why would that be? As of now, we can only speculate. Perhaps it is because clients do not have to jump through hurdles in order to gain entry and do not feel under pressure to make a commitment beyond that one session. We provide examples at the conclusion of this chapter.

Advantages That Apply to Both Health Care and Mental Health Care

Ezekiel Emanuel, an expert on healthcare ethics, and his team of researchers analyzed healthcare systems worldwide to arrive at several recommendations for improvement. Emanuel (2017) described the advantages of adopting open-access scheduling in healthcare clinics. We think these advantages also apply to mental health services:

1   When patients are seen on the same day, wait times and wait lists are reduced (Ansell et al., 2017). Emanuel also cited a Kaiser Permanente

study (Forjuoh et al., 2001) that found that implementing open-access scheduling produced a 20% drop in no-shows.

2 A second advantage was that physicians and staff were happier because patients were more satisfied with the services they were receiving (Borglum, 2014; Cohidon et al., 2019).

3 Lastly, open access benefits patients, lowers healthcare costs, and significantly reduces the use of emergency rooms and urgent care facilities (Ansell et al., 2017; Rust et al., 2008).

Implementation Recommendations

Therapists, clinic directors, and administrators are often interested in how to refine their procedures and policies when considering implementing OA/SSTs. Here, we answer some of the most common questions about implementation. For a more detailed discussion, see Slive and Bobele (2019).

No Pre-assessment

When clients can arrive without an appointment and/or a pre-assessment, how do we start a session without this information? Clinicians in "by-appointment" service delivery often consider it essential to have such information before the session begins. Yet, there is no clear evidence that such information makes a difference in treatment outcomes (Richmond, 2008). Of more concern is the possibility that clients may see it as an intrusive postponement of their treatment (Dryden, 2024). One of the main advantages of OA/SSTs is their ability to provide immediate care without lengthy waiting periods or intake processes. For many prospective clients, pre-screening barriers can discourage them from seeking assistance altogether. OA/SSTs focus on the client's presenting issues and goals that drive the session rather than adhering to a predetermined protocol driven by pre-assessments. Open-Access/Single-Session providers aim to meet the client in the moment and tailor interventions accordingly. Open-Access/Single-Session therapists adopt a strengths-based perspective, helping clients identify and build upon their existing resources and resilience. Most OA/SST services provide a brief intake form that clients can complete in less than 10 minutes. In many OA/SST services, pre-session information may consist of basic demographic information, perhaps with additional questions such as: "What is the most critical concern you would like to address today?" For example, the Community Counseling Service, where Monte teaches, uses a scaling question about a client's current level of stress along with another scaling question that asks the client how worried they are about harming themselves or someone else.

Let us also share with you some thoughts from Carl Rogers, originally published in 1957 (1992), about the need for prior diagnostic assessment before psychotherapy can begin:

> There is only one useful purpose I have been able to observe which relates to psychotherapy. Some therapists cannot feel secure in the relationship unless they possess such diagnostic knowledge. Thus, for some therapists, the security they perceive in diagnostic information may be a basis for permitting themselves to be integrated in the relationship, and to experience empathy and full acceptance. In these circumstances a psychological diagnosis would certainly be justified as adding to the comfort and hence the effectiveness of the therapist. But even here it does not appear to be a basic precondition for therapy.
>
> (p. 831)

We encourage anyone considering offering OA/SSTs to remember that our clients' needs are our primary responsibility. Rogers invites us all to consider how some of our taken-for-granted procedures may not prioritize the clients' needs over those of the therapist or their agency. Reducing pre-assessment procedures can reduce the frustration we have all seen in clients who attend a first session after enduring hurdles and wait times to get an appointment.

Follow-Up Sessions or Phone Calls

Many OA/SST services do not routinely schedule follow-up sessions or phone calls. As a reminder to the reader, our definition of Single-Session therapy encourages us to treat each session as if it could be the last while always offering the possibility of more sessions. Let us stress here that OA/SST providers routinely let clients know they are always invited and may return for another session when they decide one is needed. So, it's true that we do not routinely schedule follow-ups. Instead, follow-up occurs if and when the client chooses. We believe this is empowering for clients. We trust that our clients are the experts in their lives and can decide when the next contact would be helpful for them. In some ways, we have begun to think that the subtle message that we give our clients when we offer to schedule a follow-up appointment or even a phone call is that we don't have faith in their ability to deal with their issue or we don't have confidence that they can decide for themselves when our next contact will be. We remind clients that the effects of the session may take a day or two to begin to be experienced. We also base this practice on the research that shows that most people don't return for a follow-up visit, even when it is scheduled at the end of the first visit. The therapist reassures them that they are not being abandoned, and that future support will be as easy to access as the current session was.

We are not saying that an OA/SST service never develops ongoing relationships with its clients. Many clients return. It could be the next day, week, month, or several years later. One of our goals is for *the service* (not necessarily a specific therapist) to develop a long-term relationship with its clients. We want the client to know and trust that we will be there for them about the same or a different concern at any point in the future. This attitude provides reassurance to both the client and the community, and reinforces the message that the client is in charge.

Managing Higher Demand for Services

Some professionals have worried that opening their doors without requiring an appointment will overwhelm them with clients who take advantage of OA scheduling. While this initially worried the Eastside Family Centre, they soon realized that it might be a sign that an Open-Access service was a good idea if many people were interested. It helped them rethink their staffing patterns. One of the things that inevitably happens in mental health services is that therapists have cancellations and no-shows. When that happens, they can fit Open-Access clients into their newly available schedules. We have found that it is unusual for us to be so busy that we have to turn someone away. When that rarely happens, we tell the client that when they arrive the next time the service is available, they will be at the head of the line. In our experience, when Open-Access services begin, the demand is small and grows gradually over time. This slow startup gives an agency time to determine the optimal staffing and scheduling procedures.

We soon discovered that many of our clients are familiar with "no appointment" services. There are many examples: restaurants, barber shops, hair stylists, etc. So, being told they must wait to be seen or to come back the next day may be disappointing but rarely produces a negative reaction.

Risk Issues

Some service providers are uneasy about how to adjust their practices when clients arrive for an OA/SST session with serious risk issues. This, of course, does occur in OA/SST services. As we pointed out before, asking a simple question about risk on an intake form provides a beginning to a risk assessment. We have found it helpful to ask about harm to oneself and/or others on our intake form, providing a simple way for clients to alert us to potential suicidal issues along with other risk concerns. If the conversation requires, we address risk in OA/SST sessions in the same ways as any other professional would in any other therapy session (Slive & Bobele, 2019). This could include an extensive formal suicide risk assessment, extending the length of the session to develop a risk mitigation plan, and involving family or more intensive mental health services.

A meta-analysis by Franklin et al. (2017) examined risk factors associated with death by suicide. Their analysis concluded that the current body of research is not sufficient to justify the standard practices used to predict who is at risk of dying by suicide. Evidence suggests that suicide prevention strategies and screening in primary care settings have not been shown to reduce deaths by suicide (Zalsman et al., 2016; Milner et al., 2017). Given the lack of empirical support for extensive suicide risk assessment, a brief one-question screening on an intake form, followed up by the clinician in the interview, may be a more efficient approach. On the other hand, this ironically raises another issue: requiring clients to wait for a by-appointment session and delaying treatment with extensive preassessments may paradoxically increase client risks. We think the mere existence of an OA/SST reduces the risk to a community. The simple awareness of and availability to community members of easy access to a caring conversation may go a long way toward minimizing risk and increasing community mental health.

We have seen many clients with concerns such as suicidal thoughts who have never before had a session of counseling. Sometimes, they are concerned a mental health service will overreact to these issues. They see an open-access SST service as a way of testing us out to see if they can trust the counseling process.

Conclusion: Open Doors Are Easier to Enter

Open-Access/Single-Session Therapies represent a potential shift in mental health delivery services by offering a more available and client-centered approach. By removing barriers such as lengthy intake processes and appointment scheduling, OA/SSTs empower clients to seek support when needed most, seizing the moment of motivation and readiness for change.

This leads to a greater diversity of clientele. For example, Harper-Jaques and Foucault (2014) researched client satisfaction and outcomes at their Open-Access/SST service. They recruited as their subject pool the first 100 individual adults who arrived for a session and agreed to be research participants. Unexpectedly, 50% identified as female and 50% as male. Perhaps this option feels safer or less scary for those who have never had a previous counseling session. They can easily enter (online or by telephone or walk-in) and have a session. They are not asked to commit ahead of time for pre-assessment or multiple sessions. They are not required to return. Perhaps this allows clients to feel greater control of the situation. They know they can just try it out to see if it fits them.

We also began to notice a greater degree of culturally diverse and LGBTQ clients in our open-access service, perhaps for some of the same reasons mentioned above. We sometimes lose sight of the fact that psychotherapy was an invention that began in Europe, making it a "foreign" concept to those from other parts of the world. Some agencies providing these services offered the open-access options in multiple languages. For example, Calgary's Eastside Community Mental Health Service is in a diverse neighborhood with a significant Vietnamese community. ECMH began offering the option of meeting with a Vietnamese-speaking clinician. As of now, we are aware of no formal research that compares the degree of diverse clients using open-access services as opposed to other service delivery options. Our strong impression, though, is that we are seeing more of those clients than we had been seeing before.

The flexibility and immediacy of OA/SSTs not only benefit clients but also contribute to the well-being and job satisfaction of therapists, who can focus on meeting each client's unique needs in the present moment. As the demand for mental health services continues to grow and the recognition of the importance of mental well-being increases, the OA/SSTs model presents a promising solution to address these challenges. By embracing this innovative approach, mental health professionals can better serve diverse communities, reach underserved populations, and provide timely and effective support to those in need. While the implementation of Open-Access/SST services may require adjustments and adaptations within existing systems, the potential benefits outweigh the challenges. As the examples and research presented throughout this book demonstrate, this model has the power to transform the way we think about and deliver mental health services, ultimately improving the lives of individuals, families, and communities.

Notes

1 Pseudonyms.
2 Wellness Together Canada referred to SST as One-At-A-Time (OAAT).

References

Ahuvia, I., Mullarkey, M. C., Sung, J. Y., Fox, K. R., & Schleider, J. L. (2023). Evaluating a treatment selection approach for online single-session interventions for adolescent depression. *Journal of Child Psychology and Psychiatry, 64,* 1679–1688.

Ansell, D., Crispo, J. A. G., Simard, B., & Bjerre, L. M. (2017). Interventions to reduce wait times for primary care appointments: A systematic review. *BMC Health Services Research*, 17, 1–9. https://doi.org/10.1186/s12913-017-2219-y

Barwick, M., Urajnik, D., Sumner, L., Cohen, S., Reid, G., Engel, K., & Moore, J. E. (2013). Profiles and service utilization for children accessing a mental health walk-in clinic versus usual care. *Journal of Evidence Based Social Work*, 10(4), 338–352. https://doi.org/10.1080/15433714.2012.663676

Basnet, S., & Chaiton, M. (2024). Effectiveness of the wellness together Canada Portal as a digital mental health intervention in Canada: Protocol for a randomized controlled trial. *JMIR Research Protocols*, 13, e48703. https://doi.org/10.2196/48703

Beyer, A. L. (2024). *If therapy is too expensive, try single-session interventions.* Retrieved February 23, 2024 from https://lifehacker.com/health/what-is-single-session-therapy

Boal, A. (1979). *Theatre of the oppressed.* Pluto Press.

Bobele, M., & Ceja, D. (2020). *Érase una vez sin cita.* (Once upon a time without an appointment). In A. T. Suck (Ed.), *Psicoterapia integrativa: Una aproximación a la práctica clínica basada en evidencias* (pp. 21–30). Editorial El Manual Moderno.

Bobele, M., Cruz, S., Ceja, D., & Platt, J. J. (2018). *Therapeutic spaces in public places: Pláticas en la plaza.* A symposium was presented at the annual meeting of the American Psychological Association in San Francisco, CA.

Bobele, M., & Slive, A. (2021). An open invitation to walk-in therapy: Opening access to mental health care. In M. F. Hoyt, J. Young, & P. Rycroft (Eds.), *Single session thinking and practice in global, cultural, and familial contexts: Expanding applications* (pp. 54–65) Routledge.

Bobele, M., & Slive, A. (2025). The SST model developed in Canada and Texas for walk-in, drop-in, open-access, and virtual services. In M. F. Hoyt, & F. Cannistrá (Eds.), *Single session therapies: Why One-At-A-Time mindsets are effective* (pp. 109–123). Routledge.

Borglum, K. (2014). Five ways to optimize your patient schedule. *Urology Times*, 42(6), 25–25.

Boyhan, P. A. (1996). Client's perceptions of single session consultations as an option to waiting for family therapy. *Australian and New Zealand Journal of Family Therapy*, 17(2), 85–96.

Cohidon, C., Wild, P., & Senn, N. (2019). Practice organization characteristics related to job satisfaction among general practitioners in 11 countries. *Annals of Family Medicine*, 17(6), 510–517. https://doi.org/10.1370/afm.2449

Cornish, P. A., Churchill, A., MacKay, T.-L., & Jaouich, A. (2020). Wellness together Canada: Psychologists leading Canada's COVID-19 mental health response. *Psynopsis: Canada's Psychology Newspaper*, 42(3), 14–15.

Cornish, P. A., Berry, G., Benton, S., Barros-Gomes, P., Johnson, D., Ginsburg, R., Whelan, B., Fawcett, E., & Romano, V. (2017). Meeting the mental health needs of today's college student: Reinventing services through Stepped Care 2.0. *Psychological Services*, 14(4), 428–442. https://doi.org/10.1037/ser0000158 (College Counseling Services)

Dryden, W. (2024). *How to think and intervene like a single-session therapist*. Routledge.

Duvall, J., Young, K., & Kays-Burden, A. (2012). *No more, no less: Brief mental health services for children and youth*. Ontario, Canada: Ontario Centre of Excellence for Child and Youth Mental Health Retrieved from www.https://1library. net/document/zk8okj4z-brief-mental-health-services-children-youth.html

Emanuel, E. J. (2017). *Prescription for the future: The twelve transformational practices of highly effective medical organizations*. PublicAffairs.

Finch, E. F., Kleiman, E. M., Bentley, K. H., & Bernstein, E. E. (2023). Helpful for all? Examining the effects of psychotherapy treatment history on outcomes of single session, transdiagnostic cognitive behavioral interventions for university students. *Psychological Services*, 21(2), 347–354. https://doi.org/10.1037/ ser0000781

Forjuoh, S. N., Averitt, W. M., Cauthen, D. B., Couchman, G. R., Symm, B., & Mitchell, M. (2001). Open-access appointment scheduling in family practice: Comparison of a demand prediction grid with actual appointments. The *Journal of the American Board of Family Practice*, 14(4), 259–265.

Franklin, J. C., Ribeiro, J. D., Fox, K. R., Bentley, K. H., Kleiman, E. M., Huang, X., ... Nock, M. K. (2017). Risk factors for suicidal thoughts and behaviors: A meta-analysis of 50 years of research. *Psychological Bulletin*, 143(2), 187–232.

Harper-Jaques, S., & Foucault, D. (2014). Walk-in single session therapy: Client satisfaction and clinical outcomes. *Journal of Systemic Therapies*, 33(3), 29–49.

Harper-Jaques, S., & Leahey, M. (2011). From imagination to reality: Mental health walk-in at South Calgary Health Centre. In A. Slive, & M. Bobele (Eds.), *When one hour is all you have: Effective therapy for walk-in clients*. (pp. 167–183). Zeig, Tucker & Theisen.

Harris-Lane, L. M., Keeler-Villa, N. R., Bol, A., Burke, K., Churchill, A., Cornish, P., Fitzgerald, S. F., Goguen, B., Gordon, K., Jaouich, A., Lang, R., Michaud, M., Mahon, K. N., & Rash, J. A. (2023). Implementing one-at-a-time therapy in community addiction and mental health centres: A retrospective exploration of the implementation process and initial outcomes. *BMC Health Services Research*, 23(1), 1–13. https://doi.org/10.1186/s12913-023-09923-5

Horton, S., Stalker, C. A., Cait, C., & Josling, L. (2012). Sustaining walk-in counselling services: An economic analysis for a pilot study. *Healthcare Quarterly*, 15(3), 44–449.

Huff, C. (2017). To keep patients, some physicians get creative. *Health Affairs*, 36(12), 2040–2043. https://doi.org/10.1377/hlthaff.2017.1341

Josling, L., & Cait, C-A. (2018). The walk-in counseling model: Research and advocacy. In M. F. Hoyt, M. Bobele, A. Slive, J. Young, & M. Talmon (Eds.), *Single-session therapy by walk-in or appointment: Administrative, clinical, and supervisory aspects of one-at-a-time services*. (pp. 91–103). Routledge/Taylor & Francis Group. https://doi.org/10.4324/9781351112437-6

Kaplan, G. S. (2015). Health care scheduling and access: A report from the IOM. *JAMA: Journal of the American Medical Association*, 314(14), 1449–1450. https://doi.org/10.1001/jama.2015.9431

Lamsal, R., Stalker, C. A., Cait, C.-A., Riemer, M., & Horton, S. (2018). Cost-effectiveness analysis of single-session walk-in counselling. *Journal of Mental Health*, 27(6), 560–566. https://doi.org/10.1080/09638237.2017.1340619

McElheran, N., Harper-Jaques, S., & Lawson, A. (2020). Introduction to the special section: Walk-in single-session and booked single-session therapy in Canada. *Journal of Systemic Therapies*, 39(3), 15–20.

Miller, J. K., Platt, J. J., & Conroy, K. M. (2018). Single-session therapy in the majority world: Addressing the challenge of service delivery in Cambodia and the implications for other global contexts. In M. F. Hoyt, M. Bobele, A. Slive, J. Young, & M. Talmon (Eds.), *Single-session therapy by walk-in or appointment: Administrative, clinical, and supervisory aspects of One-At-A-Time services.* (pp. 116–134). Routledge/Taylor & Francis Group. https://doi.org/10.4324/9781351112437-8

Miller, J. K., Xing, D., Yaorui, H., & Yilin, X. (2021). Single Session Team Family Therapy (SSFT) in China: A seven-step protocol for adapting Western methods in Eastern contexts. In M. F. Hoyt, J. Young, & P. Rycroft (Eds.), *Single session thinking and practice in global, cultural, and familial contexts: Expanding applications.* (pp. 245–254). Routledge/Taylor & Francis Group. https://doi.org/10.4324/9781003053958-23-28

Milner, A., Witt, K., Pirkis, J., Hetrick, S., Robinson, J., Currier, D., Spittal, M. J., Page, A., & Carter, G. L. (2017). The effectiveness of suicide prevention delivered by GPs: A systematic review and meta-analysis. *Journal of Affective Disorders*, 210, 294–302.

O'Neill, I. (2015). What's in a name? Clients' experiences of single session therapy. *Journal of Family Therapy*, 39(1), 63–79. https://doi.org/10.1111/1467-6427.12099

Peltier, E. (2023). Need some therapy? In West Africa, hairdressers can help. *New York Times*, 173(59985), A4–A4.

Piccirilli, F. (2023). How to conduct a SST: The Canadian – Texan model. Retrieved July 31, 2022 from https://www.singlesessiontherapies.com/blog-post/how-to-conduct-a-sst-the-canadian-texan-model/

Platt, J. J. (2016, September 2016). Pedestrians as professors: Theater of the Oppressed in Mexico City. *Psychology International*. https://www.apa.org/international/pi/2016/09/pedestrians-professors

Platt, J., & Bobele, M. (2022). Therapeutic spaces in public places: Reflections on storytelling and antipropaganda dialogues in Mexico. *International Perspectives in Psychology: Research, Practice, Consultation*, 11(4), 238–245. https://doi.org/10.1027/2157-3891/a000042

Platt, J. J., & Mondellini, D. (2014). Single session walk-In therapy for street robbery victims in Mexico City. In M. F. Hoyt, & M. Talmon (Eds.), *Capturing the moment: Single session therapy and walk-in services.* (pp. 215–231). Crown House Publishing Limited.

Richmond, C. J. (2008). *A study of intake and assessment in Solution-Focused Brief Therapy.* ProQuest Information & Learning]. US.

Richter, J. R., Downs, L., Beauvais, B., Huynh, P. V., Hamilton, J. E., Kim, F., & Weigel, F. (2017). Does the proportion of same-day and 24-hour appointments impact patient satisfaction?. *Quality Management in Health Care*, 26(1), 22–28. https://doi.org/10.1097/QMH.0000000000000121

Riemer, M., Stalker, C. A., Dittmer, L., Cait, C.-A., Horton, S., Kermani, N., & Booton, J. (2018). The walk-in counselling model of service delivery: Who benefits most? *Canadian Journal of Community Mental Health*, 37(2), 29–47. https://doi.org/10.7870/cjcmh-2018-019

Robinson, A. M., Harvey, G., McDonald, M., & Honegger, T. (2021). Introducing single session therapy at a university counseling center. In M. Hoyt, J. Young, & P. Rycroft (Eds.), *Single session thinking and practice in global, cultural, and familial contexts: Expanding applications*. (pp. 143–152). Routledge.

Rodriguez, I. J. (2018). Terapia breve sin cita: Collaboration with a marginalized community in Mexico City. In *Single-session therapy by walk-in or appointment: Administrative, clinical, and supervisory aspects of one-at-a-time services*. (pp. 291–302). https://doi.org/10.4324/9781351112437-19

Rodriguez, I. J. (2022). Collaborative-dialogic practices in a single-session therapy format: A clinical example in an EAP. *Journal of Systemic Therapies*, 1, 13–27.

Rogers, C. R. (1957). The necessary and sufficient conditions of therapeutic personality change. *Consulting Psychology*, 21, 95–103.

Rogers, C. R. (1992). The necessary and sufficient conditions of therapeutic personality change. *Journal of Consulting and Clinical Psychology*, 60(5), 827–832.

Rosenthal, S. R., Sonido, P. L., Tobin, A. P., Sammartino, C. J., & Noel, J. K. (2022). Breaking down barriers: Young adult interest and use of telehealth for behavioral health services. *Rhode Island Medical Journal*, 105(1), 26–31.

Rust, G., Ye, J., Baltrus, P., Daniels, E., Adesunloye, B., & Fryer, G. E. (2008). Practical barriers to timely primary care access: Impact on adult use of emergency department services. *Archives of Internal Medicine*, 168(15), 1705–1710. https://doi-org.ezproxy.ollusa.edu/10.1001/archinte.168.15.1705

Schleider, J. L., Dobias, M. L., Sung, J. Y., & Mullarkey, M. C. (2020). Future directions in single-session youth mental health interventions. *J Clin Child Adolesc Psychol*, 49(2), 264–278. https://doi.org/10.1080/15374416.2019.1683852

Schleider, J. L., Smith, A. C., & Ahuvia, I. (2023). Realizing the untapped promise of single-session interventions for eating disorders. *International Journal of Eating Disorders*, 56, 853–863.

Shaffer, K. S., Love, M. M., Chapman, K. M., Horn, A. J., Haak, P. P., & Shen, C. Y. W. (2017). Walk-in triage systems in university counseling centers. *Journal of College Student Psychotherapy*, 31(1), 71–89. https://doi.org/10.1080/87568225.2016.1254005

Slive A., & Bobele, M. (2011). *When one hour is all you have: Effective therapy for walk-in clients*. Zeig-Tucker.

Slive, Arnold B. & Bobele, M. (2012). Walk-in counselling services: Making the most of one hour. *Australia and New Zealand Journal of Family Therapy*. 33 (1) 27–38.

Slive, A., & Bobele, M. (2018). The three top reasons why walk-in/single-sessions make perfect sense. In M. F. Hoyt, M. Bobele, A. Slive, J. Young, & M. Talmon (Eds.), *Single-session therapy by walk-in or appointment: Administrative, clinical, and supervisory aspects of one-at-a-time services*. (pp. 27–39). Routledge/Taylor & Francis Group.

Slive, A., & Bobele, M. (2019). Ideas for addressing doubts about walk-in/single-session therapy. *Journal of Systemic Therapies*, 38(4), 17–30.

Slive, A., MacLaurin, B., Oaklander, M., & Amundson, J. (1995). Walk-in single sessions: A new paradigm in clinical service delivery. *Journal of Systemic Therapies*, 14, 3–11.

Slive, A., Maclauren, B. J., Oaklander, M., & Amundson, J. (1995). Walk-in single sessions: A new paradigm in clinical service delivery. *Journal of Systemic Therapies*, 14, 3–11.

Söderquist, M. (2018). Coincidence favors the prepared mind: Single sessions with couples in Sweden. In M. F. Hoyt, M. Bobele, A. Slive, J. Young, & M. Talmon (Eds.), *Single-session therapy by walk-in or appointment: Administrative, clinical, and supervisory aspects of one-at-a-time services*. (pp. 270–290). Routledge/Taylor & Francis Group. https://doi.org/10.4324/9781351112437-18

Söderquist, M. (2023). *Single session one at a time counselling with couples: Challenge and possibility*. Routledge.

Söderquist, M., Cronholm-Nouicer, M., Dannerup, L., & Wulff, K. (2021). Making the leap with couples in Sweden: One-at-a- time mindset in action. In M. F. Hoyt, J. Young, & P. Rycroft (Eds.), *Single session thinking and practice in global, cultural, and familial contexts: Expanding applications*. (pp. 163–172). Routledge/Taylor & Francis Group. https://doi.org/10.4324/9781003053958-15-19

Stalker, C. A., Horton, S., & Cait, C.-A. (2012). Single-session therapy in a walk-in counseling clinic: A pilot study. *Journal of Systemic Therapies*, 31(1), 38–52. https://doi.org/10.1521/jsyt.2012.31.1.38

Strides Toronto. (2023). One stop talk expands access across Ontario this back-to-school season. https://www.newswire.ca/news-releases/one-stop-talk-expands-access-across-ontario-this-back-to-school-season-844772919.html

Sung, J. Y., Buggati, M., Vivian, D., & Schleider, J. L. (2023). Evaluating a telehealth single-session consultation service for clients on psychotherapy wait-lists. *Practice Innovations*, 8, 141–161.

Talmon, M. (1990). *Single-session therapy: Maximizing the effect of the first (and often only) therapeutic encounter*. Jossey-Bass Publishers.

Young, J., & Rycroft, P. (1997). Single session therapy: Capturing the moment. *Psychotherapy in Australia*, 4(1), 18–23.

Young, J., Rycroft, P., & Weir. (2014). Implementing single session therapy: Practical wisdoms from down under. In M. Hoyt, & M. Talmon (Eds.), *Capturing the moment: Single session therapy and walk-in services* (pp. 121–140). Crown House Publishing.

Young, K. (2018). Change in the winds: The growth of walk-in therapy clinics in Ontario, Canada. In M. F. Hoyt, M. Bobele, A. Slive, J. Young, & M. Talmon (Eds.), *Single-session therapy by walk-in or appointment: Administrative, clinical, and supervisory aspects of one-at-a-time services*. (pp. 59–71). Routledge/Taylor & Francis Group. https://doi.org/10.4324/9781351112437-4

Zalsman, G., Hawton, K., Wasserman, D., van Heeringen, K., Arensman, E., Sarchiapone, M., & Purebl, G. (2016). Suicide prevention strategies revisited: 10-year systematic review. *The Lancet Psychiatry*, 3(7), 646–659.

Zhu, S., Hu, Y., Qi, D., Qin, N., Chi, X., Luo, J., Wu, J., Huang, H., Wu, Q., Yu, L., Ni, S., Hamilton, K., & Tse, S. (2023). Single-session intervention on growth mindset on negative emotions for university student mental health (U-SIGMA): A protocol of two-armed randomized controlled trial. *Trials*, 24(1), 713. https://doi.org/10.1186/s13063-023-07748-5

Chapter 3

Single-Session Therapy in Three Acts

Monte Bobele and Arnold Slive

The Single-Session Mindset

The therapist's mindset and thinking about therapy are arguably the most crucial variables in effectiveness as an open-access/single-session therapy (OA/SST) therapist. Being an effective single-session therapist does not require adherence to any particular theory of therapy but does require adopting a single-session mindset. Talmon (1990) concluded his book with 14 "helpful attitudes" for SST:

> This is it; View each session as a whole, complete in itself; All you have is now; It's all here, Therapy starts before the first session and will continue long after it; Take one step at a time; You do not have to rush or reinvent the wheel; The power is in the patient; Never underestimate you patient's strengths; You don't need to know everything in order to be helpful; Life is full of surprises; Life, more than therapy, is a great teacher; Time, nature, and life are great healers; and Expect change. It's already well underway
>
> (pp. 134–135)

Since Talmon's original listing of the characteristics of the single-session mindset, or as some have referred to it, "single-session thinking," several attempts have captured the essence of the single-session mindset (Cannistrà & Hoyt, 2020; Cannistrà & Piccirilli, 2021; Hoyt, 2024; Joseph & Rajan, 2024; Porter et al., 2024; Tran, 2024). The items identified as characteristic of a therapist's single-session mindset are similar. They differ somewhat in how much detail is used in describing each item, but there is considerable overlap. Perhaps the differences result from theoretical or practice differences.

Recently, Porter and his colleagues (2024) interviewed experts in single-session therapy to identify common factors that define the single-session therapy mindset. They discovered three significant categories. The first

DOI: 10.4324/9781003351375-3

category, "About People," emphasizes that clients are the experts in their own lives, possess strengths and resources to improve their situations, and are always changing. The second category, "About Therapy," includes the belief that one session can be sufficient. It highlights the importance of the therapist getting the client moving, actively fostering hope, and maximizing each therapeutic encounter. Additionally, this category stresses that every session should have a clear beginning, middle, and end. The third category, "About Change," encapsulates the idea that change can manifest in various forms.

As you can see, there is significant consensus that therapists wishing to practice single-session therapy (SST) must adopt a mindset different from the traditional, problem-oriented one. This mindset, rooted in postmodern epistemology, rejects naïve realism and questions the validity of diagnoses and the one-size-fits-all treatment approaches favored by some conventional treatments. As a starting point, it is required that the therapist believes that good things can come from a single-session encounter. For those setting out to become SST therapists, Bob Rosenbaum, in the earliest days of single-session therapy, advised, "Training clinicians in single session therapy is more a question of inculcating a certain attitude than it is of passing on a set of techniques" (Hoyt et al., 1992, p. 77). We will now turn to the ingredients of single-session therapy that we have found helpful in applying the single-session mindset, whether in Open-Access or by-appointment settings.

The Ingredients of an SST

We previously discussed organizing an SST with an agenda or step-by-step plan (Bobele & Slive, 2025; Slive & Bobele, 2011). Although therapists may benefit from such a plan at the start of the session, we have come to understand that sessions rarely follow a predictable trajectory. Reviewing our work and those of many other therapists, we found the necessary ingredients for a successful single session. However, how they are mixed into the final recipe varies across therapists, sessions, and clients. Much like a chef prepares a dish following a recipe, the order in which some ingredients are added is essential, while others may be added when convenient or according to the chef's habits. In SST, we propose that the following ingredients are all essential: how and when they occur are decided by the circumstances of the client and the therapist.

These ingredients are based on a Stepped Care Solutions project, described in Chapter 5, to train community mental health providers in the Canadian Province of New Brunswick (Harris-Lane et al., 2023; Mahon et al., in press). The ingredients that followed were created in that project from a review of the literature on SST practices, reflecting a theoretically neutral set of principles that were important in the application of SST.[1] The following provides a general description of the ingredients and some examples of how they appear in the session along with some sample questions or statements that illustrate how to implement the ingredients. We don't make any recommendations about these ingredients' relative importance but want to emphasize that they are all essential for successful SST. The reader will note that many of the examples are drawn from our postmodern, strengths-based approaches to therapy that are heavily influenced by Solution Focused Therapy (de Shazer et al., 2021; Murphy, 2024; O'Hanlon & Weiner-Davis, 1989), Ericksonian Hypnosis (Haley, 1973), and MRI's Brief Problem-focused Approach (Fisch et al., 1982; Watzlawick et al., 1974; Fisch et al., 1982).

Single-Session Therapy in Three Acts

All experts in Pitt and Porter's research agreed each SST session should have a beginning, a middle, and an end. This logical structure reflects Keeney's (Keeney, 1990, 1991; Ray & Keeney, 1993) three-act play description of therapy:

> *Act I* is where the clients bring the opening lines, typically understood as derived from an impoverished, often painful context. *Act II* is the creation of new themes and *understandings* that are resourceful to clients and therapists. And finally, *Act III* is the prescription of *action* based on that resourceful understanding.
>
> (Ray and Keeney, p. 18)

Duvall and Béres have also applied the Three Act metaphor to Narrative Therapists' storied metaphor. The dramatic metaphor can be found elsewhere in psychotherapy, such as in Moreno's psychodrama (Moreno & Fox, 1987), Boal's Theater of the Oppressed (Boal, 1979), and recently in Narradrama (Dunne et al., 2022). We have found that this storytelling framework provides a more helpful way of thinking about the structure of an SST than the ones we used earlier. The three-act format allows the SST therapist to organize a session from any theoretical orientation and determine when and what ingredients are needed.

Act I: Emphasis on Strengths, Engendering Hope, and Expectations of Change

Act I, the beginning of therapy, includes the ingredients: *Emphasis on Strengths, Engendering Hope, and Expectations of Change.* According to

Duvall and Béres (2011), Act I, the beginning, has essentially two points of inquiry:

> 1. Points of Story: announces what this story is about, that is, what's most important to talk about. Sets the agenda to begin the therapy session paragraph; 2. Back story: develops the relevant social, cultural context. An intelligible frame in which to understand the problem slash issue.
>
> (p. 41)

The SST therapist uses the client's language, metaphors, and unique expressions to establish hope and expectancy and orient them to an SST mindset. The therapist conveys hope and belief in the client's strengths and resources and shifts the client's attention toward a more hopeful way of being.

One of our favorite cartoons depicts a physician in an exam room with a patient looking at an X-ray and saying, "There is nothing wrong with you that what is right with you can't cure." From the beginning, we train ourselves to listen to our clients. We also want to use the client's frames of reference in our conversations. In college counseling centers, for example, knowing a student's major, extracurricular interests, hobbies, favorite musicians, video games, and so on provides linguistic and metaphorical resources for the therapist. For example, in goal setting with a video gamer, instead of using ideas about slow, gradual change or step-by-step practice, likening therapy to "leveling up" might increase engagement and provide the client a way of talking about developing study habits. Likewise, with a music major, we remind them that mastering the keyboard was necessary before playing Chopin's etudes. A knitter knows that a finished scarf starts with casting on the first stitch. A brick mason knows a finished wall is created one brick at a time. Almost everyone has learned to ride a bike. Asking clients to recall the challenges in learning that skill helps them to have a way to understand how failures are learning experiences, and what felt artificial in the beginning eventually became second nature—remembering how training wheels helped and would be raised only when success had occurred at the current level.

Rapid & Positive Alliance/Joining

Carl Rogers's words about the importance of the therapeutic alliance are as accurate today as they were half a century ago: "...psychotherapy is a special kind of relationship, different in kind from all others which occur in everyday life" (1992, p. 828). The relationship between the SST therapist and their client is a unique one that changes over time but exists in the unique context of each one's understanding of the reason for them to be together in the first place. Although Rogers and many others have used the word *relationship* to describe this therapeutic ingredient, we prefer to use the word *alliance* to refer to the working-together nature of the relationship between the therapist and the client. Common factors researchers have demonstrated that this alliance accounts for approximately 40% of the variance in successful therapeutic change (Duncan et al., 2010; Lambert, 2005; Messer & Wampold, 2002).

We want to invite you to imagine yourself as a potential psychotherapy client. Alternatively, think of one of your recent clients. We don't think many people wake up one morning, yawn, stretch, and say,

> What should I do today? There is nothing on my calendar today. Nothing on my to-do list. Hmm. I've never done psychotherapy. Perhaps I should go try that today. I've got nothing better to do, and maybe I'll benefit somehow.

No! For many people, interest in talking to a counselor or therapist ranks below visiting a dentist or having a colonoscopy. Often, they arrive at our offices because of the encouragement of well-meaning friends and family, at the suggestion of their physician or other health professional. Sometimes, their spouse, parents, courts, child's teacher, or social service agencies mandate talking to a therapist.

Our clients have been struggling on their own for a long time, sometimes years, trying to deal with their problems independently. They may have sought help from friends and family. They may have read self-help books. They may have consulted physicians for medication. In short, they may have tried doing everything else instead of visiting a therapist. They may have been worried about the stigmatization of being a "mental patient." They may have been worried about making a time and money-consuming commitment with no guarantee of success. They may have tried counseling in the past and found it unhelpful. As a result, many clients arrive feeling demoralized.

SST therapists can see their role as helping to *remoralize* and uplift clients. These demoralized clients frequently arrive seemingly overwhelmed by many problems. Some clients even overwhelm their therapists with complicated collections of issues that seem to have piled up while they are hoping and trying to make things better. That is why finding out the "precipitating event," the "why now," can be helpful in the opening alliance-building stages because it gives us a specific example of the problem that has led them to our office. If the final straw, or tipping point, was their boss threatening to fire them for poor job performance, we might ask, "What would be the slightest change that would encourage the boss that you were on your way to improving your performance?"

Clients are naturally anxious at the start of a session. Many therapists are also nervous at the start of a session. We like to think of the opening moments of a session as an opportunity to lower everyone's anxiety about the start of this new encounter. For this reason, we recommend starting the conversation with topics that are comfortable for everyone. Opening with "What do you want to talk about today?" or "What is the problem that brought you here today?" are questions that put much pressure on the client right at the beginning. We prefer a slower start. We might ask about the traffic, their drive over, what part of town they had to come from, the weather, and some current events. A client wearing a professional football team cap or t-shirt would be asked about their team's recent game. One gauge of comfort in the room is that there has been a shared chuckle. We want to start building the therapeutic alliance slowly, step by step. We do not want to create hurdles to the alliance, such as introducing problem talk or limits to privacy conversations too soon. We want to avoid "confidential" information talk until the alliance is strong enough for me to propose things that would interfere with the alliance, such as the responsibility of reporting our conversation to third parties or risk assessments. So, in practices where possible, we recommend postponing that discussion for a few minutes. In doing so, it is helpful for clinicians to show a relaxed stance to clients about the passage of time, that they are not in a rush, the unspoken message being not that "we just have an hour" but rather that "we have a whole hour."

In many practices and public agencies, this elaboration of the details of informed consent occurs before the therapy session begins and may annoy some clients who are ready to start getting help with the problems that brought them to see the therapist. Having a short conversation unrelated to the problem gives the therapist some idea about the client's verbal skills and cognitive abilities. Knowing their level of verbal sophistication helps the therapist tailor the explanation of the clinic's practices and policies to the client's context, worldview, etc. For example, providing a formal explanation of the "limits of confidentiality" without knowing whether the client can make sense of our explanation defeats the purpose of having a verbal explanation. Consider the difference between the following two deliveries:

Therapist 1: I want you to know that this is a safe space to talk about anything you want. I assure you that everything we talk about here today is strictly confidential unless you tell us about threats of harm to yourself or children, older adults, or any other vulnerable population, or if another therapist has abused you. If you do, then we will have to make a report to the appropriate authorities. Do you understand?

Therapist 2: OK, before we begin talking about what you came here to talk about, I want to let you know a few things about how we work here. For the most part, anything you tell us stays between us. We won't be sharing your personal information with anyone without your permission unless we become worried that someone is being harmed. If we are worried about your safety or that of children, elders, or other vulnerable people, we may have to contact someone to help us. On rare occasions, if a judge or a court sends us a legal request for your records, we would have to turn them over. If any of these things happen that require us to share your private information, then we will let you know as soon as possible. What questions do you have about that?

The second therapist's explanation is user-friendly and conveys the same information as the first one, but in a different tone. We have been told that in agencies that require a verbal explanation of the consent form, even though the client has already read and signed a consent form, another explanation is necessary because some people sign without reading. Some people don't understand the dense legalese, and some psychotherapy clients may be cognitively impaired and need additional help in understanding what they are consenting to. We agree with all these premises. Our point is that if any, or all, of these are the case with the client sitting in front of us, then it is even more important to use language and explanations that are different from that in the written document you are trying to explain. We see this as an opportunity to strengthen the nascent therapeutic alliance by talking about our concern for the client's safety, not our reporting responsibilities. We will talk some more about these issues that were introduced briefly in Chapter (2) and provide some examples in the next chapter (Case Examples).

Another purpose of joining is that it is an assessment. Some therapists begin their sessions with a psychosocial assessment, a risk assessment, or a general screening instrument. However, in single-session therapy, joining becomes an opportunity to assess your client's strengths and resources. Those strengths and resources, called extratherapeutic factors in the common factors literature (Duncan et al., 2010), become the tools for helping clients meet their goals. We have found it helpful to assume that change has begun before our first encounter with the client. Act I also might include the SST therapist's curiosity about pre-session change and improvements that might have occurred in the days, weeks, or even months that may have passed between the referral and the first meeting with the clinician. Weiner-Davis and her colleagues happened upon this useful phenomenon several years ago when they were interviewing a family and discovered that the problem they had called about weeks earlier had been greatly improved by the time they arrived at the therapists' office (Weiner-Davis et al., 1987). Not long after that research was published, the importance of pre-session change appeared in Talmon's list of helpful attitudes: "Therapy starts before the first session and will continue long after it" (Talmon, 1990, p. 134).

An exploration of any changes between the client making an appointment or having an assessment and the start of the session is helpful for several reasons. It sets the framework of fluidity; nothing is static. Ask, for instance, "What has gotten better for you since you decided to make the call?" Then, "How did you make that happen?" Then, "What can we do today to keep you moving in that direction?" Therapists can get therapy moving much quicker by taking advantage of natural headway toward improvement. The therapist can then use this to help from one of the purposes of the SST is to help keep things moving toward improvement.

As we said earlier, by the time our clients arrived, they had been wrestling with their problems for a long time. They had been trying to resolve their problems on their own. For many, finding a therapist to talk to was a first step. We know from our own experiences that taking that step often produces relief, a sense of accomplishment, increased hope, and a slightly more optimistic outlook on their situation.

If they say things have not changed, we become optimistically curious, "How have you managed to keep things from getting worse?" We find the ability to begin to see that keeping things from getting worse is a resource, an asset that we can then explore even further. Moreover, because we are trying to take a hopeful stance, if our client says, "Not only has nothing gotten better, but it's also gotten worse since I decided to come," we gently ask how they kept them from worsening. How did they get out of bed and make their way to the meeting? We are beginning the SST, developing the idea that no matter how small, clients have resources that can be nurtured and expanded. The fact that they are talking to us, we think, is a measure of their readiness for change. The questions about pre-session change presuppose that nothing stays the same; change is always happening.

Starting the SST to Seed Hope and Expectancy

We describe how an open-access, walk-in, call-in, or by-appointment SST session works and use non-professional language. The clinician introduces the idea that one session is enough for many people. The therapist explains the policies of the organization when necessary.

The single-session therapist begins the session to seed of hope and optimism. As we have said, the most crucial idea for the therapist to have in mind that good things can happen in one session. We might communicate that to our clients by saying,

> Lots of people find that one session is enough to get the ball rolling again in their lives. During this meeting, you and I together are going to work really hard to get you back on track, taking the next step. Getting here was the first step to getting where you want to be in your life.

This opening is a simple way of communicating the hopeful, common research finding that at least half of single-session clients have found the session to be adequate for them given their current circumstances (Cait & Courtnage, 2025; Harris-Lane et al., 2023; Hymmen et al., 2013; Josling & Cait, 2018; Perkins, 2006; Perkins & Scarlett, 2008; Stalker et al., 2016; Talmon, 1990).

Some other examples of inviting the client to join us in the SST mindset and focusing on outcomes are:

When you were thinking about visiting us today, what outcome did you hope the session would have? What did you hope would change in your life?

What were you hoping you would be able to do that you haven't been doing?

What would happen later today or tomorrow that would be a sign to you that coming today was helpful to you?

What would others notice about you as a sign that this session had been helpful?

The answers are then followed up to establish behavioral, observable effects on the session. These can be thought of as mini-goals, and the therapist emphasizes from the beginning:

1 Many find one session is enough for now.
2 The goal is to get the ball rolling, get back on track, get started, or use a similar metaphor that suits the client.
3 The therapist and the client will work hard together during the session. The therapist tells the client enough about the single-session approach to plant the seeds of hope.

Remembering that clients are far less interested in therapy than we are, we rarely refer to what we will do as "single-session therapy" or even "one-at-a-time therapy." We have found that sometimes a client becomes alarmed to hear that they have arrived for what they may think is going to be the only opportunity for therapy they will have. We find it helpful to explain at the start that we will discuss if and when other sessions can happen and that they are always welcome to return in the same way for another session

Act II: Identifying Solvable Problems, Setting Achievable Goals

Following the alliance building, resource assessment, and setting the single-session stage for the client, we turn to understanding the client's problem and goal. This Act's ingredients are: Understanding the circumstances of the referral, Negotiating a workable problem, Setting Achievable goals, and Checking-in with the client about the progress of the session. According to Duvall and Beres (2011), here Act II, the middle, also has two points of inquiry: "1. Pivotal events identifying and reinterpreting the experiences that are located in the significant events in people's lives; 2. Evaluation: locating and judging the effects of problems in people's lives (p. 42)." Act II is where problems and goals are mutually negotiated. The SST therapist collaborates with clients to negotiate small goals. When clients have many problems and large goals, therapists plant the idea that small changes lead to big changes. The SST therapist invites the client to direct the session's focus and co-create attainable treatment goals.

Circumstances of the Referral

It has been helpful for us to focus on the circumstances that led to our clients seeking us out as one starting point for defining the problem that will be the focus of the session. We try to determine, as early as possible in the session, how the decision to come for today's visit was made. We understand that sometimes, clients refer themselves for therapy. We want to understand how they decided to come. It is important to understand whose idea it was. Often, someone else encouraged, referred, or required the client to come to see us. If that is the case, we want to know what the circumstances of the referral were. The Milan team's original idea about the problem of the referring person (Palazzoli, 1985; Palazzoli et al., 1980) highlighted the systemic, relational aspect of the circumstances of our clients' visits.

1 Who was the referring person?

2 What happened when they suggested the client see us?

3 What did they think we could do to help? What are they hoping the client would get out of the visit?

4 What does the client think about the referring person's concerns? How helpful do they find the referring person's advice?

Setting Achievable Goals

Many therapists are trained to begin sessions by gathering a collection of symptoms or signs of a diagnostic category to guide them in determining the problem to address with the client. Michael Yapko told a story on a podcast (Karam, 2021) about a consultation he had with Jay Haley when he was a young therapist in the late 1970s. We think this story perfectly illustrates the quandary that awaits therapists who focus on such ways of working:

> And so, I called Jay Haley, wanting to learn more about hypnosis and strategic therapy. As a student in Michigan, a very psychoanalytic program, his approach to strategic work was way outside my academic background, way outside my comfort zone.
>
> So, I got ready for my first meeting with him, and I was young and green, and I wanted to impress him with my knowledge of psychobabble and all the diagnostic nomenclature that would make me sound professional... I presented a case that, you know, here's this woman who has a borderline personality disorder with ego dystonic cognitions and she has a history of impulsive... I went through a whole bunch of terminology before I finally get to my question at the end of it, which was, "So what would you do with her?" And Jay didn't answer for the longest time.
>
> I mean, really made me squirm. I was absolutely sure I had said things that were obviously stupid, and he was trying to find a way to tell me that I was an idiot before he finally said, "I wouldn't let her have those problems." And you know, I smiled and nodded my head as if I had a clue of what he was talking about. And that was the opening round of what took me a very long time to fully grasp, which was really two main messages, many more, but two main messages. One is that *people are more than their diagnostic labels* and two, the big lesson..., *never define a problem in unsolvable terms.*

The importance of these two messages that Yapko has identified is key to successful SST. We are interested in identifying the strengths, talents, abilities, resources, skills, and problem-solving capabilities of the client that aren't represented by their diagnoses. Importantly, SST therapists avoid defining an unsolvable problem as the goal. The job of the single-session therapist is to negotiate a solvable problem with the client. We use the word *negotiate* deliberately. The therapist and the client work together collaboratively to negotiate a problem to address in the current session. Often the negotiation begins with the client's vague statement of discomfort or unhappiness. Our job is to accept that vagueness and begin to inquire about what signs of change would accompany progress in removing that discomfort or unhappiness. We are looking to affirm what the client would be able to *do* if problem was reduced or eliminated.

Our demoralized clients frequently arrive seemingly overwhelmed by many problems. They overwhelm therapists with the complicated collection of problems they may have been frequently put off and have piled up. Finding the "precipitating event," the tipping point, the straw that broke the camel's back is a way to begin to narrow down the collection. Having a clearer picture of a specific example of the problem that has led to the client's being here is important. If, for example, the final straw was their boss threatening to fire them for poor job performance, we might ask, "What would be the smallest thing that your boss would see that would encourage them that you were on your way to improving your performance?"

After establishing the circumstances for the current visit, we want to find out what the client hopes and expects. Haley (1987) advised, "If therapy is to end properly, it must begin properly—by negotiating a solvable problem..." (p. 8). Or, as Yogi Berra stated about not having a plan, "If you don't know where you are going, you'll end up somewhere" (Berra, 1998, p. 30).

What were they hoping to accomplish during the visit? We have several ways of asking this:

What were you hoping you would be able to do when you leave here that you can't do right now?

When you were driving, walking, on your way here today, what were you thinking would be better in your life when you were on your way home?

What would the person who referred you see you doing that would be a sign to them that this visit had been helpful to you?

What would your family, friends, other people in your life notice that would let them know that something was better for you.

We are looking for a small sign to them that will tell them that the visit was helpful. We are also interested in identifying small, beginning steps. Remember that in the opening of the SST we introduced our session as a beginning; now we are asking and presupposing that they will be able to DO something after the session that is a sign of that beginning. In addition to helping set a starting point for the goal negotiation, asking in this hopeful, optimistic way is another way of creating a hopeful context for the conversation.

Avoid Asking What the Biggest, Most Important, Hugest Problem Is

SST therapists think small. One of the ways we avoid starting to work on unsolvable problems is to help the client identify a small starting point. For example, you might have asked them earlier in the session what was going on when the decided to come for help, the tipping point. Using that as a starting point, ask about how they would like to have handled the situation differently. Even in a small way:

"When you decided to make this call, what were you hoping would change in your life?"

"What would be a small sign that that change was beginning to take place?"

Don't ask:

"How have you been doing lately?" This is an open invitation for a description of the unsolvable nature of the problems the client has been struggling with. The answer to this question is a step backward.

"What's the problem you are bothered with?" Again, this is the name of a problem. The therapist would need to deconstruct this with the client so that the result was a description of a desirable outcome, not the current quandary.

"What's on your mind?" So vague it's likely to be another unproductive beginning, unless it is used as a starting point for moving to a specific outcome.

"How can I help you today?" This question may be heard as asking the client to tell you how to conduct the session. It may imply that you expect the client to teach you how to do your job. Starting by focusing on the process may not be as helpful as starting with outcomes or goals. Some therapists will be more comfortable asking about the most important, biggest, main issue the client would like to work on. We think this can be an excellent way to begin the goal negotiation. Following Yapko's advice, the therapist's next step in the negotiation can be narrowing that big problem to a more workable goal or a small step.

Exceptions

We are always listening for the exceptions that the client provides us. One client told us, "I can't remember the last time I was happy." We paid attention to the implication that there was a time he was happy. So, asking him what he was doing that last time helped him describe for us in detail what he wanted to reclaim from therapy. So, little phrases like, "Most nights (or usually), I don't get any sleep" prompts us to ignore the temptation to explore what causes their insomnia and to focus instead on the implied nights when she does something different.

Variability of Problems

Psychological problems that clients present within psychotherapy can be characterized along three key dimensions: frequency, duration, and intensity. By considering these dimensions together, clinicians can develop a more comprehensive understanding of the nature and characteristics of a client's psychological issues.

1 **Frequency** refers to how often a problem occurs. Some issues may manifest rarely, such as occasional panic attacks, while others are more chronic or recurring, like daily rumination in depression. Assessing frequency helps determine the pervasiveness of the problem. When therapists have an idea about how often the problem occurs, goal setting can be cast as a reduction of the occurrence of the problem or the increase in something else the client wants.
2 With a client who is has been referred for panic attacks we have found asking how often they occur, even if an estimate can be given. We might then ask, "If they were to happen 1 or 2 times less frequently, would that be a step in the right direction toward improvement?" Then we can proceed with developing a small next step toward a goal.
3 **Duration** refers to how long a problem lasts. Some issues are short-term, such as a phobic response during a turbulent flight. In contrast, chronic problems are more enduring, such as persistent low self-esteem. Understanding duration provides another way of talking with clients about goals. We might ask how long a typical panic attack lasted, ...
4 **Intensity** reflects the severity or magnitude of a problem's impact on functioning and well-being. Mild anxiety may cause discomfort in social situations, while extreme anxiety can be debilitating and lead to avoidance. Gauging intensity helps prioritize treatment targets.

Variability across these dimensions provides opportunities for therapeutic goal-setting. For example, goals can be set as reducing the frequency of binge-eating episodes, shortening the duration of depressive episodes, or lowering the intensity of anger outbursts. This dimensional perspective aligns with the view that problems may be best conceptualized as existing along a continuum rather than present/absent categories. Talking with clients about reducing how often their problems occur, lessening the intensity of their problems, or shortening how long their problems last can be helpful in goal negotiation.

Checking In

We have found it helpful to check in with clients during the session by asking if we are talking about what they wanted and if we are providing what they were hoping for. As the session approaches its end, especially if we believe that a workable goal has been established, we ask, "What has been most helpful for you about our talk so far?" Often, clients tell us something like, "You let me tell my story," "I felt like you heard me," and "You didn't offer me stupid advice." We follow that up with the second question, "So if that was helpful to you, what do you think you'll be able to do tonight or tomorrow because of that?" You'll see that this sets the stage for suggesting a task or homework. We thank them for giving us that feedback and follow up with another question such as

What was it about (e.g., "just talking") that made you feel like it was what you needed?

What will you be able to do differently later today as a result of coming in?

What was something that stood out to you during our time together that you will take with you and start doing later today or tomorrow?

We can then ask about what they envision differently. "When would they be able to do that?" "Who in your life will notice?" We help them envision themselves following through. Often, this can lead to the planning of homework or an experiment that can be thought of as the next step.

In some clinics, it would not be unusual for the therapist and client to take a short break for the therapist to do some planning for the rest of the closing of the session. This can be a time for the therapist to organize their thoughts about what commendations, strengths and resources are going to be posed, how to refine a next step task, what referrals might be appropriate, and how to talk about options to return. SST therapists will have told the client at the beginning of the session something like, "Somewhere toward the end of the session, we might take a break." The therapist might punctuate the session with, "This might be a good time to take our break, what do you think? I would like to take some time to gather my thoughts." The therapist might add here, "Please give yourself the opportunity to relax during this break time. Perhaps you might develop an idea for your next small step. Either way, when I return, I'll ask you how your break went." As an example, on one occasion, when the therapist returned from the break, the client, who had presented with concerns about loneliness and isolation, said she had decided that when she got home, she would contact a close friend with whom she had had no contact in recent months. This idea was then incorporated into the therapist's Act III feedback. Whether or not a break has occurred, the session now turns to ACT III.

Act III: The Closing

After the goal has been identified, the therapist moves toward identifying implementable steps with an emphasis on strengths, competencies, and expectations of change producing hope. The Closing is when the therapist wraps up the session for the client. The Closing includes the ingredients: Commendations, Feedback, a plan, and next steps for the client, referrals to other providers if necessary, and information about a return visit if needed. Duvall and Béres refer to Act II as the conclusion whose points of inquiry are

> 1: Reflecting summary: reflecting on and summarizing movement that occurs in the therapy session or the overall process of therapy; 2. Receiving context: developing a new backstory context to receive changes that have developed and to accommodate the reincorporation of identity.
>
> (p. 42)

Sometimes it is helpful to open the curtain for this Act by saying something like, "We have a few minutes left in our session today. I have some ideas I would like to share with you and some ideas about next steps."

Commendations

Here, the therapist commends the client on the strengths and resources they described, or the therapist observed. As a strengths-based therapist, the SST therapist avoids using diagnostic, pathological, or problem-oriented language. They provide feedback to the client that enhances their understanding of solutions they can implement using their resources and strengths. Commendations are our report back to the client at the end of the session about what we discovered about their resources and strengths during the interview. It is different than ending a session by telling the client what was wrong with them, a diagnosis, in other words. Single-session therapists assume that what is right with the client can fix what's wrong; hence, we point out the strengths and are less focused on the shortcomings. For many clients, this is the most potent part of the interview and builds confidence and motivation to take the next step independently.

We have found that this part of the session frequently is an emotionally impactful moment for the client. Some clients respond to this positive accounting with surprise: "I never thought anyone could see that in me!" Many times, clients provide more examples of the successes and strengths that we have identified, which we take to be a sign of an improved self-concept and increased sense of self-agency.

Plan

At the end of the session, we may have an idea about a homework assignment or an experiment for the client to try to keep them on the road to
improving their lives. Tasks or homework tasks may be developed for the
client to continue the therapeutic work on their own. SST therapists highlight resources that the client may have overlooked.

Feedback and Next Steps

We always ask clients for feedback, "Did you get what you were hoping
for?" "What do you think the next steps should be?" And we never assume
that those next steps would be another appointment. Single-session therapists don't ask, "Would you like to come back next week?" If the client is
interested in meeting again, we'll ask when they think that should be. Will
they have time to try out their homework and reflect on this session and
so forth? And it's at this stage of the interview that we also might suggest
other resources that would be helpful for the client. We also make it clear
that if they make the decision to return, the decision is up to them, that
they are in charge of follow-up, and we welcome their return.

Referrals

Lastly, we may provide any appropriate referrals to community resources.
As we have seen in Chapter 2, some OA/SST services have recently added
a navigation component. Most of the time, OA/SST sessions end as a single session and that's that. Some clients might return for another OA/SST
session in the future when the time is right for them. However, some OA/
SST sessions might include a discussion of additional services, such as,
for example, ongoing sessions with a clinician, group therapy, addiction
services, and so on. In those instances, a "navigator" might be available
to assist that client in connecting to another service within that agency or
elsewhere in the community.

What We Want Them to Leave With

A Sense That They Have Been Heard

As we said earlier, it is common when we ask clients what has been helpful in the session, they tell us some variation of "You listened to me."
"I felt heard," "I was able to tell my story." This is precisely what we are
hoping for. It would be the rare client who commented on skills like asking open-ended questions, demonstrating unconditional positive regard, or

pointing out distorted cognitions as helpful. Skilled SST therapists listen to their clients. We listen in a particular way; it is not passive listening. It is active listening. We aim to listen for strengths and resources, commenting on them, and underscoring them for clients.

Increased Hope; Decreased Stress

We said earlier that clients are often anxious, demoralized, hopeless, and distressed when they arrive. We aim for them to leave their session more hopeful about their futures. We want them to be less stressed and, therefore, able to put more energy toward solving their problems.

Increased Awareness of Strengths and Resources and How to Make Use of them

One of the results of underscoring clients' strengths, exceptions to the problem, and preferred outcomes during the session is that they frequently become even more aware of them when we reflect on them during the session. We have had clients tell us that they were unaware that the strengths we saw in them were visible to other people. This enables them to leave with increased self-confidence.

A New Way to Think about Their Situation

When clients leave a successful SST, they commonly tell us that the conversation has given them insights into their situation and problems. They say the conversation led them to new understandings of their situation, often suggesting new ways to address an issue. Although helping clients achieve such insights is not an explicit goal of SST, it is a happy outcome of many of our sessions. Clients have achieved new understandings of their situations that help them take a next step in moving on with their lives.

A Plan for Their Next Step

We hope that by the end of the session, we have helped the client develop a plan and take the next step toward implementing it to accomplish the change they want to make in their lives. That plan could also include the idea of returning for another session when the timing seems right for them. Putting it this way reinforces the idea that the client is in charge. We also want the client to know, early in the session, that options for accessing other mental health services (including multi-session, by-appointment counseling) will be discussed during the session. It is most important, though, to raise that possibility in a way that does not imply an expectation, on the clinician's part, that having more sessions is preferred.

A Positive Experience with Psychotherapy

As we have said, one is the most frequent number of client visits with mental health services. Large numbers of people don't return after their first visit to a mental health clinic, even when it was not a planned single session. The data suggests that many people who didn't return got what they wanted in a single visit and saw no need for future visits. But it's also likely true that some people do not return because they didn't find the session helpful. That perception that the visit was unhelpful may have discouraged them from seeking future help when they could have used it. That's why we want people to have had a positive experience with psychotherapy in a single session visit, so that they would return in the future if needed. We hope that they will refer their friends and family for single-session services when the need arises. As SST therapists, we are nurturing the client's relationship not only with the individual provider, but with the provider's clinic, and the mental health field. The Community Counseling Service, where Monte has been for decades, routinely sees clients who have returned after dozens of years, and they have referred their family, grandchildren, and others because they had a positive experience. It is important to note that they rarely remember their original therapists' names; they remember the service and that it helped. So, in a way, we seek to develop long-term relationships with our SST clients, though that relationship is with the service rather than the individual provider.

Conclusion

This chapter provided a framework for conducting an SST session grounded on the single-session mindset. We have introduced the Three Act structure for helping therapists implement the ingredients of an SST. The Three-Act structure can be helpful in most therapeutic models we have encountered. This chapter also provides some examples, or wording, for the therapist's questions and explanations. We are not prescribing these suggestions as a script but providing them for newcomers to SST to begin making the SST mindset a part of their everyday practice. We encourage you to think about how to modify each of these examples so that they fit with your therapeutic approach, your style, and especially for each unique client that you encounter. You are now on your way to helping your clients when you have a whole hour.

In the next chapter, we will illustrate the application of the three-Act metaphor and the incorporation of the ingredients of SSTs in two challenging cases. One involved a man who had suffered an aneurysm, loss of his family, and a history of suicidal behavior; the other was a woman who consulted us several months after she was sexually assaulted in her home. We hope these examples will be helpful to you in your next steps to developing comfort and skills in SST.

Note

1 Thanks to Montana Holmes, Andrea Nava-Quintero, Leo Scaletta, and Emily Tran for their dedicated work on this project.

References

Berra, Y. (1998). *The Yogi book: I really didn't say everything I said!* Workman Publishing Company.

Boal, A. (1979). *The theatre of the oppressed.* Pluto Press.

Bobele, M., & Slive, A. (2025). The SST model developed in Canada and Texas for walk-in, drop-in, open-access, and virtual services. In F. Cannistrà, & M. F. Hoyt (Eds.), *Single session therapies: Why and how one-at-a-time mindsets are effective.* (pp. 109–123). Routledge.

Cait, C. A., & Courtnage. (2025). Implementing Single-Session Therapy. Chapter 13 in this book.

Cannistrà, F. (2020). Single session therapy: An introduction to principles and practices. Italian Center for Single Session Therapy. https://www.singlesession therapies.com/single-session-therapy/ebook-single-session-therapy/

Cannistrà, F., & Hoyt, M. F. (2020). The nine logics beneath brief therapy interventions: A framework to help therapists achieve their purpose. *Journal of Systemic Therapies, 39*(1), 19–34.

Cannistrà, F., & Piccirilli, F. (2021). *Single-session therapy: Principles and practice.* Giunti Psychometrics S.t.l.

de Shazer, S., Dolan, Y., Korman, H., Trepper, T., McCollum, E., & Berg, I. K. (2021). *More than miracles: The state of the art of solution-focused brief therapy: Classic edition.* https://research.ebsco.com/linkprocessor/plink?id=2d2b805c-b16d-3473-92dd-0862c11f984b

Duncan, B. L., Miller, S. D., Wampold, B. E., & Hubble, M. A. (2010). *The heart and soul of change: Delivering what works in therapy,* 2nd ed (B. L. Duncan, S. D. Miller, B. E. Wampold, & M. A. Hubble (Eds.)). American Psychological Association. https://doi-org.ezproxy.ollusa.edu/10.1037/12075-000

Dunne, P., Madrigal, R. D., & Afary, K. (2022). Narradrama as a three-act play. *Journal of Systemic Therapies, 41*(4), 86–108.

Duvall, J., & Béres, L. (2011). Storied therapy as a three-act play. In *Innovations in narrative therapy: Connecting practice, training, and research* (pp. 37–90). Norton.

Fisch, R., Weakland, J. H., & Segal, L. (1982). *The tactics of change: Doing therapy briefly.* Jossey-Bass.

Haley, J. (1973). *Uncommon therapy: The psychiatric techniques of Milton H. Erickson, M. D.* New York: W. W. Norton.

Haley, J. (1987). *Problem-solving therapy* (2nd ed.). Jossey-Bass. http://www.loc.gov/catdir/enhancements/fy0706/87045413-d.html

Harris-Lane, L. M., Keeler-Villa, N. R., Bol, A., Burke, K., Churchill, A., Cornish, P., Fitzgerald, S. F., Goguen, B., Gordon, K., Jaouich, A., Lang, R., Michaud, M., Mahon, K. N., & Rash, J. A. 2023. Implementing one-at-a-time therapy in community addiction and mental health centres: a retrospective exploration of the implementation process and initial outcomes. *BMC Health Services Research*, 23, 982. doi: 10.1186/s12913-023-09923-5. https://www.ncbi.nlm.nih.gov/pubmed/37700280

Hoyt, M. F. (2024). *Single session therapy a clinical introduction to principles and practices*. Routledge.

Hoyt, M. F., Rosenbaum, R., & Talmon, M. (1992). Planned single-session psychotherapy. In S. H. Budman, M. F. Hoyt, & S. Friedman (Eds.), *The first session in brief therapy* (pp. 59–86). Guilford Press.

Hymmen, P., Stalker, C. A., & Cait, C. A. (2013). The case for single-session therapy: does the empirical evidence support the increased prevalence of this service delivery model? *Journal of Mental Health*, 22(1), 60–71. https://doi.org/10.3109/09638237.2012.670880

Joseph, J., & Rajan, S. K. (2024). Evolution of single-session therapy: A bibliometric analysis. *American Journal of Psychotherapy*, 77(2), 71–78. https://doi.org/10.1176/appi.psychotherapy.20230054

Josling, L., & Cait, C.-A. (2018). The walk-in counseling model: Research and advocacy. In M. F. Hoyt, M. Bobele, A. Slive, J. Young, & M. Talmon (Eds.), *Single-session therapy by walk-in or appointment: Administrative, clinical, and supervisory aspects of one-at-a-time services.* (pp. 91–103). Routledge/Taylor & Francis Group. https://doi.org/10.4324/9781351112437-6

Karam, E. (Host). (2021, February 12). Michael Yapko (No. 46) [Audio podcast episode]. https://rss.com/podcasts/aamft/134503

Keeney, B. P. (1990). *Improvisational therapy: A practical guide for creative clinical strategies*. Systemic Therapy Press.

Keeney, B. P. (1991). *Improvisational therapy: A practical guide for creative clinical strategies*. Guilford Press.

Lambert, M. J. (2005). Early response in psychotherapy: Further evidence for the importance of common factors rather than "placebo effects" *[Article]. Journal of Clinical Psychology*, 61(7), 855–869. https://doi.org/10.1002/jclp.20130

Mahon, K. N., Harris-Lane, L. M., King, A. C., Bobele, M., Churchill, A., Cornish, P., Goguen, B., Garland, S. N., Jaouich, A., & Rash, J. A. (Under Review). Evaluating provider training in Stepped Care 2.0 and one-at-a-time services among mental health and addiction providers. *International Journal of Mental Health Systems*. [Ref# cd41436f-1ea2–4d94–990b-f06640dfd7c3].

Messer, S., & Wampold, B. (2002). Let's face facts: Common factors are more potent than specific therapy ingredients. *Clinical Psychology: Science and Practice*, 9(1), 21–25.

Moreno, J. L., & Fox, J. (1987). *The essential Moreno: Writings on psychodrama, group method, and spontaneity*. Springer.

Murphy, J. J. (2024). *Solution-focused therapy*. American Psychological Association. https://doi.org/10.1037/0000370-000

O'Hanlon, W. H., & Weiner-Davis, M. (1989). *In search of solutions*. W. W. Norton.

Palazzoli, M. S. (1985). The problem of the sibling as the referring person. *Journal of Marital & Family Therapy*, 11(1), 21–34.

Palazzoli, M. S., Boscolo, L., Cecchin, G., & Prata, G. (1980). The problem of the referring person. *Journal of Marital & Family Therapy*, 6(1), 3–9.

Perkins, R. (2006). The effectiveness of one session of therapy using a single-session therapy approach for children and adolescents with mental health problems. *Psychotherapy: Theory, Research & Practice*, 79(Pt 2), 215–227. https://doi.org/10.1348/147608305X60523

Perkins, R., & Scarlett, G. (2008). The effectiveness of single session therapy in child and adolescent mental health. Part 2: An 18-month follow-up study. *Psychology and Psychotherapy: Theory, Research & Practice*, 81(2), 143–156. https://doi.org/10.1348/147608308X280995

Porter, S., Pitt, T., Eubank, M., Butt, J., & Thomas, O. (2024). An expert understanding of the single-session mindset. *Journal of Systemic Therapies*, 43(3), 1–25. https://doi.org/10.1521/jsyt.2024.43.3.02

Ray, W. A., & Keeney, B. P. (1993). *Resource-focused therapy*. Karnac Books.

Rogers, C. R. (1992). The necessary and sufficient conditions of therapeutic personality change. *Journal of Consulting and Clinical Psychology*, 60(5), 827–8322.

Slive, A. B., & Bobele, M. (Eds.). (2011). *When one hour is all you have: Effective therapy with walk-in clients*. Zeig, Tucker & Theisen.

Stalker, C. A., Riemer, M., Cait, C. A., Horton, S., Booton, J., Josling, L., Bedggood, J., & Zaczek, M. (2016). A comparison of walk-in counselling and the wait list model for delivering counselling services. *Journal of Mental Health*, 25(5), 403–409. https://doi.org/10.3109/09638237.2015.1101417

Talmon, M. (1990). *Single-session therapy: Maximizing the effect of the first (and often only) therapeutic encounter*. Jossey-Bass Publishers.

Tran, E. (2024). *The mindset in action: Exploring the practicality of the single-session mindset* (Publication Number 31149186) [Psy.D., Our Lady of the Lake University]. ProQuest Dissertations & Theses Global. United States, TX.

Watzlawick, P., Weakland, J., & Fisch, R. (1974). *Change: Principles of problem formation and problem resolution*. W. W. Norton.

Weiner-Davis, M., de Shazer, S., & Gingerich, W. J. (1987). Building on pretreatment change to construct the therapeutic solution: An exploratory study. *Journal of Marriage and Family Therapy*, 13(4), 359–363.

Chapter 4

Single-Session Therapy with Complex Cases

Monte Bobele and Arnold Slive

One of the most frequent questions clinicians new to single-session therapies (SSTs) ask is, "How do you handle a client with significant signs of
risk?" Our answer to that question is,

> Exactly the same way you would handle risk in any other service deliv-
> ery model. You assess for risk and then aim to be helpful to the client
> so that the danger of harm is greatly reduced because of your conver-
> sation with them. The session may or may not end with a referral for
> additional services.
>
> (Slive & Bobele, 2019, p. 19)

In other words, the therapist's job is to assess for risk and assure, to the
extent possible, that their client will be safe when they leave the therapist's
office.

Over 30 years ago, I published a paper (Bobele, 1987) that reported
using brief systemic therapy to treat two cases of life-threatening behaviors. Although we were not calling it single-session therapy yet, I understood that those opportunities to be helpful might be my last. Those two
cases and others since have convinced me that responding genuinely and
empathically with the client and addressing their presenting concern first,
hearing them out, and establishing a working alliance first leads to more
effective safety planning because when clients' needs are prioritized, the
likelihood that the risk of subsequent suicide or other adverse outcomes is
reduced by the end of the session. In other words, safety planning can be
based on where the client is at the end of the session, not at the beginning.

Therapists' concerns about risk and risk assessment may result from
the increased litigious atmosphere in the United States and other countries. However, the negative impact on clients of routinely assessing for risk
has recently become apparent. (Harris & Goh, 2017; Pisani et al., 2011).
Clients will likely be put off by having a therapist pull out a form and
ask questions that might seem to ignore their request for immediate help

DOI: 10.4324/9781003351375-4

because of the crisis. In some ways, this is akin to the care a patient receives when they arrive at an ER. They are treated first, and paperwork is delayed until the patient is out of danger. This chapter presents two examples of cases where risk was evident in the interview.

Starting the Interview

Frequently, the initial part of the first encounter with any client, Act 1, whether risk is or is not an issue, is making everyone in the room comfortable. Anxiety, apprehension, and other impediments to developing a successful therapeutic alliance are inevitable at the beginning of therapy. As we noted in the previous chapter, an early task in the therapy session is for everyone's anxiety to be reduced – this includes the therapist. Perhaps the therapist's comfort level is more important than we have considered. If the therapist is worried about the client's safety or suicidal threats, the therapist's anxiety may severely damage the therapeutic alliance. Clients in crisis may be best served by a therapist who exhibits a calm, accepting demeanor from the outset. Beginning a therapy session with a ritualistic, impersonal suicide assessment and clinical talk about limits of confidentiality, especially in cases where harm is an issue, is paradoxically likely to raise anxiety and impair the development of a helpful working alliance.

The only significant difference is that the SST therapist does not abandon the idea that this may be the last and only opportunity to help this client. Such situations remind us of the importance of being as helpful as possible in the current session.

Suicide

No other circumstance arouses worry and skepticism in encountering SST work than those around the perceived risk in working with clients who have talked about or attempted to die by suicide. I think the concerns stem from two main quarters: the therapist's responsibility to "do no harm" through action or inaction that might result in the death or injury to their client; the second has to do with the fact of the litigious/risk-adverse climate we practice in nowadays. Researchers have found that people who have a relationship with a therapist are less likely to die by suicide. People who never seek the help of a therapist are at the highest risk. This fact is well-known and perhaps has justified widespread mental health awareness programs to offer assistance. Several studies, however, have reported on the disappointing failure of our suicide prevention programs to reduce the ever-rising deaths. Of course, there are many factors contributing to the increase, but increased mental health awareness programs may have resulted in the over-pathologization of ordinary everyday problems in living as "depression" rather than sadness or disappointment. Worry and pre-test jitters are self-diagnosed as anxiety, or more specifically, "test anxiety." This may be attributable to evidence of increasing diagnosis creep. Diagnosis creep, also known as concept creep, is the process of broadening the definition of a disease or mental illness, often by expert panels. This can lead to a broader range of conditions being considered disorders or less severe problems being diagnosed.

Organizing SSTs with at Risk Clients

Often, therapists, perhaps out of a sense of urgency, reach for their preferred suicide risk assessment device, but the evidence such screening devices, mainly the Columbia-Suicide Severity Rating Scale (Simpson et al., 2021) reduce suicides is equivocal (Milner et al., 2017; Zalsman et al., 2016). We recommend that the most important initial task for the therapist is establishing an effective working alliance. We suggest that the results of any risk assessment are likely more reliable and valuable to the clinician if they are obtained after a solid therapeutic alliance is developed so that clients will be more comfortable sharing their thoughts and intentions about hurting themselves candidly.

Complex Multi-Problem Example

Act I: Emphasis on Strengths, Engendering Hope, and Expectations of Change

José, a Mexican American in his early 40s, walked into the Community Counseling Service one morning. He apologized for arriving later than expected for his walk-in session. He had ridden his bicycle about 5 miles to the clinic. On his intake form, he wrote that about four years earlier, he had suffered an aneurysm that left him partially paralyzed, unable to walk or talk, and cognitively impaired. Obviously, he had improved considerably by the time I met him. He called the CCS for information about walking in, he rode his bicycle, which required considerable motor coordination and balance, and throughout the session, he carried on a coherent conversation with me. All of these were evidence not only of his improvement but also of his strong motivation or readiness for change. At times, he struggled to find the right words or properly construct his sentences, but he always made himself understood. He was aware that his speech was confusing at times and apologized. José was a man carrying a considerable number of when he arrived. In fact, he later said he felt like he had a "ton of bricks" on his shoulders: trouble with rehab, a wife who divorced him and was not helpful during his recovery, money worries because he couldn't work, and difficulty connecting with medical assistance (he had been disappointed with medical care earlier).

Note that the early moments of the session were intended to put José at ease and reduce any unease he might have been experiencing as much as possible. Two years earlier, José had been told about the CCS by Orlando, a friend and co-worker at the hardware store where he had worked for nearly 20 years. He told me that he had been thinking about coming for help for the last two years, but finally, today, he decided to come in. The following transcript has been lightly edited to reduce the length and give the reader a sense of how the conversation flowed through the three acts of the SST:

Monte: Hello!
José: How are you, sir?
Monte: I'm good. I'm Monte Bobele. Yeah, you can call me Monte.
José: Monte. How are you doing, Monte?
Monte: And, what should I call you?
José: You can call me José.
Monte: Okay. Nice to meet you, José. Um, I'm uh, I- I heard that you rode your bicycle here today.

I use openings like this to begin building a therapeutic alliance around the client's everyday strengths and resources, such as riding a bike several miles to our clinic following the aneurysm we knew about from his intake materials. This is also designed to start the conversation with a strengths-based atmosphere rather than starting with asking about what the problem or issue is that he is interested in addressing. I also introduced humor into the interview by teasing him about the "fibbing" he did:

Monte: And how far away from here do you live? I'm still thinking about that bike ride over here.
José: Off Preston.
Monte: ...that's what, about five miles?
José: Yeah, well, okay, I'm- I'm- I'm fibbing a little bit. I'm fibbing a little bit.
Monte: Oh, we're starting off on the wrong foot already.
José: Well-
Monte: (laughs).
José: ...okay, I... now, now, I rode most of the way, but I got on the bus.
Monte: Ah.
José: Once I got tired, I put the bike on the rack. And I rode the bus. But I rode most of the way.
Monte: My hat's off to you.

After I highlighted his resourcefulness in using his bike and the bus to arrive, José continued by telling me about some of the problems that contributed to his coming for the visit. I wanted to postpone the problem talk for a bit more to introduce him to the CCS's operations and briefly introduce him to the SST mindset:

Monte: Let me- let me stop you, because I need to hear all of that and I want be sure that you have an opportunity to let me know about that. I wanted to tell you just a few things about how we work here, or how I work here. Um, this is our walk-in service that you've come to today. You didn't have to have an appointment and that was probably a good idea for you.

José: Yeah.

Monte: If in the future you want to come back after we get done talking, we can arrange for you to have an appointment to see somebody again or you can walk back in again.

José: Yeah.

Monte: But one- one thing that we find is often people who come to our walk-in service uh, find that when they leave, they've gotten some good ideas about getting back on track with their lives.

José: Right, I gotcha.

Monte: We'll see where you are at the end of the hour with that.

José: Exactly. I know that I have resources, but I just need a little help.

Monte: Okay. Like a little shove?

I made a mental note of his saying he had "resources." I reflected that José had introduced the idea of working toward a small change in this session, "a little help." When I asked early what he had been hoping for, perhaps what he was thinking on the ride over, his initial response was, "Just talking like we are now." I next wanted to find out how he decided to come to the CCS. We sometimes call this the circumstances of the referral. This can lead to an exploration of his social network and other resources. It can provide us with information about his understanding of his situation:

Monte: Well, let me ask you this. Who told you about this place?

José: Okay, and thank you for asking, that's a great question.

Monte: (laughs) Oh, thanks.

José: I worked at Rio Grande Lumber Company...for, uh, off and on, for a period of 20 years, so-I was a flooring salesman. I would sell carpet, vinyl, tile, ceramic tile. I- I was, a- a jack of all trades, master of none, you know? If they needed me in the plumbing department, I would sell plumbing. I would sell

	paint. You know, in 20 years, you- you learn a little bit about everything. I was, I was like Tim the Tool Man[1], you know.
Monte:	Like Tim the Tool Man (laughs).
José:	Yeah, so, you know. So, a- a- and they became my family. Okay, to make a long story short. Uh, one of the plumbers there, his name is Orlando. His wife... And I didn't know this, I worked with him for over 20 years, and I didn't know that his wife was a graduate from Our Lady of the Lake.
Monte:	So, Orlando told you that this was a place where people learn how to be therapists? And, I have a team that's working with me. I don't know if he said anything to you about that.
José:	Yes, yes.
Monte:	Oh, he told you all about that?
José:	Yes, he told me be open. No holds barred. So, I'm going to do that. I'm going to- I'm going to... Because I trust him. He's a great guy. He told me he went through marriage counseling-

With this revelation, José leaned forward and whispered, delivering this confidentially as if this was still a sensitive topic for Mexican American men. I took it to mean that he thought that receiving counseling or talking to therapists was still shameful among some men.

Monte:	It sounds like he's been a real good friend. Has he been there 20 years too?
José:	Off and on like myself, yes.
Monte:	You're a pretty loyal employee.
José:	Yeah. Yeah, well they were a very, very loyal company. U- u-um...They've been good to me, they're my family. You know I don't want to bite the hand that feeds me. It didn't seem right because they- they- they- they- they let me go you see I was on vacation when the aneurysm occurred, I was on vacation- I was supposed to come back on that Monday, and it happened on Sunday.

José was eager to get on with the session and was uninterested in my ideas about what was vital for him to know about the CCS policies and procedures. José was not unusual in this; perhaps I was overly diligent about ensuring he understood how the CCS worked. I wanted to be sure that José understood that other people were participating in the session before he revealed sensitive personal information. This case illustrates that in some cases, clarifying consent items and other business is not as important to the client as talking with someone about what is troubling them. He had been waiting two years for this opportunity and was anxious to get on with it. I was also aware that the trainees observing the mirror expected me to demonstrate how I explain consent informally.

When explaining the nuts and bolts of the clinic's operation, the paperwork, and other such items, I try to use the client's language and experiences to make them more understandable. I used his hospital experiences to this end. I likened my team to the ones he had in the hospital and during his recovery. He told me, "I'm down with that," when I pointed out the camera and microphones that enabled the team to participate. He waved at the camera, saying, "I have nothing to hide." Concerning the consent form, he explained to me that he did sign it but that it was difficult for him, still, to write because of his neurological problems. We discussed that momentarily, and then I let him move us into Act II, where solvable problems are negotiated and goals for the session are collaboratively created.

Act 2: Identifying Solvable Problems, Setting Achievable Goals

José: You know, I've gotten to that point where if I don't grab my life right now, if I don't take a hold of my life and start doing something, nobody's gonna do it for me. 'Cause that's what it's about. Like for for years I've been on my own and so, it's like I've been in shackles. It's been like I've been in prison.

Monte: Sounds like one of the things that you lost, in addition to your motor skills, was your family?

José: Yeah, well, yeah. Yeah, my wife. It was mainly my wife. My daughter, she's awesome man. She takes care of me. She looks out for my wellbeing.

José clarified that although he referred to her as "my daughter," Eve was his 12-year-old granddaughter. Eve's mother, José's daughter, according to José, was a heavy drug user and was unreliable. The session continued with José telling me how, despite his losses, he still felt fortunate:

José: And I'm sure you hear this story a lot. The thing is, okay, I lost everything. All right. I should be thankful I have been blessed because, you know, all the people do tell me, "You're blessed. You don't even see it." Like my face didn't go to the side, you know?

José grimaced and pointed to illustrate how the facial paralysis he had escaped might have looked:

José: I've come, yeah, I've come aways, but I've done it. Because I did it. Nobody - nobody helped me.

Monte: Where did you get all that strength?

I intended for this question to encourage an elaboration of the strengths he had demonstrated and invite him to identify other resources that were available to him. I had kept in mind his earlier comment that he knew he had resources. He told me that he had a twin sister who had also suffered an aneurysm ten years earlier. Unfortunately, she never recovered, and José's family had to withdraw life support in accordance with her DNR orders. He told me how he started taking better care of himself after her death because he wanted to honor her memory.

Here José is alerting me to the seriousness and complexity of the problems by telling me, "Uh, uh, uh, it- it's-... a real long story. And- and-and I... it's probably gonna take a couple sessions." He was not unusual in expecting that therapy was likely to require several visits. I used this opportunity to return to the stage setting I had been doing very slowly in Act I. I was going to try to begin to negotiate the problem we would address and what the outcome of the session would be:

Monte: So, when you're riding over here this morning, and you must have been thinking about coming...

José: I've been nervous. I've been trying to get over here for a year. But last night I couldn't sleep. It- th- it- I'm sorry, Monte, if I'm making it difficult for you...it's difficult for me.

Monte: Yeah, I'm- I'm sure it's more difficult for you. Well, let me ask you th- this, uh, José...when you were riding your bike over here this morning, what- what- what were you thinking would be one small thing that would make your life better as a result of coming here today?

José: Talking about it. What we're doing it now. I feel a ton of bricks off my shoulders. Already. When I was riding over here. I- I couldn't wait to get over here. But, uh, it's really nice meeting you. And- and just having you hear me out. It- it's- it's worth a lot. Believe it or not. It's worth a lot.

José had already experienced pre-session change. He finally overcame the obstacles that kept him from coming for help. The availability of the walk-in option eliminated any hurdles that might have discouraged him from taking the next step in his recovery by coming to the CCS. The session had already moved him along another step or two. This vague goal of "talking about it" was an acceptable beginning of our goal negotiation:

José: I had a brain- a brain aneurysm back in uh, late 2014. I was 44 years old. I was very active. After all the medical bills and every-thing, it came out to $200,000 plus in medical bills. Well, I had a good insurance. I had insurance, and it reached its limit. And so, it was time for therapy and uh, whoops. It was said, "you have no more funds, José." So, I told my wife, at the time, I told her with my last paycheck from work, go buy me a bike and I've been riding my bike since then.

Monte: That's amazing.

José: Yeah. Eh, y- you know what? Now that I think about it. It is.

My comment highlighted the new strength he had revealed about his determination to recover. His response illustrates how powerful such a comment can be in ordinary therapeutic conversation. He gave me examples of the life he wanted to return to. He cataloged the slow steps to recovery he had made. Several new resources come to light: his musical talents, his generosity, his becoming sober, his financial and familial responsibilities, and his determination to walk again:

José: And so as soon as I was just determined that I wasn't gonna go out that way, man. That was like, no man, there's no way! I was learning drumming, you know? I love to drum. I love drumming and so I wanted to get back on my drums, which I have but it's not the same. Too much- too much shit's going on in my life that the depression just, just kicked in hard.

Monte: Wow.

José: You know, from having everything to nothing. From losing my girl, my kids. You know, I was the kinda guy that – I'll give you the shirt off my back, man. You know. I'm not gonna change who I am.

Monte: It's gotta be tough to have lost all of that and still be so generous you'd give somebody the shirt of your back.

José: My motor skills are shot. I just started talking a couple years ago.

Monte: That must have been a lot of hard work.

José: It's like learning how to walk. And, literally, walk.

Monte: It's like being a baby all over again.

José: Exactly. Like the saying goes, you gotta crawl before you can walk.

José: I was just starting off in drumming. I was one of those late bloomers. Well, you know, I didn't know I had the skills. I come from a long line of musicians. And I always was the black sheep of the family. But it took me too long to find my skills, because I was too busy having a good time. Too busy working. Uh, uh, uh, I did a lot of partying, man, in my day.

Monte: Really?

José: I did a lot of drinking, smoking, I did a lot of drugs.

Monte:	Wow. So, you were a professional partier?
José:	(laughs). Yeah, and you know what? You know what, Monte? I had it together. Bills got paid. I took care of my family. But it wasn't, I didn't have it together. I thought I had it together. When I was a kid, my dad was in a Mexican band. He was a mariachi. He was in a Mexican kind of band. I was like, uh, that- that wasn't my scene. I went to rock and roll. You know me, with the long hair, of course.
Monte:	What did he play?
José:	He played trumpet. Yeah, all through high school and through the army. He would take me with him. And the drummer in his band... When I saw the drums, it was like, "Oh, my gosh!" I was like, "Wow!" You know, it was like seeing those seven angels. I got hooked, yeah.
Monte:	What kind of band did you want to play with?
José:	I love rhythm and blues, man. And I still have my drum set. It's the only thing that I have. But of course, it's put up. You know, beautiful. 14-piece pearl, metallic blue. Oh, I it to death. It's the only thing that I that I kept without losing it.
Monte:	So, what did the doctors say about you playing drums again?

José explained that he has been unable to obtain disability benefits because he had not found a doctor to verify his condition. He revealed that his wife, who was supposed to help manage his care during his aneurysm recovery, neglected her responsibilities because she was having an affair. As a result of her neglect, it took him considerable time to regain his ability to speak clearly and articulate these events. José then revealed that his granddaughter Eve, whom he thought of like a daughter, discovered his wife's affair through social media. She showed José on his phone, demonstrating the technological skills that José lacked with modern phones. Despite being devastated by this discovery, José maintained a strong facade when Eve told him and assured her that he was okay while internally, he was heartbroken. His discovery of his wife's affair explained why she had been neglectful during his recovery from the aneurysm, which he managed largely on his own through faith, without professional medical support that they could not afford.

Strengths-Based Suicide Assessment

At this point, the strength of the therapeutic alliance is strong. José has been open about his struggles with his family and his health and was now ready to tell me about the crisis of faith that he had reached after he left the hospital. José responded with a number lower than 3 when asked how worried he was that he or someone close to him was in danger of hurting themselves, so I had not inquired about risk earlier in the session:

Monte: How were you able to overcome all of those setbacks?

José: Faith. As soon as I got out of the hospital, I started going to church. I'm glad because, you know. If it wasn't for God, for faith, I wouldn't be here talking to you right now. I was so suicidal.

Monte: Really?

José: I thought of ways how to do it. I said, "Let me just, you know what, I'll walk in front of a bus. And it'll, whoa, take me out." I, but with my luck, (laughs and gestures to the unaffected side of his body)-

Monte: You'd be paralyzed on the other side?

José: [Laughing and leaning forward] Thank you!

Monte: Right?

José: Yeah. (laughs). So, I felt out..., I go, "Man, I'm screwed." (laughs).

Monte: By then you could walk well enough to get in front of the bus?

José: (laughs). Yeah. I'm like, "I'll just take that leap of faith." I go, "But with my luck, I'm gonna be paraplegic." (laughs). I say, "No, that ain't gonna work."

Monte: OK, did you have a plan B if the bus didn't work out?

José: Oh, well, the other thing was to get in my daughter's [Eve's mother] truck and siphon the hose, and put in the window from the exhaust pipe of the truck. And carbon monoxide, and I'd go to sleep.

Monte: Ah, okay. Yeah.

José: But then I said, "Man, I don't want to do that to Eve." What if she's the that finds me? And then, she's got that guilt. I can't do that to her. So, all these things are going through my head.

Monte: Did you have a plan C?

José: Oh, the other plan was a train.

Monte: Oh?

José: Falling in front of the train, and, whew- [pantomimes cutting his throat with his hand]... decapitate me.

Monte: Mm-hmm.

José: Uh, every time I did it, I swear to God, I did that three times. The train wouldn't pass by. (laughs).

Monte: Oh, really? You were actually standing there waiting on the tracks?

José: Oh man, I was just waiting. It was 100 degrees. I'm dying out there, the heat.

Monte: Well, that was the point, right?

José: (laughs). But I wanted to go fast.

So, at this point, I have cataloged his three previous attempts. Clearly, he had the means and intent in the past but did not succeed. His concern about his granddaughter was a robust inhibiting factor. There still might be a plan D, so I wanted to assess the current threat:

Monte: So, how close are you to thinking about doing that now?

José: I won't do it. You know why? Something happened. Something happened.

Monte: What happened, José?

José: I took, uh, I took over 40 pills. Muscle relaxers. I had them in my bag. I was like, "Why don't I just do that? That way when the train comes, I'll be easier. I'll be whatever..."

Monte: Uh-huh. You'll be unconscious?

José: Yeah. Yeah. So, I took them. Nothing happened. I waited, nothing happened, nothing happened, nothing happened. That whole day. The stupid train didn't pass by. So, you know, uh-

Monte: And you'd taken 40 muscle relaxers? Man, you're some strong character to be able to take...

José: Well, check this out. I take the muscle relaxers. I felt so bad, that's why I'll never do this again. Like I said, I'm letting it all out. I'm not suicidal. And I won't do it again. Because whatever happened, there is a God, because, that night...Okay, I took the 40 pills. Nothing was happening. Three hours go by. I'm dying out there in the heat. Nothing's happening, nothing's happening, nothing's... I'm not feeling nothing. So, I catch the bus to my daughter's. She says, "Dad, you could stay here. Dad, stay here." And I'm like, eh, whatever, you know. I'm just... I'm a wreck. I said, "No, just, maybe I'll sleep it off and I'll never wake up." I wasn't supposed to wake up.I wake up in the middle of the night. I had to go to the bathroom. I don't know how I made it. The bathroom was... I- I guess maybe five feet away. I had to crawl to the bathroom. They were kicking in.

Monte: Oh?

José: Oh, man, I was... call it scared straight, I don't know, but, that night I made a deal with God. I said, "Okay, if I wake up in the morning. I'll never do this again. I swear, God. I promise You, Jesus Christ. So, help me, I'll never do this again." I woke up, Monte, like nothing. I wasn't dizzy. I woke up like nothing had happened.

Monte: So, God touched you there?

José: In more ways than one. Because, okay, I had lost faith. All right. At that point, I had lost faith. Because you're not supposed to do that. But that day right there, He kicked me in the ass. He said, "You belong to Me." Uh, I don't care what I go through from here on-... I don't care what I go through. I'll never do it again.

Monte: That's an inspiring story.

José: It's the reason that I cry over it, because it- it's the embarrassing. And- and, uh, I feel- I feel a lot of, uh, gratitude. You know? How could I just think of myself when there's people out there that are going through worse?

Monte: Most- some people would say that you've been through the worst.

José: I've been through some shit, Monte, but, you know, I go to AA meetings. And, you know, when you hear everybody's stories they had, it's like, selfish. How could I be so selfish? But I can't talk there like I'm talking to you right now? I can't do that. I just feel better, I feel good talking to you. Thank you.

Monte: Okay.

José: I feel I feel real good. I feel real good. Man. I got too much on my bucket list that I still want to take care of, you know?

Monte: You know José, it sounds to me like you've come back from death two or three times in your life.

José: You read my mind.

Monte: You know?

José: You read my mind!!

Monte: Wow. You came back from the aneurysm. You came back from the - the train tracks. What else?

José: A lot.

Monte: You keep bouncing back.

José: I keep bouncing back. And you know what's crazy? I've seen a lot of death. I've seen a lot of death. Uh, I was in- I was in- in car accidents, where I saw the people on the other side perish. I- I've- I've taken courses in CPR, you know, to try to help people. In- in- in case, uh, something was to happen. Which, I don't know man, I- know- I know I'm not ready to go. I know I'm okay.

Monte: Sounds like when God signed you up to be on His team, He had some plans for you.

José: Yeah.

Monte: You know?

José: Yes.

Monte: So, what do you- what do you think?

José: I think you're right. I think you're absolutely right. I just, uh, man, Orlando told me this- this was gonna be just like this, man. And I really appreciate you for just -to hear me out. I really appreciate you.

The significant points of suicide assessment and safety planning occurred in this session. The careful reader will have spotted them. Commonly, suicide assessment involves assessing the presence of suicidal thoughts, history of previous attempts, specific plans, access to lethal means, absence of protective factors, and mental health problems. All of these were evaluated in the interview, and I thought they did not rise to the level of imminent danger for José:

Monte: Sounds like that you haven't had lately a lot of folks to talk with.

José: No.

Monte: Um, you have your friend, from Guadalupe Lumber. Tell me his name again.

José: Orlando. But I don't really talk to him. Yeah, you know, and we all got problems.

José: Yeah, we all got problems, you know, but, uh, my problem is financial. When you take away a man's ability to be a man financially. I mean, I had my own place, when people needed a place to stay. I had the place. I say, "Hey, there's a three-bedroom house." I live by myself. I had it going on. I was the go-to guy. Yeah. I had a good stable job. Sure, I worked from paycheck to paycheck, but I still had it going on. My bills were paid. I had vehicles. But, man, I lost it all.

By this point in the interview, I thought we had sufficient resources and strengths to begin building a plan with José. So, I returned to a variation of a question that I had asked earlier about what he wanted to have better in his life:

Monte: I'm wondering, what do you think tonight or tomorrow, when you get home, when you're thinking about the talk that we've had today, what are you thinking that you might be doing differently or thinking about differently?

José: Trust. Trusting the doctors more. Because before I didn't trust doctors.

Monte: Sounds like they haven't done a lot to earn your trust.

José: Hmm. Well, they have now. You know, God puts people in our path for a reason. But it's up to us, you know? He gives us this [pointed to his head] He gives us a brain. It's up to us, how we use it. You know? Have you heard that joke?

José told me the old story about the man stranded on the roof of his house surrounded by rising flood waters. He declined the offer of assistance from a rescue crew in a rowboat, a large motorboat, and finally, a helicopter. Each time, the man assured the rescuers that "God has my back." The man eventually drowned. When he reached heaven, he asked God, "Why didn't you save me?" God replied, "I sent you a canoe, a motorboat, and a helicopter. What more did you want?"

José: You know what, I'll tell you what, Monte. Uh, God hasn't taken my humor.
Monte: I'm really impressed. Because you've been through so much that I imagine if you didn't have a sense of humor, you would be screwed up.
José: I give that to the church.
Monte: So because of coming here and some thinking that you've been doing, maybe you're going to trust doctors more so.
José: Yeah. Definitely.
Monte: What- what are you going to do with that trust now?
José: Uh. I'm gonna definitely, uh, I tell you what, man. Uh, I see my purpose. I see my purpose. Okay. Just the way people are helping me, I want to help. I'm gonna- there was a movie where if I do my good deed, maybe that person will do his good deed.
Monte: *Pay it Forward*?
José: That's what I'm gonna do.
Monte: Okay. So, do you have in mind what the first step's gonna be?
José: Hit the hospitals. Maybe, uh, a get a dog. A puppy. And, you know, a lot of people, when I was at hospital, I was the youngest one there. But there was a lot of elderly people that they didn't have anybody. They didn't have anybody to go see them. They didn't have anybody just to talk to.

José told me that when he was in the hospital, he was impatient to recover, disagreeable with the staff, and eager to recover fully, go back to work, and start playing his drums again. He and many of the other patients were also very lonely and had few visitors. He had the plan to go visit patients in rehabilitation hospitals with a dog to cheer them up:

José: Four years later, I didn't think I'd be here. Talking to you, telling you that this was tough. Man, crazy. Just crazy.

Monte: I really admire how hard you've worked these last four years to get your life back on track.

José: And, Monte, I appreciate what you're telling me, man. Why didn't my old lady tell me that. You know, for what I've gone through. If you would have gone to my house before, it looked like a golf course. Wouldn't just sit there and watch TV all day and be a couch potato. I have to do something. So, the yard looked like a golf course.

José revealed that his former wife was 10 years older than him and would tell her relatives that she had married a young man to care for her. She resented him after he became disabled because she had to go back to work to support them both. She was not supportive and eventually was unfaithful to him. When Eve showed him that his wife was having an affair, he confronted her. She denied it, claiming that José's aneurysm had affected his "sanity":

José: Telling me that I was crazy, that I was imagining these things, when Eve's telling me.

Monte: You might have had a brain aneurysm, but you didn't get stupid. (laughs).

José: Exactly. Hey, I was born, but I wasn't born yesterday. So, but the good thing is, through all this, Monte, I tell you, God works in great, great ways.

Monte: If God has a football team; it sounds like He drafted you to be on His team. And He made a good draft pick.

Check-in Prelude to Closing Act II

Ordinarily, I begin to bring the curtain down on ACT II by asking two questions. The first is some variation on "José, what has been helpful for you so far in this session today?" Clients often respond with things that made the session meaningful, such as "I felt heard and listened to." I then follow up with a second question, "Great! And because you felt heard and listened to, what are you going to be able to do when you leave here today? Maybe even this afternoon?" The client's answer often begins a plan to reinforce at the end of Act III. As you will see, José was way ahead of me:

Monte: We're getting kinda toward the end of the time that we have. And usually, what's helpful for me is to go talk to my team who's been listening to be sure I have- have covered everything that we probably need to talk about. And see what kinds of ideas they have and kind of what they think. I'm not going anywhere. I want you to stay right here.

José:	I understand. I just want to thank you. For hearing me out, because, you know what? Feels good. I feel good. And so, when I leave today...I'm gonna leave with a positive attitude.
Monte:	So, what's the first thing you're gonna do when you get home as a result of that positive attitude?
José:	I'm gonna call Orlando. (laughs).
José:	But, you know what? Uh, I'm headed that way. I'm probably gonna stop by 'cause that's my old job. And to me, those people are family. You know when you've been somewhere, employed at a place so long, after a while you meet some great people when you consider family after a while. And Orlando, he's just, he's a great friend. And I really appreciate the advice he gave me. I'm gonna look at it as a pay it forward. I'm looking at everything as progression and going forward with my life. I'm not going backwards.
Monte:	No, that's clear.
José:	And what I was gonna say, real quick, before we go, before we end this, that-uh, uh, that thing with my marriage and everything, it was a blessing. What she did, what she did to me, the hurt that she caused, she did me a favor. Because I know, I know that there's somebody out there that's better for me. That's gonna take good care of me. But, in the process, what doesn't kill will make you stronger.
Monte:	You know, a very famous person said that. Yep. Yeah, he was a German philosopher. I think his name was Nietzsche.
José:	And you know it is so true.
Monte:	Well, listen, I'm coming back in just a few minutes after we are done consulting together.

Act 3: The Closing

Monte:	Okay. Well, I have to tell you that, um-
José:	I'm pretty screwed up, right?
Monte:	Yeah, yeah. You're probably the most screwed up guy I've seen today.
José:	(laughs).
Monte:	But you're the only one I've seen today.
José:	(laughs).
Monte:	Well, José, you know, if a guy had been through what you had been through and wasn't screwed up, I'd really be surprised.
José:	Thank you.
Monte:	But what does surprise me is you've been through what you've been through and you're not screwed up.

José:	It's normal, right? It's, I mean, for a guy who's gone through what I've gone through, that's what I was trying to tell her-
Monte:	Yeah.
José:	...that she's- she's... she's ghetto. She's heartless. She's just heartless. So-
Monte:	Well, you're not the heartless one though.
José:	Yeah.
Monte:	Yeah, I mean, you're a guy with a- with a huge heart.
José:	I try to be.
Monte:	Yeah. Yeah, my team was saying that they are blown away by what a strong man you are. How you've been able to keep coming back and coming back and coming back.
José:	But-
Monte:	And, lots of men who've been through the losses that you've had...
José:	I'm just...
Monte:	Your sister...
José:	...used to bad news. I'm used to bad news. Damn, when is it gonna stop being so bad? When is it gonna start being good news? I mean-
Monte:	It sounds like you've got a plan-
José:	Yes.
Monte:	...to start turning some things into good news.
José:	Yeah. I do have a plan. A grand plan.
Monte:	Yeah. And- and we all admire how strong-
José:	Thank you.
Monte:	...you have been. And you- you know, and I know, that it's hard for men to kind of talk about these sorts of things.
José:	It's taken me a whole year.
Monte:	...it's taken you at least a year. Yeah. You've been-
José:	I've been told about this place. And Orlando's been on my butt. He goes, "José." You know what that dude, Monte? When he told me he goes, "José, I- I- I had to take, uh, marriage therapy." And I looked at him and that's what did it. That's what- that's what did it. That's what opened the door. I said, "Okay."
Monte:	So, when you talk to Orlando later today, what are you gonna tell him was helpful about being here today?
José:	I'm gonna hug him.
Monte:	Okay.
José:	I'm gonna tell him thank you, that he's a good friend. Good, loyal friend. You know, in this world, if you have one friend, you're very lucky.

Monte:	Yep.
José:	But if you got two, man!
Monte:	(laughs).
José:	You're damn lucky. (laughs). Well, let me tell you, Monte, what you do. If nobody ever tells you, I'm gonna tell you. Thi- what you do, right now, you may not think it's a lot, but it is.
Monte:	Well, I appreciate that.
José:	All right? So- so, by the end of the day, when you go home… give yourself a pat on the back, man. Because, let me tell you, it's hard do what you do. I- I- I- I couldn't do what you do.
Monte:	Man.
José:	I'm gonna tell you right now, I'm a selfish fucker when it comes to certain things. And I am a little selfish.
Monte:	Are you?
José:	I'm trying to… yeah, I think I am.
Monte:	You know, well, I can't take all the credit. I've got a team that's really helpful here too.
José:	Cool. Good. Thanks to the team.
Monte:	Yeah.
José:	I know what it is to be a team. There is no- there is no I in team.
Monte:	(laughs). That's true. Well, listen, José, I'm gonna have to turn you loose. Um-
José:	Let me tell you, man, thank you for your time.
Monte:	Well, anytime you want to come back, you can come in like you did today. You can just walk in without an appointment.
José:	Thank you bud. Thank you bud.
Monte:	Or you can call, uh, let's see, I think we give you a copy of this and the phone numbers on here. If- if something happens… outside of business hours, there's, uh, an emergency number that you can call there.
José:	I- I think I'm headed in the right direction.
Monte:	I think you are too. Maybe… maybe you'll come back in a few weeks and just let us know how you're doing.
José:	You know what? Monte, will you be here so I can talk to you? Because you will be the person I would want to talk to. I- I don't want to talk to anybody else because I feel like- like, uh, we broke some ground. A- a- and-
Monte:	Well, it was everybody on my team… has heard your story. So, anybody on my team would be familiar with what's going on with you.
José:	All right. I understand that.
Monte:	Okay, so, if I'm available, I'd be happy to talk with you. We're like a medical clinic you take who's available.

José: Monte, again, thank you for your time, man.
Monte: All right. You be careful on that bike.
José: Thank you. I will. I will. Thank you.

José never returned to the CCS, but I never forgot him. I frequently used this session as an example of doing a strengths-based interview when it would have been easy to overlook Jose's strengths and focus on his sadness, loneliness, and life-threatening history. A couple of years after this session, I received some informal follow-up about Jose. At a professional meeting, one of our former doctoral students approached me, saying, "I have some information about your former client, José." I just smiled and nodded and tried not to compromise my promise to José to keep our meeting private. She went on, "My husband, Orlando, worked with José. He referred José to the CCS." I just smiled and nodded:

> Orlando came home from work the day Jose met with you. I know it was you because José told Orlando he had talked to 'that dude, Monte' at the CCS. Orlando told me it had been a long time since he had seen José as animated. He seemed to be getting back to his old self. The two walked around the workplace, José greeted some of his former colleagues.

"She went on to say that José had been regularly coming by and having coffee with the crew and telling them stories about how people reacted to the little dog he takes to a couple of rehab centers here in town." I smiled, thanked her for the information, and asked her to thank Orlando for telling her about José's progress. I winked and added, "Tell Orlando to tell José, 'That dude, Monte' said hello."

Trauma

The best practices for working with sexual assault survivors, particularly from a trauma-informed care perspective, have been extensively discussed in recent empirical studies and literature reviews (Chalmers et al., 2022; SAMSA, 2014). Trauma-informed care (TIC) emphasizes understanding, recognizing, and responding to the effects of all types of traumas. It aims to avoid re-traumatization while promoting a pathway for healing. Creating an empathetic and validating environment is crucial for survivors of sexual assault. Practitioners should respond with empathy, validation, and respect when survivors disclose their experiences. This involves offering support, resources, and referrals to services that can address the survivor's immediate and long-term needs while maintaining confidentiality and respecting the survivor's autonomy. Trauma-informed care advocates for a strengths-based approach that highlights survivors' resilience, coping mechanisms, and personal strengths to boost confidence and foster empowerment that aids survivors' recovery. Single-session therapists work collaboratively with clients to establish achievable personal growth and development objectives. This collaboration and negotiation of workable goals helps the client regain a sense of self-agency and enhances their engagement and commitment to the healing process. Ensuring easy, open access to care is vital. It is helpful for these clients to have easy access to therapy without navigating a maze of intake procedures, forms, waitlists, and inconvenient appointments.

The following case example illustrates how the principles of trauma-informed care were implemented in an OA/SST. The transcript has been modified for simplicity of presentation. For instance, I combined the two Latina therapists into one to make the dialogue simpler to follow.[2] I will refer to the therapist as Alyvia. Susan (a pseudonym), a Latina in her early 40s, came to the CCS during the walk-in hours. She had been attacked and raped in her home by a man who had been working as a contractor.

Act I: Emphasis on Strengths, Engendering Hope, and Expectations of Change

History of Previous Therapy

Susan told us that following the attack, she had received help from a therapist several months earlier at an agency that provided free services for victims of such attacks, but the funding had run out after several visits. She told the therapist that the services had been helpful, but the therapist's approach had been long-term, and when the grant funding ran out, Susan had no other resources to tap into:

Joining

Susan: That's where the assault in April happened, and so, I honestly don't even know. I'm freaking out. Like, nothing feels right. I started working again this month, and it's not the same, and it's actually kind of depleting me a lot. And I had been making progress, so I'm like, okay, I'm scared. That's why I need to talk to someone, because I don't know what's next.

Alyvia: You were making progress?

Susan: I was, but it just seems to kind of have regressed. But I also did kind of throw myself into work. So, I wasn't putting myself first again. So obviously that's the thing.

In the opening moments of the session, Susan alludes to pre-session improvement—improvement following the assault several months earlier and the present. She also clarifies that she is looking for help finding out what's next. The therapist followed up on her comment about working and found she had had a successful career as a restaurateur over the last few years. The therapist explored Susan's background further, looking for additional resources and strengths in Susan's past. Therapist did not respond to the "regressed" comment but instead chose to continue asking about Susan's background. This gave Susan an opportunity to modestly describe her educational history:

Alyvia: And where did you go to school?
Susan: Umm first bachelor's was at [prestigious university] in New York City, and then I did a few certifications and stuff in Europe, and then I was at [another prestigious university], and then another one, and then I got a Fulbright and worked down in Peru for a while.
Alyvia: You've been having all this experience with education all over the world.

Here, the therapist underscores Susan's expertise, and it leads to her elaborating on her interests and motivations:

Susan: I love cultures and traveling and learning and everything. It's just, I guess that frustrates me even more because I know what I've accomplished and what I've done, and now I can barely leave my bedroom because I'm so freaked out all the time. So, yeah. It's nice to remember, though, that I did live.

Susan goes on to describe why she walked in the clinic that day. She paints a vivid picture of the circumstances that were the final straw, so to speak, that led her to walk in that morning:

Susan: But this week, I'm accepting and realizing that I don't feel happy there. I don't feel comfortable. I'm constantly, I lock... It's like a fortress. Cameras everywhere, lock everything, and every single noise, I'm still jumping up.
Alyvia: That makes sense. You want to make sure that your home, where you lay your head down at night, and feel safe.

The therapist agrees with Susan's wisdom in looking to feel safe and acknowledging the effect of the terrible experience she had undergone:

Susan: Yeah, that was my thing. I wanted to go back and stay there, and I didn't want that to be taken from me. And it's really hard for me to accept and admit that I can't function at my peak, or my potential there and it's a sacrifice that I have to make and a compromise. I'm pretty pissed off about it.

Act 2: Identifying Solvable Problems, Setting Achievable Goals

Susan's description of her desire to be back to functioning at a peak provides a glimpse into what her preferred future for herself might be. It opens the door for the therapist to ask about that future. Twelve minutes into the session, she asks for Susan's goals for the session using Susan's image of "replenishment." Note that the time frame for this mini-goal is in the immediate future:

Alyvia: I think you have every right to be pissed off. And thank you, too, for sharing your previous experience of counseling. If we were to replenish you today, and you get in the car, and you're driving back home and...You know, just kind of just reflecting on the conversation we're having...What would you be doing afterwards? Maybe in this... Later today, maybe even tomorrow when you wake up that would tell you that today was a good use of your time?

Susan: I could breathe. And I could not have to every couple of hours, I realize how tense I am. And I want some sort of relief not to have to focus on just being still and being okay with just being still. Because I... It's like, crazy in my head constantly. And I'm tired. I just want just even just like a second of just like, just forget everything, you know? And I can't

Alyvia: Well, if you woke up in the morning, and you open your eyes and look around the room. And you had forgotten everything, what would be different? What would be the first thing to tell you that you weren't thinking about what had happened in April?

Susan: I would actually get up and not try and hear every noise, and think what's on the other side of the door? Or check... My routine - as I wake up and immediately check all my cameras and just... I don't want to live like, I don't feel like being undead is alive, and I miss being alive.

Now, the therapist begins to flesh out what Susan would be doing if she were to start to make the changes she is longing for.

Alyvia: What else has been helpful for you to push through and keep going? I think that's what, 7 months or so.

Susan: I finally stopped counting the days. So that's, I guess, a good sign. It was like every single day I knew how many days to the minute.

Alyvia: About how long ago was that when you stopped counting the days?

Susan: I don't even know anymore. I guess it's been probably about a month, maybe. I inundated myself with... herbal teas. I got really into ritual, like, teas, and making sure that I had a morning tea, and what it was going to help, because I don't like medications. I don't like chemicals. Like what I eat, you know, and my food journey and all of that stuff. And I'm like, okay. So, I grow a lot of stuff.

Susan turns to a new description of her preferred self.

Susan: I forced myself to make sure I had my hands in dirt at least once a day. Or, doing something with my plants or my garden, my yard. And, like, I don't have that routine anymore. And I think that's what's really messing me up. Because forcing myself to work, and then that's not bringing me... It's not fruitful. So, I'm neglecting all of that.

Susan elaborated on what used to give her peace:

Susan: But those little rituals like DIY, face masks, hair masks, just like those little self-care things soaking my feet. Just very, very simple. And now I'm not doing anything. And it's been pretty detrimental. But, yeah, just small daily rituals that a lot of people maybe take for granted. That was really getting me through. And now it's like, I don't have time or I don't have the energy, the motivation. I had no motivation. That's the word. So...

The therapist seized the opportunity to ask about exceptions to Susan's lack of motivation, which led Susan to providing more examples of how she is already making small improvements:

Alyvia: And when's the last time you've, you know, been outside putting your hands in dirt or doing a DIY face mask?

Susan: I haven't done a mask for hair. And we could tell probably like 2 months, 3 months. Yesterday, I forced myself I threw the ball 3 times for my dog. That was all I could take.

Alyvia: How were you able to get yourself to do that?

Susan: I got home from work, and it's just that guilt of knowing that he's just been there and having to, you know, see me like that. So, it was just, like, for him. I needed to, I forced myself. So, before I even went inside the house, I just threw it a couple of times. And then I felt, like, super exposed. And vulnerable. And freaked out. And went back in… And went inside.

Now, despite minimizing the previous day's success, she goes on to describe another recent example of self-care.

Susan: And I did make myself a tea this morning. That felt nice. That was, like, sounds so lame right? But it felt so, like, because 'cause it forced me to wash some dishes. And it forced me to kind of clear my counter space. And for me, cleanliness and everything makes me feel so good. I think that, too, has just been weighing on me, and I just see, like, dust and things just collecting, and I'm by myself always. So, it's not like I can ask anyone. It's sheer willpower and, like, forcing myself.

The therapist followed Susan's lead and asked her to imagine continuing to behave counter to the ways that she dislikes:

Alyvia: With it being so nice today, what could be something you might do?

Susan: I wish I would go ride my bike, but that requires me to get a new tube, and so I don't really want to…

Alyvia: Yeah, that might be too much for today, you've already done so much.

Susan: My to-do list has not changed. Like, it just… I can't knock anything off my to-do list. And it's like, I want to do this and that, And then it's like I get all overwhelmed, and where do I start? And then I'll start something and not finish it, and I'll start something else, not finish it. Susan: And then it adds, like, five more things because I started this, now I have to do that. I would probably like to just, like, clean my bedroom. Or maybe even just, like, clean my kitchen and prepare something to eat. That would be amazing.

Susan has arrived at setting her own achievable, small goal here. And goes on to express her current discouragement by saying that she felt that she was not living her life:

Susan: I don't recognize myself, and that's scary as hell.

Alyvia: Sounds like you don't know this Susan.

Susan:	Yeah, I used to be a real Bad Ass! (laughs).
Alyvia:	Really??
Susan:	Yeah, I got desperate yesterday for the first time. Like I said, I hadn't had any of those kind of really intrusive thoughts. And yesterday it did. And I was like, "Holy shit. I'm..." I'm slipping into somewhere where I don't want to be and where I can rationally, like, you know, remove myself and look and observe and be like, not healthy.
Susan:	If it was someone else, I would so be like, "Go get help." So that's what... I'm trying to flip that lens to myself now.
Alyvia:	For yourself, yeah.
Susan:	And it's not extreme. It's not, like, dire, but it's enough to be, "to know, I need to..."
Alyvia:	Putting it into action.
Susan:	Yeah. I need to do something now before it does get extreme, which I allow things to get. So, yeah.
Alyvia:	It's really wise to know that about yourself. You're so attuned. Knowing what you need to get, even when it's really hard.
Susan:	It sucks because I'd rather be a little bit more ignorant, like. No, just kidding. I rather not feel or see certain things. But it's like "Damn it!"
Alyvia:	Like ignorance is bliss?
Susan:	Yes! Yes! I always say that. Oh, I'm so stupid. No, I'm just kidding. That sounds bad, but you know.
Alyvia:	I'm just thinking right now about when you leave here today and maybe something that you might be able to do differently. So small. And I don't want us to have you go and fix your bike. That's too much. But maybe something different, or maybe just...
Susan:	I already feel like I can breathe. By the way, I really appreciate y'all.
Alyvia:	How were you able to tell that you feel like you could breathe right now?
Susan:	Ummm, I literally just took a deep breath.
Alyvia:	I heard it. It sounded nice. It made me want to take a deep breath.
Susan:	It made me feel... I don't know. That was like a genuine laugh, and that was genuine joking. But like... You know that like sisterhood. But it just felt... I feel safe, and I really appreciate ya'll making me feel that. I never, ever feel safe anymore. I hate-- Sorry.
Alyvia:	I'm wondering, how do you know when you're safe? Like, what does that feel like? How are you able to pinpoint "this is safety?"

Susan:	There's like a warmth.
Alyvia:	Mmm.
Susan:	Just like umm… Like… Like a warmth inside, like, you know like when you're in your grandparents' house or when your mom's… when she's cooking. Or when you're watching the sunrise. And it's just like that quiet peace. And… I value those moments so much, and that's what I miss the most. It's like being able to find that at any time. Being able to tap into that anytime and not have to purposely mindfully reach that point. Like, I do this exercise to allow myself to sleep of, like, thinking of. Every single muscle and relaxing it, you know? Because I'm so tense, so wound up. And literally, like, I've never played stupid games on phones. Like, I now do that just to, like just to stop all the thoughts. And so, yeah, when I can breathe. And then I remember to breathe, because it's like short breaths all the time, I guess, because then when I do, I'm like, "Oh, whoa." Like today the doctor, when they make you, they do the stethoscope "Whoa, I haven't breathed that deep in I don't know how long!" And she's like, "that's not good." So, yeah.
Alyvia:	You can take some deep breaths in here?

The supervisor called in to suggest the consultation break because, at this point in Act II, the therapist had reached a goal – returning to the earlier "Bad Ass" Susan by implementing a plan to return to her routines and make a list to keep herself on track:

Alyvia:	They suggested that now might be a good time to take a break. They said that they could tell how much we were just, like, you know, creating and building this list and how we're setting up that game plan.
Susan:	Yeah. Okay. Sure.
Alyvia:	Well, and before I do that, Susan, I wanted to know: What has been most helpful about talking to us today?
Susan:	Honestly, I feel like no judgment. And I feel like y'all get it. Like… And you're not asking, like ridiculously remedial questions, or like stupid things, or like convoluted…I don't know. I struggle finding therapists and counselors. Because I'm like, "Are you serious? Did you really just pull that out of a textbook, right now?" You're actually following me, and you're letting me go in my direction. But also guiding it, and I don't know, it works. Thank you!
Alyvia:	Sometimes, I explain that trying to find a therapist is trying to find that good fitting shoe. You know, some shoes - they look good, but they just might not be as comfortable. I am glad we

were a good fit to help you today and got that idea started of a
game plan - pen to paper.

Susan: Yeah, I guess I wrote very little bit on that little questionnaire.
I feel like you all actually really made it that focus of... Okay,
"what do we do to replenish and how to get a productive day?"
So, I appreciate, I feel listened to, and I feel gotten, so that for
sure. Thank you.

Alyvia: And now that you got that feeling of being understood and
"You get it." What will you be able to do with that later?
Maybe later today?

Susan: Function. And know that there's like a light. There's, there's...
Things can get better, and things will. I just have to show up.
And it was hard to show up today, and I did.

Alyvia: You did it, yeah. And you showed up twice. Right? We were on
a different team this morning. Yeah...So showing up twice and
going to see your mom.

Susan: Yeah. And it hasn't been bad. You know? And it's like, okay,
I can push through. And I think things will get better. Now I
have faith again that things will get better, because I was just in
this numb mode for the past several months of like, is this life
now? "Is it always going to be like this?" I was already kind of
accepting it. But then yesterday, I just got so disgusted with the
thoughts that I was having that I refused to give up.

Alyvia: What a beautiful thing to have. Yeah, we'll go step out for a little bit just to meet with the team and bring back some of their
feedback.

Susan: Cool.

Act III: The Closing

The team began reflecting on the many resources and strengths that Susan
had revealed during the interview. They produced a lengthy list for the
therapist to convey to Susan. They discussed how to reinforce her plan to
make a list of things to keep her focused on staying busy. As you will see,
the therapist's intended agenda for the closing was derailed by Susan, who
provided her own closing. And you will see, the commendations were the
most critical part of the closing in this case. There was no need to reinforce
the plan, because Susan articulated it so clearly before and after the break.
Susan was satisfied with the help she had received in the brief single session
opportunity that she had taken:

Alyvia: Hi Susan, I'm back. I met with our team, and they just had
so many really great things to say that they noticed in our

	conversation. So, would it be okay to share a few of those things with you?

Susan: For sure. I'm curious.

Alyvia: One of the things that really stuck out to me… one of the people on the team, you know, they said the word that came to their mind was "powerhouse." Susan is such a powerhouse. So impressive. And someone threw in, "an unstoppable powerhouse." They were just so impressed with how much you're a go getter. You own all these businesses, and you know what you need and how to get it. And even today was a perfect example of that. Of recognizing, you know, that there's some changes that you wanted to make, or you're ready for that. And you came in here, walked in, nothing can stop you.

Alyvia: Right, right. Yeah.

Susan: Yeah, that's cool. That's really cool.

Alyvia: And the team also commented, just seeing where you are today, considering what happened 7 months ago with the attack. they were just like, blown away. WOW, I don't know if many other people would be in the same position of almost on this path of just getting this old Susan back And they said, "She might disagree with that. She might disagree with that, and that's okay." But they were like, many people just wouldn't be where you are today after experiencing what you did. Only 7 months ago, too.

Next, we see that Susan agreed with this assessment of her capacity to bounce back quickly and elaborated on it and provided more examples. She also repeated her pre-session improvement example of how she had quit counting the days that had passed since the assault had occurred:

Susan: Yeah, that actually is something like when you asked about my mom, my mom said that, like, even a month after I was already trying to just be normal again. She's like, "Take it easy, relax." So that, that kind of resonates with me. I keep trying to remind myself, too that, like ok, I think that's why I stopped counting the days, because it felt, like so long, and I was almost putting this pressure on myself. Like, I should already be normal again, or I should already have fixed this And, like, because I am so solution based. It's, like, hard for me to accept and realize that there's no, like, permanent solution. I'm just going to have to learn how to navigate. And, like, so… I definitely can see that, and I appreciate that because I do kind of pride myself. Like, I don't want to just slump over and give up. I refuse to. and that was supposed to be like, my parents were like, "Come home now." It was just insane. I was at Battery Park. That's where I was going to college. I just moved there, and they're like, "This is a sign, you just come back home." And I don't know. That's when that kicked in for me. That's when I can literally remember the very first time, like I refused to give power to change my life without me deciding it. And I think that's what this has just really shaken that with me. It was just like, the fuck? Like, I did not choose this. And so now I'm realizing - I appreciate that feedback, because now I'm realizing, too, that I do have the ability to choose going forward, how and what to do. And I had been feeling pretty powerless, and I'm realizing that there is power in that decision making and choices, so I actually really, really appreciate that feedback.

Alyvia: I'm sure they're saying back there like, "Wow, she's even more of a Badass." You know?

Susan: I never knew that anyone else could see that about me or understand that. And, so that's really kind of cool, and I appreciate it.

Alyvia: We only have a couple of minutes left and want to be respectful of your time. We have a survey here like when people might go into your restaurants to rate their meals or rating their experience. This is about how the session went for you. Like I said, I'm sure you have plenty of experience of rating a restaurant. Your feedback is really important to us. Is there anything else that you think that we could have done to make the session even better for you, today?

Susan: I've actually never had a first session where I actually feel like I know what I want to do. And I feel like – I'm literally, I'm, like, shaking. I'm excited, and I can't even. This now is happy tears, but, like, I'm just Wow. I didn't expect didn't know what to expect. You know. It's awful but, "it's free" and, you know, things like that, I don't know. But it, umm, gosh, thank you all for, like, offering this and doing this. Like, I have light at the end of the tunnel, and I was really scared. I'd never feel this excitement. I'm excited now. It's like I feel like I made such a huge breakthrough in a freaking hour. It's insane. I'm pretty surprised and impressed, and I'm just so grateful. I'm excited, and I haven't felt that in a long time.

Alyvia: Beautiful. It might have been, exactly what you needed on the one day you needed it. In our experience, we definitely see that people continue to take the next steps and continue to go forward. So, if you ever do find yourself wanting to come back here, We are here, and just like you did today, you found us,

Susan: you walked in, you might call after taking a couple of days, or weeks, and kind of just enjoying this experience of happiness.

Susan: Yeah, I want to ride this for as long as I can. That's what I tend to do. Who knows what I will tell you another time. No, I'm just kidding. Thank you so much. Really, really, really truly. It's crazy. I'm still kind of flabbergasted at how effective this was. Thank y'all!

How the Principles of TIC were Implemented

Susan's case exemplifies the core aspects of single-session therapy with a survivor of sexual assault and trauma. These shared elements underscore the therapeutic approach, techniques employed, and Susan's experiences during the session. Susan's experience illustrates how a successful single session of therapy can incorporate the guidelines for trauma-informed care through a comprehensive approach that supported Susan's recovery from a sexual assault. Alyvia fostered an *empathetic and validating environment*. She *actively listened* to Susan's concerns, *validated her emotions*, and *provided a safe space* to express herself freely, which Susan said helped her feel understood and supported. Adopting a *strengths-based approach*, Alyvia encouraged Susan to *identify her resilience, coping mechanisms, and personal strengths*, which boosted her confidence and *fostered empowerment*. *Collaborative goal setting* was also evident as Alyvia worked with Susan to establish achievable growth objectives, giving her a *sense of agency and ownership*. *Reflective listening* further deepened the therapeutic alliance, allowing Alyvia to summarize Susan's experiences to ensure understanding and encourage exploration of her emotions and challenges. Therapist also *acknowledged the profound impact* of Susan's expertise, validating her struggles with shock, anger, and loss of joy. Recognition of her self-care practices, like herbal teas, gardening, and DIY projects, underscored her positive coping mechanisms while acknowledging the challenges of maintaining these routines. Finally, Alyvia emphasized that healing is a continuous process, validating Susan's realization that her recovery required ongoing self-awareness and acceptance.

Conclusion

In this chapter, I have offered two examples of how a single-session therapist can effectively manage complex cases, particularly those involving suicide risk and trauma. Our OA/SST work emphasizes that risk assessment should not overshadow the therapeutic alliance. Establishing rapport and addressing clients' immediate concerns should precede formal risk evaluations. José's case demonstrated how SST can effectively address a complex case involving several simultaneous presenting problems, including suicidal ideation. The therapist focused on highlighting the client's strengths, building rapport, and allowing José's narrative to unfold naturally rather than immediately jumping to risk assessment protocols. The case illustrated three fundamental principles in managing risk: First, therapeutic effectiveness stems from genuine engagement rather than rigid adherence to assessment protocols. Second, clients are more likely to disclose risk factors after establishing trust. Third, identifying and amplifying client strengths can help reduce immediate risk and build resilience.

Susan's case demonstrated how single-session therapy can effectively support trauma survivors through a trauma-informed approach that emphasizes strengths, fosters agency, and validates experiences. Through careful attention to Susan's self-identified strengths – her education, entrepreneurial success, and determination – the therapist helped transform her self-perception from feeling "undead" to reconnecting with her identity as a "powerhouse"[1][2]. The session highlighted three fundamental therapeutic principles: creating a safe, empathetic environment for free expression, utilizing a strengths-based approach that builds upon existing coping mechanisms, and implementing collaborative goal-setting to empower actionable recovery steps. Susan's dramatic shift from hypervigilance and isolation to excitement about her future challenged conventional assumptions about trauma treatment, showing that meaningful therapeutic progress can occur within a single-session. This case exemplified how trauma-informed SST can provide immediate, meaningful support while honoring survivors' autonomy and natural capacity for healing.

In conclusion, this chapter challenges the conventional wisdom that complex cases require multiple sessions. It shows how meaningful therapeutic work can happen in a single session when the therapist maintains a strengths-based perspective while remaining attentive to risk factors.

Notes

1 *Home Improvement* an American popular sitcom in the 1990s, starring Tim Allen as Tim "The Toolman" Taylor, centered on a television host and his family.
2 We thank Olivia Hinojosa Galvan and Alyssa Arredondo for permission to share their work.

References

Bobele, M. (1987). Therapeutic interventions in life-threatening situations. *Journal of Marriage and Family Therapy*, *13*(3), 225–239.
Chalmers, K., Dussault, N., & Parameswaran, R. (2022). Encouraging trauma-informed care of sexual assault survivors. *Academic Medicine*, *97*(8), 1103. https://doi.org/10.1097/ACM.0000000000004369

Harris, K. M., & Goh, M. T. (2017). Is suicide assessment harmful to participants? Findings from a randomized controlled trial. *International Journal of Mental Health Nursing, 26*(2), 181–190. https://doi-org.ezproxy.ollusa.edu/10.1111/inm.12223

Milner, A., et al. (2017). "The effectiveness of suicide prevention delivered by GPs: A systematic review and meta-analysis." *Journal of Affective Disorders, 210*, 294–302.

Pisani, A. R., Cross, W. F., & Gould, M. S. (2011). The assessment and management of suicide risk: State of workshop education. *Suicide and Life-Threatening Behavior, 41*(3), 255–276.

Simpson, S. A., Goans, C., Loh, R., Ryall, K., Middleton, M. C. A., & Dalton, A. (2021). Suicidal ideation is insensitive to suicide risk after emergency department discharge: Performance characteristics of the Columbia-Suicide Severity Rating Scale Screener. *Acad Emerg Med, 28*(6), 621–629. https://doi.org/10.1111/acem.14198

Slive, A., & Bobele, M. (2019). Ideas for addressing doubts about walk-in/single-session therapy. *Journal of Systemic Therapies, 38*, 17–30.

Substance Abuse and Mental Health Services Administration (2014). *SAMHSA's concept of trauma and guidance for a trauma-informed approach*. Rockville, MD: Substance Abuse and Mental Health Services Administration.

Zalsman, G., Hawton, K., Wasserman, D., van Heeringen, K., Arensman, E., Sarchiapone, M., Carli, V., Höschl, C., Barzilay, R., Balazs, J., Purebl, G., Kahn, J. P., Sáiz, P. A., Lipsicas, C. B., Bobes, J., Cozman, D., Hegerl, U., & Zohar, J. (2016). Suicide prevention strategies revisited: 10-year systematic review. *The Lancet Psychiatry, 3*(7), 646–659. https://doi.org/10.1016/s2215-0366(16)30030-x

Chapter 5

Implementing Open-Access Therapy in the Province of New Brunswick

Katie Burke and Bernard Goguen

Setting the Stage

If you are reading this book, it is likely that you have some interest in and understanding of single-session therapy (SST) or the concept of open-access services. There are several books and journal articles that describe examples of how these services can be delivered and the benefits they can bring to clients (Slive & Bobele, 2011; Hoyt, 2018; Hoyt & Bobele, 2019; Dryden, 2021). In New Brunswick, Canada, these services are being referred to as One-at-a-Time Therapy (OAAT) and were implemented as part of a large-scale system transformation. This chapter will focus on the change management and the operational processes involved in the implementation of One-at-a-Time Therapy within a broad continuum of addiction and mental health services in this Canadian province.

Like most other jurisdictions, New Brunswick's public Addiction and Mental Health Services were characterized by lengthy wait times and difficulty accessing services when needed. While this can be partly attributed to lack of resources, it was also due to some aspects of the service delivery model. Prior to 2022, individual counseling services were largely based on an ongoing, long-term therapy model with very few, if any, brief and structured interventions.

Prior to implementing OAAT, the typical process and outcome when someone reached out to seek help or was referred for services was as follows: the individual was scheduled for an intake assessment appointment, detailed information was collected, and then they were generally referred for individual counseling and placed on a waiting list. The time spent on waiting lists varied depending on the level of need, but as all clinicians had full caseloads, it was also dependent on another person exiting services for a mental health clinician to become available (Figure 5.1).

In this former service delivery model, everyone who sought help was triaged, assessed, and prioritized based on presenting severity of need and

DOI: 10.4324/9781003351375-5

Client Journey Process Before OAAT

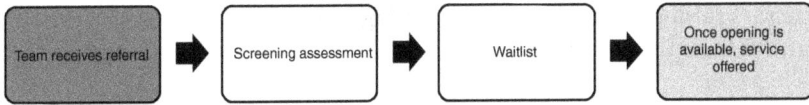

Figure 5.1 Client journey "before" state, depicting standard processes before therapeutic intervention

risk. Most would wait anywhere from several weeks to many months to be assigned a clinician, including those who would have likely found relief through brief therapeutic intervention accessed on an as-needed basis.

The New Brunswick Addiction and Mental Health Services Landscape

New Brunswick is a province on the east coast of Canada with a population of about 825,000. It is largely rural with three larger cities that have populations of slightly over 100,000 each. There are three main partners involved in the public addiction and mental health system in New Brunswick. The Department of Health (DH) is responsible for the overall planning, funding, and monitoring of the addiction and mental health continuum of care, while the two Regional Health Authorities (RHAs), Horizon Health Network and Réseau de Santé Vitalité, have the mandate of delivering Addiction and Mental Health Services.

The province is divided into seven health zones, with one of the two RHAs taking responsibility for delivering services in each zone. Together, the two RHAs employ approximately 1,700 employees in their Addiction and Mental Health Services. Primary service provider employee groups include Nurses, Psychiatrists, Physicians, Psychologists, Social Workers, Occupational Therapists, Licensed Practical Nurses, Nurse Practitioners, Human Service Counsellors, Attendants, Peer Support Specialists, and Recreation Specialists. There are also Directors, Managers, and Administrative Professionals. 19 Community Addiction and Mental Health Centers are located across the health zones to ensure provincial access to services and programs. These Centers offer a wide range of services and programs including assessment, case management, psychoeducation, community outreach, family services, pharmacological treatment, individual therapy and group programs, ongoing recovery support, and various specialized programs for issues such as personality disorders or complex trauma. Services can be brief or more long-term, depending on the needs and engagement levels of the individual, and are identified as being for adults (19 years and above), or children and youth (under 19 years of age). Many private mental health practitioners, NGOs and not for profit agencies also provide various forms of addiction and mental health service delivery, support, and navigation.

The Need for System Transformation

Between 2015 and 2019, Department of Health employees, including one of the authors, conducted three service reviews and consulted key Regional Health Authority partners, various stakeholders, and people with lived experience who were using public Addiction and Mental Health Services. These consultations brought to light key areas of need, including system improvement and modernization and an interconnected continuum of evidence-informed services.

The feedback, observations, and resulting recommendations of these consultations laid the groundwork for the creation of the Department of Health's Inter-Departmental Addiction and Mental Health Action Plan for 2021–2025 (New Brunswick Department of Health, 2021). Five overall goals were defined through the Action Plan: Improve Population Health, Improve Access to Care, Intervene Earlier, Match Individuals to Care, and Reduce Drug-Related Impacts.

To immediately improve access to care, priority was given to implementing One-at-a-Time Therapy in the province's Community Addiction and Mental Health Centers. As a low barrier, open access point of entry, this type of service had been identified as a missing component to the New Brunswick continuum of care. It was expected that OAAT would be an effective means of providing early intervention as well as guided navigation to more specialized or long-term services when needed. With the necessary resources, training, and process changes in place, clients seeking help could be offered a therapy appointment as a first step instead of completing an intake questionnaire and being placed on a waitlist. Clients would be able to return to this service if they felt the need to talk to someone again, and those requiring more specialized or longer-term treatment could be navigated more effectively to other services on the continuum of care.

OAAT in a Stepped Care Continuum

As psychologist Kurt Lewin wrote, "There is nothing so practical as a good theory."[1] New Brunswick's implementation of OAAT is best understood in the context of an overall plan and framework for system transformation and improvement. Based on the work of Dr. Peter Cornish and his creation of Stepped Care 2.0 (Cornish, 2020), the Department of Health, Horizon Health Network, Reseau de Santé Vitalité along with key community partners, stakeholders, and people with lived and living experience started to co-design a Stepped Care continuum for Addiction and Mental Health Services in the province at the time of publishing this book chapter.

While our aim in this chapter is to share our experience with the implementation of open-access OAAT services, a brief description of Stepped Care will provide helpful context and understanding of OAAT's intended place in a client-centered continuum of services. In a Stepped Care system, services populate the continuum in alignment with a variety of step levels based on service intensity and level of client engagement needed. The model includes both formal and informal services, as well as flexible, open-access care options with minimal assessment, such as One-at-a-Time Therapy (Stepped Care Solutions, n.d.; Mental Health Commission of Canada, 2023) (Figure 5.2).

New Brunswick needed system-wide transformation to address increasing demand for services and province-wide barriers to timely access. After considering various systems and frameworks for provincial Addiction and Mental Health Services, the Department of Health identified Stepped Care 2.0 as the client-centric care model that would guide the necessary changes to make care available to all, not just those in crisis or with severe symptoms.

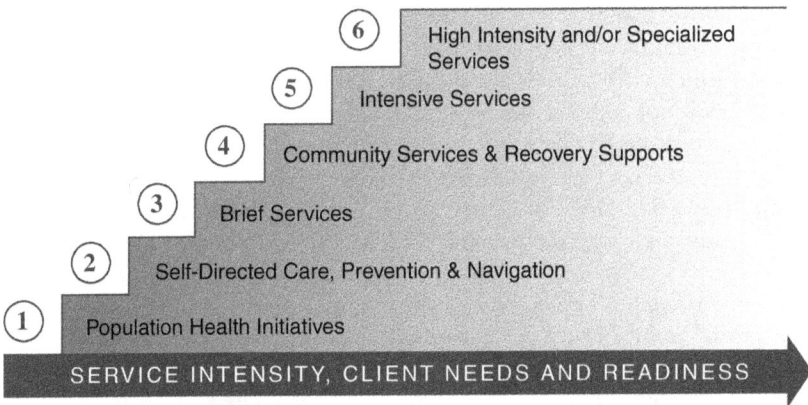

6 High Intensity and/or Specialized Services
5 Intensive Services
4 Community Services & Recovery Supports
3 Brief Services
2 Self-Directed Care, Prevention & Navigation
1 Population Health Initiatives

SERVICE INTENSITY, CLIENT NEEDS AND READINESS

Figure 5.2 Stepped care model example, adapted by the New Brunswick Department of Health

Implementing One-at-a-Time Therapy

By the start of 2021, New Brunswick's Department of Health was ready to establish OAAT as an integral service in the provincial continuum of care. The vision was to drastically reduce wait times and the number of clients on wait lists by removing procedural bottlenecks and making low-barrier, rapid-access mental health support available in every region. To move together as a province, full commitment was needed from all the key stakeholders.

A central tenet of change management is that organizational change comes from individual change (Prosci, n.d.). In *The Gift*, psychologist Edith Eger writes

> We do not change until we're ready... But readiness doesn't come from the outside, and it can't be rushed or forced. You're ready when you're ready, when something inside shifts and you decide, until now I did that. Now I'm going to do something else.
>
> (Eger, 2020)

In other words, readiness to adopt a new clinical mindset and service delivery model couldn't simply be imposed through a top-down directive. Hundreds of employees including Directors, Managers, Clinical Leads, and front-line Clinicians across the province had to feel prepared to shift and decide "Until now I've done that. Now I'm going to do something else."

The challenge was to build shared readiness and capacity for change in seven health regions under two distinct health authorities with different working languages. To be successful, planning had to be responsive to the people whose changed behavior was most needed to make One-at-a-Time Therapy a reality. To help with this, a change management specialist was hired to join a core project team led by the Department of Health Directors of Addiction and Mental Health in Adult and Child & Youth Services, alongside a seasoned portfolio manager and senior health consultants.

To start, the core project team brought together a provincial working group made up of Directors and regional Managers as assigned implementation leads for every Community Addiction and Mental Health Center and both RHAs. In May 2021, the provincial working group for Adult Services formed, and collaborative planning began to implement OAAT as an essential point of access for clinical intervention and system navigation at times of need. Taking a phased approach due to the scale and scope of change in this initiative, Child and Youth teams kicked off under the same project framework nearly one year later, in March of 2022.

Over the next 18 months, provincial working groups and local service teams invested significant time and effort toward integrating OAAT services into all Community Addiction and Mental Health Centers and Child and Youth teams in the seven health zones. This involved learning new clinical and administrative approaches, reviewing and adapting processes, and creating new work aides and guiding documents. The scope of work accomplished by the provincial working groups during the implementation phase included but is by no means limited to:

- Recruiting and hiring dedicated OAAT Leads to provide on-the-ground clinical support and mentorship in all seven health zones.
- Creating an employee training program to develop shared understanding of Stepped Care and One-at-a-Time Therapy principles and applications.
- Developing Administrative Guidelines to establish OAAT service delivery standards and promote a consistent client and care provider experience.
- Participating in process mapping and client journey exercises to help determine how best to integrate OAAT into operations.
- Contacting waitlisted clients to offer appointments and inform them that open access services were now available when and if they should need to talk to someone.
- Educating long-term clients on the availability of a new open-access therapy option, as a potential alternative or additional support to their regular treatment program.
- Taking part in operational risk and readiness assessments.
- Assisting in promotions and stakeholder engagement efforts to help raise awareness among care partners.

The project team applied a change management framework (Association of Change Management Professionals, 2019) to help guide planning in a way that recognized and honored the individual change process as the foundation for collective transformation. As key elements of the strategy:

Vision Alignment was a starting priority, including developing a clear common understanding of project context, objectives, expected benefits, and general timelines. The core team developed a project charter at this stage to clearly outline the scope of the initiative with target outcomes and key performance indicators to help answer the question – *What specifically are we trying to achieve, and how will we know if we've been successful?*

Clear Roles and Responsibilities were established to help set expectations, secure accountability, and provide a structure for important direction, collaboration, support, and flow of information between the provincial working group members and the local teams responsible for implementing and sustaining the new service on the ground.

Risk and Readiness Assessments were done throughout the lifecycle of the project to paint a vivid real-time picture of on-the-ground challenges, strengths and resources that might help or hinder successful adoption and benefits realization. As an example, some identified barriers were unclear direction, misunderstandings, and concerns about the new approach, while notable strengths included early adopters and champions.

Communications and Stakeholder Engagement plans prioritized managers and leaders to ensure they had a good understanding of the changes taking place and were well supported in order to lead these changes within their local teams.

Phased Training was designed to build awareness of the reasons for the initiative and expected benefits, knowledge of One-at-a-Time Therapy principles and their place within a Stepped Care continuum, ability to apply these approaches as a clinician or administrator, and finally, reinforcement practices to promote a culture of ongoing feedback and learning.

Adoption and Resistance Management plans were informed by continual stakeholder assessments that helped identify and find appropriate ways to address the root causes of resistance to adoption.

One helpful approach was leveraging early adopters first—this was done by finding and promoting success stories, supporting and encouraging champions to lead the change, and giving others a chance to learn from examples and proceed when ready. Another was being extremely open to feedback—this meant project leaders setting a tone with collaborators at all levels that their questions, concerns, ideas, and on-the-ground realities were valid and important to the success of the initiative. For the project team, a third helpful piece of adoption and resistance management was mobilizing formal leaders to help remove critical barriers and reduce risks to benefits realization as these were being flagged. For example, securing funding for new dedicated OAAT positions to increase staffing capacity and providing targeted coaching and support to team leaders struggling with implementation were key strategies in resistance management.

Implementation Challenges and Successes

Building a comprehensive Stepped Care continuum has the potential for transformative change that can address persisting issues around access to Addictions and Mental Health Services. It's worth noting that for the first phase of work involving OAAT implementation in New Brunswick, the speed expected for an initiative of its size was very ambitious from the outset. Involved teams were rightly concerned about whether they could be successful in leading and adopting the targeted province-wide changes in the timeline set out.

Even so, the implementation initiative for OAAT did successfully meet timelines and even exceeded target metrics for waitlist reduction. Some

Managers expressed deep gratitude that the project was made a priority when it was, as it led them to make more effective use of their services during a time of strained resources and significant pandemic-related absences.

In a post-implementation review, all seven health zones were assessed for their status with operationalizing OAAT. Despite undertaking the initiative while faced with staffing shortages and the COVID-19 pandemic, teams all showed movement toward a standardized approach to situating open access services in the continuum of care and a shared understanding and belief in the value of a "one at a time" clinical approach. The emergence of local champions and informal communities of practice providing peer mentoring and support, self-reported increased job satisfaction among clinicians, and feelings of being more effective in their work were also observed.

In terms of challenges, several shared themes surfaced, including alignment of front door processes and client navigation experience during first contact between all Community Addiction and Mental Health Centers. Four months post-launch, there was still uncertainty about how to properly direct clients upon receiving a new referral or walk-in. Teams still needed guidance around when and how to direct a client to OAAT vs. intake and the review team found that inconsistent information and language was being used in some cases with the client. For example, re-directing the client before providing support or giving overly complicated descriptions of treatment options in an effort to give the client choices were observed.

Possibly because of the challenge of getting the right messages across about OAAT and its place in a Stepped Care continuum, clinicians also reported that many new and existing clients were resistant to trying the open access service (OAAT) and would rather wait for an assigned clinician. Some care partners were also skeptical of the client-led, "one at a time" approach and were concerned about their referrals not being given the level of care they believed they needed. There was a mindset change being asked of clients—to consider a rapid access, on-demand approach to therapy that doesn't necessarily require long-term commitment to an assigned clinician—as well as for clinicians and care partners, who were being asked to not automatically assume future sessions would be wanted or needed. Instead, conversations were shifting toward prioritizing clients' current needs and readiness and the potential for small steps to lead to meaningful change.

After the provincial post-implementation review, the core project team developed recommendations to help guide iterative improvement. These recommendations included:

1 All teams across the province consistently introduce OAAT as the main point of access to Addictions and Mental Health Services.
2 Remove eligibility criteria from the conversation with the client.

3 Provide all teams with front-door speaking points that are clear and consistent with the new process.
4 Keep newly added Clinical Lead positions dedicated to supporting and sustaining OAAT and enable them to dedicate time to a provincial Community of Practice.
5 Integrate OAAT into all Addiction and Mental Health Services (i.e., not just within segmented service delivery teams) to develop system-wide understanding and capabilities in Stepped Care and "one at a time" approaches, making smoother navigation possible for clients to move up, down, in or out of the continuum of care depending on their current needs.
6 Update overarching Addiction and Mental Health Operational Guidelines to support and align with the addition of One-at-a-Time Therapy and a Stepped Care approach.

Preliminary Results

No one service will meet the needs of every client—a robust continuum of low-to-high-intensity care is required. But preliminary data and feedback heard from clients has been encouraging: as a rapid access, client-centered, and strengths-based intervention option, OAAT seems to be making a positive difference in people's ability to access services. (Figures 5.3-5.9).

The initiative to roll out One-at-a-Time Therapy in New Brunswick formally started in May 2021 with Adult Services teams and continued the following year with the province's 44 Child and Youth Integrated Service Delivery teams, in a phased approach to making low barrier, rapid access care available to all age groups. Within two years:

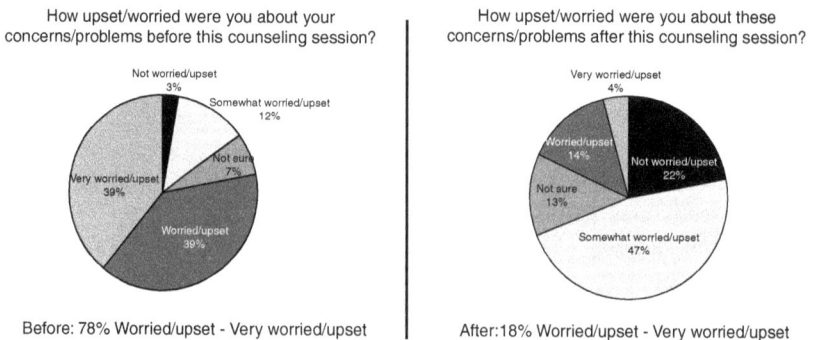

How upset/worried were you about your concerns/problems before this counseling session?

Not worried/upset 3%
Somewhat worried/upset 12%
Not sure 7%
Very worried/upset 39%
Worried/upset 39%

Before: 78% Worried/upset - Very worried/upset

How upset/worried were you about these concerns/problems after this counseling session?

Very worried/upset 4%
Worried/upset 14%
Not worried/upset 22%
Not sure 13%
Somewhat worried/upset 47%

After: 18% Worried/upset - Very worried/upset

Figure 5.3 Client satisfaction feedback from 927 surveyed adult One-at-a-Time Therapy (OAAT) clients showing a significant reduction in feelings of worry/upset before and after the counselling session

How satisfied are you that this session helped you to develop
a plan to address the concerns/problems?

	Not satisfied	Somewhat satisfied	Not sure	Satisfied	Very Satisfied
	1	2	3	4	5
■ Total	0%	3%	5%	42%	50%

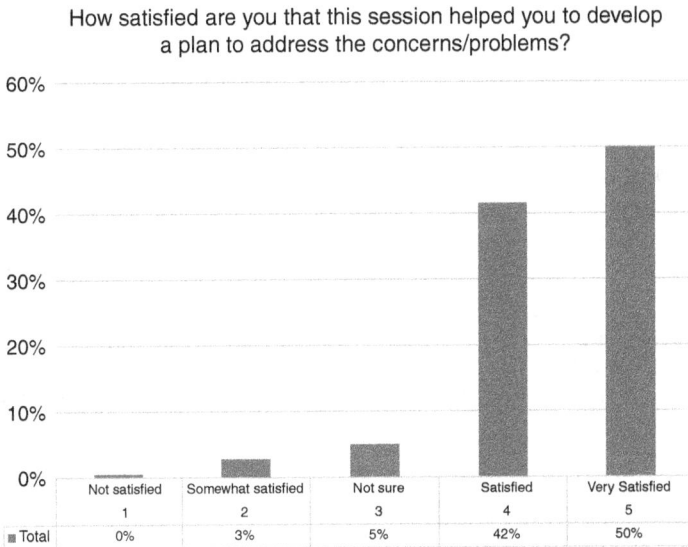

92% Satisfied/Very Satisfied

Figure 5.4 92% of 927 surveyed adult One-at-a-Time Therapy (OAAT) clients reported feeling satisfied or very satisfied with the session's effectiveness in helping them develop a plan to address their concerns

**How satisfied are you with the plan
you and the therapist developed?**

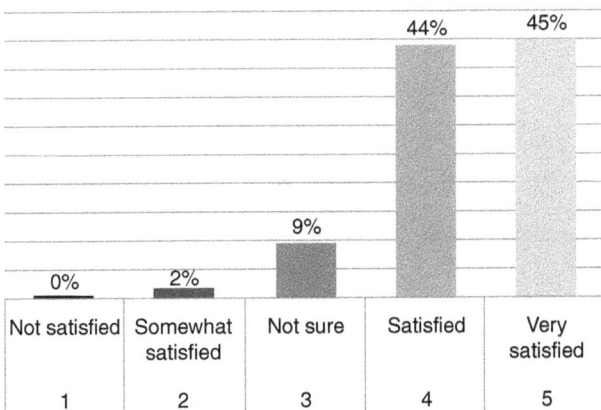

Not satisfied	Somewhat satisfied	Not sure	Satisfied	Very satisfied
0%	2%	9%	44%	45%
1	2	3	4	5

Figure 5.5 89% of 662 surveyed child and youth One-at-a-Time Therapy (OAAT) clients reported feeling satisfied or very satisfied with the plan developed with their therapist during the session

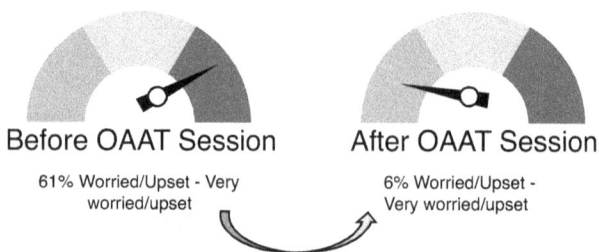

Before OAAT Session

61% Worried/Upset - Very
worried/upset

After OAAT Session

6% Worried/Upset -
Very worried/upset

Figure 5.6 Client satisfaction feedback from 662 surveyed child and youth One-at-a-Time Therapy (OAAT) clients showing a significant reduction in feelings of worry/upset before and after the counselling session

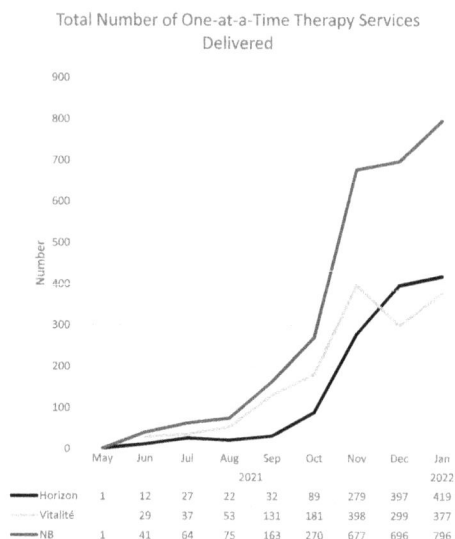

Total Number of One-at-a-Time Therapy Services
Delivered

	May	Jun	Jul	Aug	Sep	Oct	Nov	Dec	Jan
					2021				2022
Horizon	1	12	27	22	32	89	279	397	419
Vitalité		29	37	53	131	181	398	299	377
NB	1	41	64	75	163	270	677	696	796

Figure 5.7 Early service delivery data from New Brunswick Adult Services teams reflects the integration of One-at-a-Time Therapy (OAAT) from time of launch

- Over 900 provincial Addiction and Mental Health Services employees became trained in Stepped Care and "one at a time" approaches.
- All 19 Community Addiction and Mental Health Centers and 44 Child and Youth teams in the province were offering rapid access One-at-a-Time Therapy.
  - Over 1,900 OAAT sessions were provided to clients,

Waitlists Before and After One-at-a-Time Therapy Implementation (Adult Individual Services)

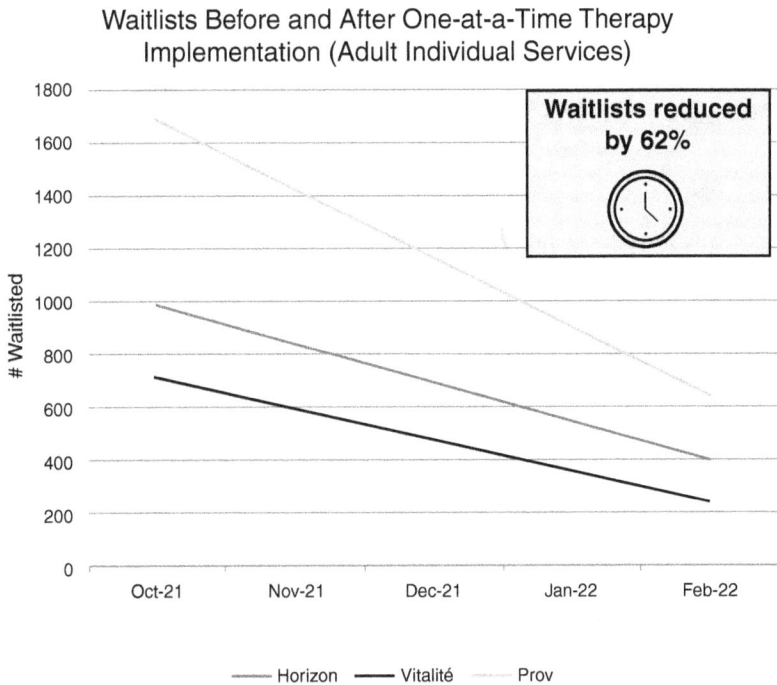

Waitlists reduced by 62%

Legend: Horizon — Vitalité · · · Prov

Figure 5.8 Early data indicates a 62% reduction in adults waiting for individual services four months after integrating One-at-a-Time Therapy (OAAT) into New Brunswick's continuum of care

Waitlists Before and After One-at-a-Time Therapy Implementation (C&Y Individual Services)

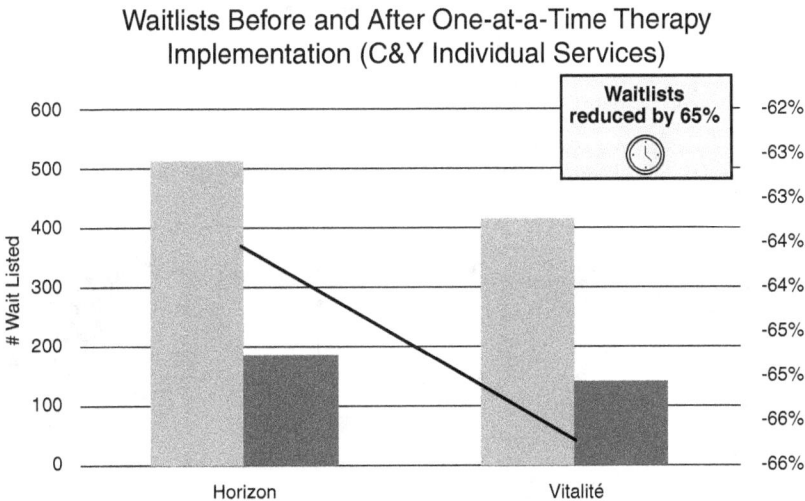

Waitlists reduced by 65%

-62%
-63%
-63%
-64%
-64%
-65%
-65%
-66%
-66%

Figure 5.9 Early data from Child and Youth Services teams reflecting OAAT integration and waitlist reduction from time of launch

- Waitlists for Child & Youth Services were reduced by 65% and Adult Services by 62%, and
- 90% of nearly 2,000 surveyed clients had reported feeling "satisfied" or "very satisfied" with their OAAT session.

Client Stories

Before this initiative, the client journey process in New Brunswick looked like this (Figure 5.10).

After the work laid out in this chapter, the new client journey process is as follows (Figure 5.11).

The difference may appear small in a flow chart, but to individuals making the effort to seek help, offering clinical intervention at the first point of contact can mean the difference between waiting weeks to months, and receiving therapy at the time when their motivation for change is the strongest.

Client Journey Process Before One-at-a-Time Therapy

Figure 5.10 Client journey process before the introduction of One-at-a-Time Therapy

Client Journey Process With One-at-a-Time Therapy

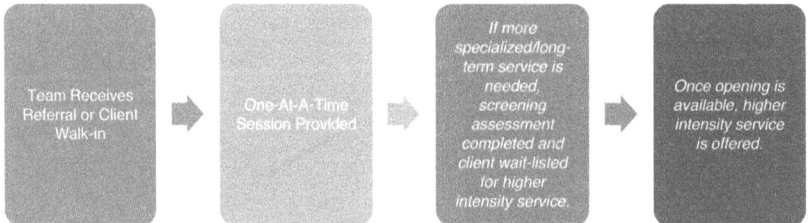

Figure 5.11 Client journey process with One-at-a-Time Therapy in the continuum of care, showing earlier therapeutic intervention

Some actual case examples can help illustrate common client experiences now that OAAT is integrated into the New Brunswick continuum of care as a point of easy access and navigation:

Client Journey Example: André

André is in his late 60s. He had never sought mental health support before and had no history at all in the system, but having recently had some challenges, he spoke with his family doctor, who recommended OAAT. André called Addictions and Mental Health Services on a Friday and was offered an appointment first thing Monday morning. During the session, André's counselor provided psychoeducation tailored to his concerns, including information about general symptoms and what one might expect concerning anxiety and depression. He was provided information on options and potential next steps. At the end of the appointment, André felt he understood his situation better and had a plan for how to proceed. André reported feeling validated and that he didn't know that talking to someone would be so helpful and provide such a sense of relief. He expressed feeling relieved to know about this service and that he could come back anytime. André came in, received OAAT, and left feeling relieved and encouraged, knowing he can self-refer anytime.

Client Journey Example: Jeanine

Jeanine came in for an intake appointment for higher-intensity services. She completed the screening and was referred to a wait list for individual counseling and psychiatry. While waiting to be connected to an assigned clinician and psychiatrist, Jeanine arrived for several OAAT sessions. As standalone sessions, these appointments were arranged at Jeanine's discretion (i.e., she reached out when she felt she needed to talk to someone about her situation) and she was seen by the available clinician on rotation each time. Afterward, Jeanine reported feeling better and feeling supported. She felt grateful the service exists and is available while she's waiting for the next steps with psychiatric care planning, and she self-reported some improvement in symptoms because of accessing OAAT. Jeanine needed more intense, longer-term support, but some preliminary work was being done to reduce symptomology and risk of worsening condition while she waited.

Client Journey Example: Raquel

Raquel called Addictions and Mental Health Services and spoke to someone on duty. She was invited to come in for an OAAT appointment and was informed that if needed, this could lead to an intake for a more specialized service or assignment to a long-term clinician. Raquel met with an OAAT clinician and shared that she was upset about her school situation. She was feeling overwhelmed, like she didn't know how to keep everything under control. At the time of the session, Raquel was on leave from school and felt she couldn't go back. She was struggling with feelings of stress and inadequacy. Through discussion, it came out that she had previously overcome substance use issues, and the focus of the conversation shifted to how she had overcome these difficulties in the past. Raquel began to explore her capacity to make decisions and trust herself. Together, she and her counselor developed a plan with some specific next steps that she felt would be achievable and make a difference in helping her feel things were more in control. She had lost sight of her resilience and achievement in working through hard times in the past and felt renewed hope and strength for moving forward. At the end of the appointment, she was informed she was welcome to come back anytime if she felt she needed more help, which she did one more time.

Client Journey Example: Nathan

There was a turning point in the middle of Nathan's OAAT appointment where it became clear he had no confidence in his ability to rely on his strengths to improve his situation. Nathan was not sleeping, not eating, and didn't seem to have enough resources to be able to self-mobilize. Based on the in-session assessment, the OAAT clinician determined that Nathan was at an elevated risk for suicide, and together, they opted to complete an intake assessment then and there. Nathan's session ended with a plan to access OAAT three to four times while waiting for an assigned clinician and with him being reassured that this open-access therapy service would be available for him if/when he is ready to step back down from this higher-intensity care plan.

What Some Other OAAT Clients in New Brunswick Are Saying

"This is the first time I have left with a solid plan with timelines and objectives. [The therapist] was able to really identify succinctly where help was needed."

"The session was much more productive and helpful than I expected!"

"She listened and kept me on focus with what can help today. I'm ready to make changes."

These case examples and testimonials highlight the variety of issues and situations where having OAAT in a continuum of care can improve the client experience and improve timely access to services.

Sustainability and Reinforcement of OAAT in New Brunswick

As with any change, the risk was that individual clinicians or even full teams would revert to familiar approaches instead of continuing to develop comfort and competency in the new mindset and processes. To prevent this, reinforcement measures were planned early in the project. Post-launch, the provincial working group transitioned from implementation phase to reinforcement and sustainability phase, with four pillars leading ongoing support and monitoring:

1 **Ongoing Training:** Training isn't a one-and-done exercise. A wealth of knowledge had been developed in New Brunswick, and this could be called on to continue developing abilities and reinforce skills in applying OAAT concepts in Addiction and Mental Health Services. To promote ongoing learning and development after the implementation phase, routine training programs were embedded into operations to help guide Clinical Leads and Managers in guiding new and seasoned staff toward confidence in and shared understanding of One-at-a-Time Therapy and Stepped Care.

2 **Clinical Leads and Champions:** An important part of the sustainability and reinforcement of OAAT was hiring Clinical Leads for the service in all regions, for both Adult and Child and Youth Services. These leaders provide accessible clinical guidance and encouragement to all team members as it relates to OAAT and its role in a Stepped Care continuum. Champions also emerged to support the initiative and promote full adoption of the changes within their regions. These are team members who enjoy developing their skills in OAAT and have an enthusiasm and willingness to play a role in continuous improvement and day-to-day peer support.

3 **Community of Practice:** A community of practice (CoP) was established to help clinicians stay current by exchanging knowledge, experiences, evidence, and resources related to OAAT, as well as provide professional development value through a strong shared understanding of OAAT service delivery within a Stepped Care continuum. Clinical Leads in the province hold regular CoP meetings to help sustain and reinforce system changes and promote full adoption of best practices through continuing support to clinicians.

4 **Measure, Evaluate, and Manage:** Key targets and success indicators were defined in early stages of planning and outlined in the OAAT Administrative Guidelines. Protocols were established for ongoing monitoring, including a self-service dashboard depicting real-time data, standardized fidelity assessments, and assigned ownership for ongoing direction and re-direction when needed at the team, regional, and provincial levels.

Without a good sustainability and reinforcement plan, this high-potential initiative was also at high risk for failure. A failed OAAT implementation could have included known clinical and system-level benefits not realized, months of investment wasted, the responsibility for success left on the shoulders of individual clinicians and clinical leads, an inconsistent client experience, and an essential step in New Brunswick's Stepped Care continuum not becoming engrained. Shared ongoing commitment to clinical supervision, communities of practice, onboarding protocols for new employees, and strong leadership by senior management to monitor and evaluate OAAT within the continuum of care was the insurance needed to avoid a worst-case scenario.

One year post-launch, in the Fall of 2022, OAAT fidelity assessments were conducted in adult Addiction and Mental Health Services in all seven health zones. During this process, in-person visits or virtual interviews were led by three evaluators, including two Department of Health file leads and a Horizon or Vitalité Clinical Lead. Clinical Leads, Managers, and Clinicians in each zone completed questionnaires and interviews, and randomly selected client files were audited. Scored reports were provided back to each zone, and action plans were prepared by teams based on the feedback and recommendations in their evaluation.

This fidelity scale assessment has since been established as an annual process, important for reinforcing positive trends and best practices and flagging risks to sustainability. After the first year of OAAT in New Brunswick, highlights included the accessibility of OAAT in many regions virtually or by telephone, walk-in, and by appointment, and increased promotion of OAAT to new clients as well as existing clients who may only need occasional support. It also brought into focus areas for close attention and potential course-correcting, such as not over-relying on OAAT when it is clear that higher intensity services would be more helpful to the client and finding ways to address recruitment and retention challenges.

Don't Try This at Home (without Reading This Chapter)

OAAT is now offered in all Community Addictions and Mental Health Centers in New Brunswick. There is no lengthy assessment and no waitlist. Individuals can book a rapid access appointment, usually within 1–3 days, or walk-in and talk to a therapist about the issue that is currently affecting them. No further appointments are scheduled, but the individual is welcomed to come back anytime when and if they need more or other services. This is a significant change from the previous common scenario of intake assessment and placement on a waitlist, with very little regard for a person's actual needs and readiness.

The implementation of OAAT services in New Brunswick was far from perfect, but it was successful and continues to be so, well over a year after its initiation. The project team had no secret sauce, but they did learn a few things that were essential to the process and the transformation that took place. First, creating or demonstrating the need for change was a necessary ingredient. In New Brunswick, this boiled down to two clearly articulated issues: (1) People not being able to access services when they need it and (2) the addiction and mental health system being difficult to navigate. Having a clear vision and plan, with visible and committed engagement from senior leadership, was a key ingredient for a successful large-scale implementation of this nature.

Second, creating the right partnerships and effective working relationships was paramount. For OAAT implementation in New Brunswick, the key partners were the Department of Health, Horizon Health Network, Reseau de Santé Vitalité, Memorial University, and Stepped Care Solutions. This collaborative combination provided effective system planning, service delivery and operational knowledge, research capability, subject matter expertise and, above all, mutual accountability and motivation to see the initiative succeed.

A strong and motivated implementation project team was also vital. This team should be diverse and include people with clinical expertise, leaders who can make things happen, people who can collect and use data, people who have expertise in project management and change management, people who have in depth operational knowledge, and a few champions who really believe in OAAT. To reassure service providers that OAAT would not create an additional workload demand, positions for new employees were created in every health zone, in particular clinical supervisors, who could support and grow OAAT and play a leadership role in their regions. From here, having a detailed project plan with a project charter, work breakdown structures, deliverable timelines, project reporting, a communication plan, and a feedback loop to continually adjust strategy helped keep the implementation on track and headed in the right direction.

Early adopters sharing their success stories was highly impactful in fostering belief and creating a positive momentum throughout New Brunswick around the implementation. An informal pilot OAAT implementation was begun in Campbellton, a smaller health zone in the northern part of the province, about 8 months prior to the provincial implementation. This was led by two key early adopters, a local Manager and a Psychologist. Their enthusiasm, leadership, and foresight were instrumental in creating initial procedures, documents, client journeys, supervision processes, etc., that were immensely helpful in the provincial implementation. The result of their work was the initial success story.

Finally, believing it to be equally important, the project team also remained committed to understanding and acknowledging voices of dissent, as there are always important factors there to consider that help lead to necessary adjustments and improvements.

If we were to do this again, and *yes* we would, we certainly would do a few things differently. While expediency is sometimes necessary, we were likely too ambitious in our timelines and implementation process. This led to regularly having to look back and adjust, change the message or a procedure, etc. In a large-scale change management project, it's a certainty that some things will be missed or not foreseen. However, having a realistic and appropriate timeline can make implementation go much smoother.

Lastly, a key principle of change management is overcommunication. Even knowing this and talking about it regularly, our project team still did not communicate often and clearly enough, not to our partners and not to the public. Even when we thought we were providing detailed information to those involved in the implementation, we realized that sometimes the message was not received or not clear enough. Effective project communication falls into the "easier said that done" category.

The Transformative Power of OAAT

The evidence continues to grow and demonstrate the positive impact that OAAT can have on individuals as they work toward making meaningful changes in their lives to achieve improved relationships, reduce stress, or simply feel better about themselves. What is at this time less clear and less studied is the impact that the implementation of OAAT can have on a large scale and broad continuum of care. While OAAT has been shown to reduce waiting lists and increase access (Mental Health Commission of Canada, 2023), other potential impacts on the overall system are less understood.

We have come to believe that OAAT needs to be a key feature of a Stepped Care Continuum of Services. OAAT can be an open-access brief service and, when indicated, an entry point to more intensive or specialized addiction and mental health services. While OAAT has been shown to reduce waiting lists, increase access, and provide early intervention, we have only begun to consider and understand its potential impacts on the overall continuum of care.

Perhaps the most unexpected yet welcomed outcome has been the sense of hope and renewal it has created in many clinicians. "OAAT has re-ignited my pilot light," said one Addiction and Mental Health Services worker. "In 17 years in mental health I have not had job satisfaction like this. I believe in the model wholeheartedly." A clinician in another region similarly credited One-at-a-Time Therapy with re-igniting her fire after a long career in Addiction and Mental Health Services and reflected "the large majority of people we see are surprised we can see them so quickly." In another part of the province, a clinician felt relief that these changes in the New Brunswick mental health system mean that she can always start with an open-access approach. If, during a conversation, it seems that longer-term or more specialized services are needed, the appointment ends with the necessary next steps to help navigate the client in that direction. "Clients leave with a plan that is co-created, something in their hand that they feel empowered to move forward with, knowing they can come back," she shares. "People get so caught up in their deficits, they completely lose sight of the wellness side. OAAT has allowed me to step out of pathologizing and step into *What are you doing that's working that we can build on?*"

As mentioned, the system-wide implementation of OAAT also led to the creation of a dedicated Community of Practice (CoP) for clinicians and clinical leads, something that was not previously widely used in New Brunswick's Addiction and Mental Health Services. Clinicians are reporting that the CoP has led to valuable knowledge exchange and feelings of increased connectedness with others who do similar work.

While still in early stages of development and full incorporation into the system, the addition of OAAT provides an opportunity to communicate to the public that there is hope and that services are available and accessible. It can also lead to dialogue about different levels of need and help dispel some of the common belief that long-term therapy is needed for anyone experiencing a substance use or mental health challenge:

Providing OAAT as a first step as opposed to the screening questions/intake is a much better service for the client. We are meeting with them at the right time when they are most ready and are providing them with a set of coping skills that they can use immediately rather than placing them on a wait list.

– *Clinician's testimonial*

Summary

The provincial implementation of OAAT in New Brunswick has had a bigger impact than we ever could have imagined. We initially thought it would improve access and reduce waiting lists, as it had done in other jurisdictions (Mental Health Commission of Canada, 2023). It has done that and much more.

While only the first step in adopting a Stepped Care continuum for Addiction and Mental Health Services, the addition of OAAT to the existing continuum of care has created hope that the system is improving. Clinicians who are involved in OAAT delivery are reporting increased satisfaction in their work and feel they are really making a difference in immediately helping people when they need it the most. The next steps will include exploring how outcome measures can help clients feel empowered to choose the care pathway that will best meet their needs and improve their quality of life. Isn't that what client-centered mental health care should be about?

Note

1 Lewin, K. (1951). *Field theory in social science: Selected theoretical papers* (D. Cartwright, Ed., p. 169). Harper & Row.

References

Association of Change Management Professionals. (2019). *Standard for change management.* Retrieved from https://www.acmpglobal.org/page/the_standard

Cornish, P. (2020). *Stepped care 2.0: A paradigm shift in mental health.* Springer International Publishing.

Dryden, W. (2021). *Single-session therapy and its future: What SST leaders think.* Routledge.

Eger, E. E. (2020). *The gift: 12 lessons to save your life.* Rider Books.

Hoyt, M. F., & Bobele, M. (Eds.). (2019). *Creative therapy in challenging situations.* Routledge.

Hoyt, M. F., Bobele, M., Slive, A., Young, J., & Talmon, M. (2018). Walk-in and by-appointment single-sessions now and in the future. In M. F. Hoyt, M., A. Slive, J. Young, & M. Talmon (Eds.), *Single-session therapy by walk-in or appointment: Administrative, clinical, and supervisory aspects of one-at-a-time services.* (pp. 369–379). Routledge/Taylor & Francis Group.

Mental Health Commission of Canada. (2023, April 19). *Stepped care 2.0.* Retrieved from https://mentalhealthcommission.ca/what-we-do/access/stepped-care-2-0/

Mental Health Commission of Canada. (2023, June 13). *Partnering together for person- and family-centric care.* Retrieved from https://mentalhealthcommission.ca/resource/stepped-care-nwt/

New Brunswick Department of Health. (2021). Inter-Departmental Addiction and Mental Health Action Plan: Priority areas for 2021–2025. https://www2.gnb.ca/content/dam/gnb/Departments/h-s/pdf/en/MentalHealthandAddictions/inter-departmental_addiction_and_mental_health_action_plan.pdf

Prosci. (n.d.). 5 Tenets of Change Management. Retrieved from https://www.prosci.com/resources/articles/5-tenets-of-change-management

Slive, A., & Bobele, M. (2011). When one hour is all you have: Effective therapy for walk-in clients. Zeig, Tucker & Theisen Inc.

Stepped Care Solutions. (n.d.). SC2.0 Model. Retrieved from https://steppedcaresolutions.com/methodology/

Chapter 6

The Eastside Community Mental Health Service

The Evolution of a Walk-In Single-Session Service to an Open-Access Mental Health Hub

Janet Stewart, Nancy McElheran and Dan Neuls

History of the Walk-in Single-Session Service

Wood's Homes, in Calgary Alberta, Canada, is a community based, not-for-profit Mental Health Centre constantly seeking to improve how youth and families access community-based mental health support. This is accomplished, in part, by attending to the experiences of clients in order to identify gaps in service. With more than 40 programs and services located in selected communities across Alberta, Wood's Homes is nationally and internationally recognized for its innovative approach to service development and delivery. In the late 1980s, the Eastside Family Centre (EFC) and the Community Resource Team (CRT), both Wood's Homes community-based programs, were developed in collaboration with the diverse cultural and economic communities in northeast Calgary (Slive et al., 1995). These initiatives were implemented in response to the evident decrease in both health funding and mental health resources for families in those communities in particular. The services were designed to reduce risk and distress while providing community service by diverting clients from hospital emergency rooms (Stewart et al., 2018). Both services were developed in collaboration with key community members who offered ideas about where these services could be conveniently located to maximize accessibility, keeping in mind ways these services could meet the community's diverse cultural and economic needs. Over time, the programs have grown to provide reliable and seamless service delivery of both single sessions of therapy and family crisis support to children, youth, individuals, and families in moments of need.

Since its inception, the EFC was the first walk-in therapy service in Canada with no appointment or fee required. The CRT was the only community-based service in Calgary providing mobile family crisis support that focused on youth and their families. Clients were able to access

DOI: 10.4324/9781003351375-6

both programs at moments of need, as opposed to the more common experience of being placed on a wait list.

In 1987, before the development of the EFC, CRT implemented a telephone crisis response line for families with high-risk parent-child relationships; these parents were also connected to the Wood's Homes' Stabilization program that provided a much-needed 3–5 days out-of-home respite experience for families where there was a perceived risk of physical or verbal violence and /or family breakdown. CRT supported these families before and after their participation in the Stabilization program.

CRT, now called the crisis counseling team (CCT), continues to provide crisis services to individuals and families in the community with, or without, connection to the Stabilization program. Its services have expanded beyond a telephone response to include text messaging and instant messaging as well as face-to-face meetings in a family's home or elsewhere in their community. Typically, counselors talk with clients on a one-at-a-time basis and offer appropriate crisis intervention ideas for them.

A community advisory group evolved from the original stakeholders' group, as noted above, to include community representatives such as police, business owners, and school personnel who assisted in determining the geographic location of the service. This group also assisted in setting the walk-in hours for the EFC and in the promotion of the CRT. Hours established for the walk-in at that time (six days a week: from 11 a.m. to 7 p.m. on weekdays and 11 a.m. to 5 p.m. on Saturdays) were based on the feedback received from the community (Clements et al., 2011). The emphasis on meeting community needs with highly accessible services has been central to both the EFC's and CRT's focus and mandate. The EFC approach to a single-session delivery system has been replicated in various provinces across Canada in ways that are unique to their particular needs. The EFC single-session therapeutic approach has been described extensively in previous journals and books (McElheran et al., 2020; Stewart et al., 2018; Slive et al., 2008).

Four key areas of need were:

1 The response to community needs, as noted above.
2 The development of the infrastructure to support clients walking in to see a therapist at moments of need chosen by them.
3 The therapeutic approach that fits with this type of service.
4 The teaching, training, and supervision offered to multidisciplinary graduate students and community professionals.

The original design of the ESFC reduced hurdles to accessing services. The practicalities of this process, once clients were on-site, included a receptionist introducing them to forms that ask specific questions as to their need of the moment, the ranking of their current distress, and the answering of questions about their current emotional state (e.g., symptoms of anxiety and depression). The intent was to assess risk, from the client's perspective, and to ascertain their concern(s) that could then be followed up in their session. Clients were also asked to indicate their hoped-for outcome from their session. Some of the forms referenced above are modifications of those developed by Duncan et al. (2004) and are utilized in many similar services across the country (McElheran, 2021).

The single-session approach, also called one at a time (OAAT), is grounded in research that has demonstrated that clients often come for only one session, that rapid change is both possible and common in the human experience, and that a strengths-based approach to client problems can uncover as yet-to-be-discovered abilities and capacities for change and growth (Hoyt et al., 2021; Bloom, 2001; Talmon, 1990). Central to the Eastside's single-session/OAAT therapy approach is the specific theoretical principles of systems theory and thinking that stress the importance of the context in which problems and their solutions occur, brief/solution-focused ideas that support consultation and collaboration with the client, narrative ideas that reveal undiscovered strengths and the client's theory of change (Slive et al., 2008; Lipchik, 2002; Hoyt, 1998; White & Epstein, 1990).

The format for OATT/single sessions at the EFC is guided by the work of the Milan group (Boscolo et al., 1987) and consists of the following five parts: (1) a pre-session team consultation focused on the client's presenting concern(s); (2) the session itself in which the client and therapist create a collaborative context where they discuss the presenting issue(s) and the hoped-for outcome from their session; (3) an inter-session consultation where the therapist meets with the consulting therapy team regarding the client's concern to create possible interventions; (4) an end-of-session conversation with the client that offers new ideas and perspectives regarding the concern and which aligns with the client's hoped-for outcome; and, (5) a post-session de-brief where the therapy team meets to discuss whether they believe they met the client's need and to propose ideas should the client's return. A single-session summary note highlights the key elements of the session.

A team of experienced therapists that is either watching from behind a mirror or over video offers guidance to the therapist conducting the session. The therapist often takes a break during the session to consult with the team. The team also teaches, trains, and supervises graduate students and community professionals from various disciplines. Students have the opportunity to hear multidisciplinary perspectives regarding a particular client's situation, while community professionals find it useful to participate to learn the single-session approach to therapy and to experience, firsthand, the benefits of teamwork. Students from the disciplines of social work, psychology, nursing, psychiatry, family therapy, family medicine, and genetics have been welcomed at the EFC and have found supervisors eager to support their learning needs. Shift coordinators, who are experienced clinical supervisors in their own right, guide each team in the therapy process while being mindful of the quality of service being delivered (Stewart et al., 2018).

Opportunity for Change

The EFC and CRT clients consistently reported significant decreases in overall levels of distress after their sessions, as well as satisfaction with the immediacy of the service. Many clients reported that they had sought services from both EFC and CRT instead of going to their family doctors and emergency rooms or not getting help anywhere at all. CRT clients reported they had called other services, but the crisis counselors at the Eastside were the first to respond immediately. This approach was consistent and positive until 2019.

While clients' overall satisfaction was consistently positive, the data indicated a need for ongoing support. Specific feedback from clients highlighted the need for a more personal or "warm" referral to additional resources as opposed to the usual less personal practice of a "cold" referral, i.e., being told about a service and given a phone number. Clients often requested ongoing support as they navigated an often-complex mental health system. Clients reported difficulty following up with recommendations for services because of language or cultural differences as a major reason they were not getting the care they needed at the right time in the right place. Complicating the accessibility issue was a significant and unanticipated transition in funder priorities that required an immediate revision of both programs. As an outcome of this financial shift, and in keeping with client feedback, the program leadership group saw the need for the transformation for both the EFC and CRT programs. Blackstaffe (2020) conducted an environmental scan (Blackstaffe, 2020) that included reviews of funders and grantors' priorities in the community. The outcome was the identification of new and different service delivery models and innovative strategies that had the potential to maintain immediately accessible mental health support in the community. As a result, amid a global pandemic and 30 years following the initial launch of these individual programs, Wood's Homes responded again to the needs of the community.

The 72-hour Pivot

In March 2020, both EFC and CRT were impacted by the health restrictions placed on the Calgary community by provincial and federal governments in response to the rapid spread of the COVID-19 pandemic. In keeping with its mandate to meet community needs, the leaders, clinicians, and counselors of EFC and CRT created new ways to deliver services that fit the needs of clients while at the same time adhering to the public health mandate to minimize interpersonal contact. Previously inconceivable decisions were made to immediately suspend all in-person therapy sessions as well as in-home family crisis visits. After over 30 years of experience with a walk-in, face-to-face, single-session team approach, and an in-home mental health crisis support model, counselors and clinicians alike made the necessary adaptations to meet the anticipated significant mental health challenges of youth, individuals, couples, and families during an unprecedented global event.

The Launch of Virtual Services

Fortunately, members of the core Eastside therapy team had previous telehealth service experience, as did the CRT crisis counselors who led the way with their experience in providing immediate mental health support over the phone and via text and instant messaging. Armed with an abundance of highly skilled, intelligent, and committed staff and some reasonably adequate desk phones, the EFC launched a single-session phone therapy service, identified as the "call option" on March 23, 2020. Initial plans called for the therapists to continue to ask clients to complete the walk-in information forms over the phone prior to the phone therapy session, thereby staying as true to the origins of the walk-in service as possible. This proved to be unmanageable as each session instantly became exhausting for both clients and therapists because of the added time each session required. The next step was for CRT to collaborate directly with the therapy teams to support the new phone therapy services. The CRT crisis counselors began to do intakes with the therapy clients over the phone and gather the client information that would previously have been completed by the client when they walked into the EFC. This new "intake" process provided clients with a "first contact" experience that offered immediate connection and support while generating the information needed for the subsequent therapy session. Clients were booked for an immediate appointment, at a time coinvent for them the same day, that enabled the therapy teams to continue providing the high quality, efficient services they had previously offered. Clients reported significantly improved satisfaction with the ease of this intake process and the subsequent therapy they received.

As the core therapy staff group at the EFC became comfortable with managing and delivering this new version of the former system, a new idea emerged, one that would require another pivot. The EFC began offering online video sessions in addition to the phone sessions that were now in full swing. Clients were given the option of either a by-appointment telephone or a video session. Both modalities were supported by the therapy teams; both were guided by the session format created for the walk-in service; intakes for virtual sessions were also completed by the crisis counseling team. But as you will see next, the new technology presented a challenge.

Teamwork Makes the Dream Work

While a multidisciplinary team approach had been central to the services offered at the EFC, that essential team approach was at risk during the early stages of the pivot to virtual therapy services. EFC's traditional in-person-paper-pen intake process was one of the barriers to overcome. This challenge was complicated by the fact that staff, students, and community volunteer therapists all shared computers to complete session documentation. Another challenge was that in our team approach, consultation teams typically sat together in-person in small meeting rooms.

The EFC faced challenges in maintaining the team-based treatment model. Significant investments of time, energy, and finances by management, clinicians, and the Wood's Homes IT Department were essential. New funders were necessary to improve the technological infrastructure. These supported the continuation of the team consultation model as an integral part of the new open-access virtual single-session therapy service while ensuring privacy for all concerned. The result was the addition of new computers and cell phones, cutting-edge video conferencing screens, upgrades in program servers, storage, and computer networks as well as the development of virtual service delivery processes and procedures that linked the team and the client consistently from wherever both were located. All therapists, consultants, students, and residents were asked to complete declarations acknowledging they would maintain a confidential therapy working area in their remote location and follow guidelines for the responsible use of the new technology.

Benefits of the Pivot

One significant benefit of this investment was creating a seamless, accessible, technology-enhanced therapy service where clients continued to be offered individualized, integrated, and rich therapy sessions. Instead of picturing a multidisciplinary group of professionals in one room co-developing impactful and fitting interventions (picture the opening credits of the 1970s American television show "The Brady Bunch"), now team members for the day could be seen on the computer screen from the shoulders up using Zoom technology.

Videoconferencing invitations stretching from the beginning of the therapy day to the end were sent to all therapy team members. Team members joined from across the city at their remote locations or from the Eastside office when that was feasible. The therapeutic consultation and intervention processes that were previously developed continued for each youth, individual, couple, and family seeking single sessions of therapy.

Another unexpected benefit and outcome of working in this manner was a significant increase in the number of clients for whom psychiatric consultation was deemed advisable since these particular psychiatrists were able to watch sessions from locations that fit them. Currently, psychiatric consultations occur every weekday, compared to two to three days a week prior to the introduction of virtual services.

Thirdly, at a time when the number of mental health practicum opportunities plummeted in the Calgary community due to health restrictions related to COVID-19, graduate students at the EFC completed their practicums and experienced enhanced learning opportunities, receiving intensive training in virtual therapy service delivery as well as learning a single-session/OAAT approach to therapy.

Lessons Learned from the Transition

Clients continued to report high levels of satisfaction with the use of a team approach. The team was frequently thanked during the satisfaction survey process. This finding aligns with previous research that indicated that clients were particularly complimentary of the team approach (Stewart et al., 2018). The combined training and experience of the clinicians in both single-session therapy and basic telehealth readily adapted to a virtual world.

The importance of having accessible, flexible, and immediate mental health support for clients and the community in moments of need has never been clearer than during the past 3 years. Providing single sessions of therapy both over the phone and via sophisticated and highly confidential video conferencing systems proved to be of value, particularly because there was a dearth of this type of service during the initial stages of the pandemic. Most of these new forms of therapeutic support aligned with the prior experiences and outcomes of offering a walk-in single-session therapy service: clients come once, come for several sessions over a brief period of time, or return later to address new or different concerns.

Other findings were more specific to the therapists and management group at the EFC, who were concerned they might lose the close bonds they had forged in-person once they were required to move to remote ways of conducting their work. It was a challenge for some therapists, and a welcome change for others, to conduct single-session work from a remote location. At the same time, some of the therapy staff struggled to find meaningful connections to the team in the virtual spaces where they found themselves. These differing experiences were often articulated by clients, with some questioning when the Centre would return to in-person therapy and others expressing worry that virtual sessions might stop.

It could be argued that the pandemic has helped to challenge some of the more traditional notions regarding the meaning of connection. What the therapists came to understand was that they are responsible, in collaboration with the client, to create the best possible connection regardless of the medium used. This notion has been supported in the bulk of the literature that underscores the importance of brief/single-session approaches to therapy, in which the engagement with the client, regardless of the context, becomes critical to the client's perceived success of the therapy itself (Slive & Bobele, 2011).

Evolving to a Permanent Hybrid Service Delivery Model

With the lifting of COVID-19 restrictions, we began exploring how, when, and if a return to in-person walk-in single-session therapy and in-home crisis family support was safe for clients and staff. Clients were reporting satisfaction with virtual services for several reasons: e.g., day and evening appointment times fit school and work schedules for individuals and families; travel time was eliminated; time spent waiting to access a walk-in session on busy days was reduced; accessibility for clients in rural locations was improved as was accessibility for disabled or handicapped clients and those with pronounced social anxiety. In addition, therapists expressed comfort in forming virtual connections with their clients. Some indicated they preferred providing virtual services for some of the same reasons clients did, such as reduced travel time and the convenience of doing therapy in their own home. However, as stated above, some clients also regularly asked when in-person sessions would be available. Given all of these considerations, opening access to in person single-sessions of therapy, including in-person, virtual, telephone, and text-based, resumed at the Eastside in May 2022.

Developing an Open Access Mental Health Services Hub

Despite the accessibility and availability of programs such as the EFC and CRT, there are an estimated 1.6 million Canadians with unmet mental health care needs each year (CMHA, 2018). The Eastside Community Mental Health Services (ECMHS) HUB was launched in November 2020 in response to client feedback, noted above, which conveyed their experiences struggling to maneuver within complex mental health systems. As a result, both the EFC and CRT were re-positioned as a mental health services hub, bringing the service delivery option of one-at-a-time crisis counseling and single-session therapy under one umbrella, while adding new and different ways of opening access to a single-session service in a broader way than was previously conceived.

The HUB Service Delivery Model

Calgary community-based researchers have identified the establishment of integrated service "hubs" as a means to address challenges in the sector (GermAnn et al., 2018). Hubs can address insufficient attention to the front end of mental health support – times when clients are ready for general mental health information, early crisis resolution, and/or accessible therapy services. Services organized in a hub format can connect families, youth, and individuals with the right level of care, at the right time, addressing their most urgent needs while supporting them through a continuum of care. Community-based integrated mental health services are advocated by both international organizations (World Health Organization [WHO], 2013) and national organizations as a solution to fragmented and insufficient mental health care (Bostock & Britt, 2014).

The ECMHS chose to conceive the program's Hub model as a "one stop shop" location offering system navigation, crisis counseling, and one at a time/single-sessions of therapy.

The environmental scan completed for the ECMHS (Blackstaffe, 2020) noted above discovered that other centers, nationally and internationally, tend to provide integrated mental health services in primary care medical settings targeted to youth. The new ECMHS, by contrast, was developed as a Hub for all ages – adult individuals and couples as well as youth and families in response to local community needs. In addition, there was a growing trend for single sessions of counseling/therapy to be co-located with other social services (Cornish et al., 2020).

The Hub Model in Action

System Navigation services can be found in Canada at a variety of locations. Calgary, at the time of the environmental scan, did not have an in-person mental health system navigation service. System navigation services, first introduced in the 1990s within primary care settings, are intended to link clients and families to primary care services, specialist care, and community-based health and social services to provide comprehensive patient-centered care (Valaitis et al., 2017). Walking with clients on their mental health journey and throwing light on a growing and complex mental health care system is being identified as a key component of mental health support services.

The ECMHS systems navigation service addresses this identified need by providing support for a seamless transition to other resources. Along with assessing the need and best fit of community programs, navigation services address the individual circumstances, social and community-related factors, and living conditions consistent with the Social Determinants of Health (Dahlgreen & Whitehead, 2021).

The ECMHS regards system navigation in a hub setting as facilitating open and equal access to services for clients to ultimately achieve the "highest attainable standard of health" (WHO, 2013). The ECMHS system navigators provide (1) immediate counseling support to reduce client distress; (2) conduct need and risk assessments, and (3) initiate immediate community referrals in collaboration with the client and support timely access to the ECMHS crisis counseling and single-session therapy services.

An addition to the three components of the ECMHS Hub model of service delivery noted above is an intervention called a "Caring Contact." A caring contact intervention following a single session of therapy occurs when a client expresses suicidal ideation and intent as a presenting concern expressed in their session. This intervention was developed to align with new standards outlined in The Canadian Journal of Psychiatry to ensure the safety and well-being of clients (Links et al., 2019). In addition to the risk of suicide or self-harm, ECMHS therapists initiate caring contact when a client presents at medium- to high-risk for domestic violence and/ or where child protection may be required or where a client is significantly isolated.

The need for a caring contact intervention is determined during the inter-session consultation among the multidisciplinary team members and presented to the client during the end-of-session conversation. Therapists collaborate with the client to determine the safest and/or best time for the call to happen. Therapists also explain who will be calling, either ECMHS therapists or crisis counselors. Crisis counselors provide services throughout the day and into the evening hours up to 11:00 p.m. seven days a week. As a result, there is considerable flexibility as to when this service can be delivered. The therapist shares demographic, contact, and presenting concern information about the client to the crisis counseling team, with permission from the client when possible. Each caring contact includes the following:

Assess current risk; review safety plan; identify any barriers to the safety plan; provide crisis counseling to reduce any current distress; and answer any additional questions based on referrals or suggestions provided by the therapy team.

If risk remained high following a caring contact intervention, counselors and therapists arranged external support from local police or ambulance services. Evaluation and client satisfaction data collection is in its infancy and will be the next step in the development of this intervention as part of the ECMHS hub.

Case Example

Ramona Lopez[1] was referred to the Eastside Community Mental Health Service Hub by her family physician. Earlier that day, during her appointment with her physician, Ramona described high agitation most days over the past two weeks, inability to focus, and difficulties with getting and staying asleep. She told her physician that she was very worried "something awful" might happen. Ramona's doctor suggested she use Eastside's accessible service to talk about her symptoms before considering medication or any other intensive support. ECMHS is close to a municipal train stop and is easily accessible to Ramona. When Ramona arrived at ECMHS, the receptionist welcomed her to the service and explained the steps of the process. They started with a scale on which she ranked her needs and level of distress. Romana was asked to indicate on the new Hub intake documents which service she thought would best meet her needs and be the most helpful – including system navigation, crisis counseling, and one-at-a-time therapy.

After taking only about 15 minutes to complete the various forms, Ramona returned them to the front desk. The receptionist noted there were two concerns for Ramona: the anxiety her physician was referring her for and her worries about the stability of her current living arrangements. She also responded to the questions about risk: that violence in her life might be something important to talk about today. The receptionist informed Ramona her forms would be reviewed by a system navigation staff member who would then assist her further. The system navigation staff member invited Ramona into a private counseling room. It was noted by both the receptionist and the system navigator that Ramona had indicated she had a problem that she wanted to talk about with a therapist and was also wondering how she could receive help regarding her living arrangements somewhere in her community.

After reviewing the informed consent with Ramona, the system navigator spoke with her about her conversation with her doctor and her expectations for the visit. The systems navigator described both services that Romana was interested in, specifically, including how a single session of therapy could address her symptoms of anxiety as they affected her current functioning and how system navigation could refer her to the appropriate community services. The system navigator was also curious about the violence in Ramona's life. Ramona told him that she did not feel comfortable telling her doctor about an incident. Roman described her relationship as becoming less and less physically safe and that she was grabbed by her upper arms and shaken by her boyfriend 3 times before coming to the ECMHS. She did not tell her doctor because she was embarrassed, but she was hopeful that Eastside could help. She intended to leave her boyfriend, but leaving was complicated because she had co-signed the apartment lease. The system navigator relayed the more detailed information obtained in Ramona's system navigation session with the therapy team.

While Ramona was meeting with her therapist, the system navigator simultaneously began exploring immediate possibilities for domestic violence support in the community: he determined the procedure Ramona would need to follow to apply for a service called "Safer Spaces for Victims of Domestic Violence" that would permit her to be removed from the lease. Following the therapy session, the system navigator again met with Ramona and provided information about the support available to her. Ramona booked a follow-up system navigation session for the next day so the system navigator could help her connect with the resources. At that time, they would also draft the letter required from a registered health professional to support receiving the specific help Ramona needed regarding her living situation.

Ramona received the right support from the right teams as the therapy team provided her with an opportunity to explore her feelings and identify effective coping suggestions to manage her immediate anxiety along with an invitation to return for additional single sessions of therapy when she thought one would be helpful. The system navigator focused on her instrumental needs: her living arrangements and additional support to access expert domestic violence support in the community. At the end of the session, Ramona reported a high degree of satisfaction with the team approach and a significant reduction in her distress from pre-session level of eight compared to a post-session level of distress 3.

The New Hybrid Model

On the first open access/walk-in day after three years, the ECMHS provided five single-session/(OAAT) therapy sessions and one walk-in crisis counseling session. Prior to the onset of the COVID-19 pandemic, single-session therapy was the only service available to clients when they walked into the main location in a northeastern neighborhood of Calgary. The ECMHS, as a newly developed Mental Health HUB, now offers a combination of open access/walk-in single-session therapy, system navigation, and family crisis counseling. Currently, in-person open-access walk-in single-session therapy, family crisis counseling, and system navigation are available twice a week, and virtual single-session therapy services are offered twice a week. Both in-person and virtual single-session therapy services (or hybrid days) are offered twice a week. Evidence consistently shows that clients like to the option to choose when and how they will come for therapy. In 2022, 85% of ECMHS single-session therapy clients reported a reduction of distress following an intervention, 86% reported high satisfaction with the intake process, 87% reported high satisfaction with the team approach, and 94% reported feeling heard, respected, and understood.

Library-Based Support Counseling and Navigation

As part of its new Mental Health HUB service, the ECMHS plans to extend its reach to select community locations. In 2020, ECMHS in partnership with the Calgary Public Library launched the *Wellness Desk* – an open-access space for therapeutic conversations, launched in 2020. The Wellness Desk aligned completely with ECMHS' years of experience providing accessible one-at-a-time mental health support in the community. ECMHS' crisis counseling team (CCT) currently delivers mental health and addiction support at three different libraries across the city.

Access to the library-based services is straightforward. As noted by the staff at the *Wellness Desk*, there are very few barriers short of coming through a door. One library staff member commented that we are there to support people who have historically avoided mental health support for various reasons. Using the Warm Transfer approach, as noted above, CCT crisis counselors complete an intake and provide a crisis service. This crisis service could be followed by an immediate appointment for single-session therapy (virtual or in-person for a client seen at the Wellness Desk, ensuring access to all services, including single-session therapy and/or system navigation at the ECMHS Hub) or system navigation as required.

In Conclusion, We Are Now an Integrated Ethnocultural Team

Forty percent of ECMHS clients identify as having diverse cultural backgrounds, with language, race, gender, or immigration and newcomer experiences often constituting barriers to accessing mental health services. Canadian Mental Health Association (CMHA) is clear: "There are consequences for the inadequate and inequitable treatment of mental illness" (CMHA, 2018). Over the past two years, the ECMHS has responded to the calls for change in Canadian society to address structural racism in mental health service delivery. The ECMHS leadership group has intentionally developed an integrated ethnocultural team of mental health service providers by modifying hiring and training processes for CCT crisis counselors and Hub clinical therapists. Language and cultural proficiencies were identified as qualifications at the same level as other training and experiences. An ECMHS crisis counselor stated in 2021, "We are now the clients we see." The definition of barrier-free and open-access mental health services at ECMHS is now clearly defined as ethnocultural, gender affirming, and equitable as well as immediate and no-cost to the client.

Note

1 A pseudonym.

References

Blackstaffe, A. (2020). *Eastside Family Centre & Community Resource Team: Possibilities for Integrated Services. Unpublished Manuscript.* Wood's Homes Research Department.

Bloom, B.L. (2001). Focused single session psychotherapy: A review of the clinical and research literature. *Brief Treatment and Crisis Intervention,* 1(1), 75–86.

Boscolo, L., Cecchin, G., Hoffman, L., & Penn, P. (1987). *Milan Systemic Family Therapy: Conversations in Theory and Practice.* New York: Basic Books.

Bostock, L., & Britt, R. (2014). *Effective approaches to hub and spoke provision: a rapid review of the literature.* Social Care Research Associates. Retrieved from www.alexiproject.org.uk

Canadian Mental Health Association (CMHA). (2018). *Mental Health in Balance: Ending the health care disparity in Canada.* https://cmha.ca/brochure/mental-health-in-the-balance-ending-the-health-care-disparity-in-canada/

Clements, R., McElheran, N., Hackney, L., & Park, H., (2011). The eastside family centre: 20 years of single session walk-in therapy. In A. Slive, & M. Bobele (Eds). *When One Hour is All You Have: Effective Therapy for Walk-in Clients* (pp. 109–127). Phoenix, AZ: Zeig, Tucker & Theisen

Cornish, P.A., Churchill, A., & Hair, H.J. (2020). Open-access single-session therapy in the context of stepped care 2.0. *Journal of Systemic Therapies,* 39, 21–33.

Dahlgreen, G., & Whitehead, M. (2021). The Dahlgren-Whitehead model of health determinants: 30 years on and still chasing rainbows. *Science Direct,* 199, 20–24.

Duncan, B.L., Miller, S.D., & Sparks, J. (2004). *The Heroic Client: A Revolutionary Way to Improve Effectiveness through Client-Directed Outcome Informed Therapy.* San Francisco, CA: Josey-Bass.

GermAnn, K., MacKean, G., & Butler, B. (2018). *Exploring mental health services and supports for children, youth and families in Calgary: A report to the United Way of Calgary & Area.* United Way Calgary office. Retrieved from https://www.thesocialimpactlab.com/wp-content/uploads/2018/10/United-Way-Exploring-Mental-Health-Services-and-Supports.pdf August 20, 2020.

Hoyt, M.F. (Ed.) (1998). *The Handbook of Constructive Therapies.* San Francisco: Josey-Bass.

Hoyt, M.F., Young, J., & Rycroft, P. (2021). Single session thinking and practice going global one step at a time. In M. F. Hoyt, J. Young, & P. Rycroft (Eds). *Single Session Thinking and Practice in Global, Cultural, and Familial Contexts: Expanding Applicants* (pp. 2–26). New York: Routledge.

Links, P.S., Eynan, R., & Shah, R. (2019). Are new standards for assessing and managing suicidal patients needed in Canada? *The Canadian Journal of Psychiatry*, 64, 400–404.

Lipchik, E. (2002). *Beyond Technique in Solution-Focused Therapy*. New York: Guilford Press

McElheran, N. (2021). The story of the eastside family centre: 30 years of walk-in single session therapy. In M. F. Hoyt, J. Young, & P. Rycroft (Eds). *Single Session Thinking and Practice in Global, Cultural and Familial Contexts: Expanding Applications* (pp. 125–132). New York: Routledge.

McElheran, N., Harper-Jaques, S., & Lawson, A. (2020). Introduction to the special section: Walk-in and single session and booked single-session therapy in Canada. *Journal of Systemic Therapies,* 39, 15–20.

Slive, A., & Bobele, M. (2011). Walking in: An aspect of everyday living. In A. Slive, & M. Bobele (Eds). *When One Hour is All You Have: Effective Therapy for Walk-in Clients* (pp. 11–22). Phoenix: Zeig, Tucker & Theisen.

Slive, A., McElheran, N., & Lawson, A. (2008). How brief does it get? Walk-in single session therapy. *Journal of Systemic Therapies*, 27, 5–22.

Slive, A., McElheran, N., Oakander, M., & Amundson. (1995). Walk-in single session: A new paradigm in clinical service delivery. *Journal of Systemic Therapies*, 14, 3–11.

Stewart, J., McElheran, N., Park, H., Oakander, M., MacLaurin, B., Jing Fang, C., & Robinson, A. (2018). Twenty-five years of walk-in single sessions at the eastside family centre: Clinical and research dimensions. In M. F. Hoyt, M. Bobele, A. Slive, J. Young, & M. Talmon (Eds). *Single-Session Therapy by Walk-in or Appointment: Administrative, Clinical and Supervisory Aspects of One-at-a-Time Services* (pp. 72–90). New York: Routledge.

Talmon, M. (1990). *Single Session Therapy: Maximizing the Effect of the First (and Often Only) Therapeutic Encounter*. San Francisco, CA: Jossey-Bass.

Valaitis, R., Carter, N., Lam, A., Nicholl, J., Feather, J., & Cleghorn, L. (2017). *Implementation and maintenance of patient navigation programs linking primary care with community-based health and social services: A scoping literature review. BMC Health Services Research*, 17(1), 116. https://bmchealthservres.biomedcentral.com/track/pdf/10.1186/s12913-017-2046-1

White, M., & Epstein, D. (1990). *Narrative Means to Therapeutic Ends*. New York: Norton

World Health Organization (WHO). (2013). *Mental Health Action Plan 2013–2020*. Geneva: WHO.

Chapter 7

Walk-in Together
Online Therapy for Families, When and Where They Want It

Lynda Moore, Aaron Knuckey, Nick Barrington, Kelly Tsorlinis, Elizabeth George, Karen Story, Eliza Hartley, Jennifer McIntosh and Jeff Young

Introduction

This chapter describes an online, walk-in, single-session family therapy service called *Walk-in Together* (WIT). WIT was launched and piloted by The Bouverie Centre in response to the overwhelming demand for timely mental health services during the COVID-19 pandemic. In this chapter, WIT is situated within the single-session, walk-in, and telehealth literature, the delivery model described, pilot data presented, and outcomes and client feedback shared. Operational and clinical considerations are discussed, illustrated by examples of the work. The chapter concludes with a discussion about potential wider applications.

Walk-in Together: A Response to Overwhelming Demand[1]

At the end of 2019, devastating bushfires ravaged Australia, followed by the COVID-19 pandemic. These crises exacerbated a pre-existing unmet demand for accessible, affordable, responsive mental health services (Australian Bureau of Statistics, 2015; Australian Institute of Health and Welfare, 2021; Slade et al., 2009; Senate Select Committee on Mental Health and Suicide, 2021) and underscored the fact that addressing the tension between overwhelming demand and inadequate service capacity would "require new approaches to service provision" (Young, Rycroft & Hoyt, 2020, p. 215).

Underpinned by the ethos and principles of single-session thinking (Young & Rycroft, 2019), WIT combines the immediacy of in-person walk-in models (Bloom & Tam, 2015; Miller & Slive, 2004; Stewart et al., 2018; Young, 2018) with the additional accessibility and clinical possibilities afforded by an online mode of service delivery.

DOI: 10.4324/9781003351375-7

Locating WIT within Single-Session and Walk-in Services Internationally

Walk-in services have their origin in Medical Emergency Rooms and Free Clinics in the 1960s in the US (Hoyt et al., 2018). In 1990, Arnie Slive and colleagues at Woods Homes Eastside Family Centre in Calgary, Canada, pioneered walk-in single-session therapeutic services after a series of community consultations found people wanted accessible services with no unnecessary paperwork and procedures, delivered in non-stigmatising contexts such as shopping centres and provided when needed most, such as Friday evenings and Saturdays (Slive et al., 1995).

Since then, walk-in therapy services have expanded across Canada (Young, 2018) and other parts of the world (Levin et al., 2018). Supported by a growing body of evidence (Harper-Jaques & Foucault, 2014; Hartley et al., 2023; Hymmen et al., 2013; Josling & Cait, 2018; Lamsal et al., 2018; Miller and Slive, 2004; Stalker et al., 2015), walk-in services are designed to meet client need at the time help is sought (Horton et al., 2012; McElheran et al., 2020; Slive & Bobele, 2011; Stalker et al., 2012). Clients are seen immediately, with few intake criteria and minimum red tape. Assessment does not follow lengthy, standardised proformas but occurs in response to what is needed to help the client get what they want from therapy. Consistent with the data from single-session therapies more generally, (Bloom, 1981; Boyhan, 1996; Campbell, 2012; Hoyt et al., 2021; Talmon, 1990), client outcomes are positive and satisfaction with walk-in sessions is high (Harper-Jacques & Foucault, 2014; Hartley et al., 2023; Hymmen et al., 2013; Miller, 2008). Many clients find one session enough to create sufficient momentum for change in the client's prioritised area of need (Hoyt et al., 2021), thus liberating precious resources for clients needing more intensive or longer-term interventions (Slive & Bobele, 2019; Young & Jebreen, 2019).

WIT sessions are guided by single-session thinking (Young et al., 2020), following the ten core elements of The Bouverie Centre's single-session family therapy approach (Rycroft & Young, 2021): negotiating a client-led outcome, establishing clients' priorities, finding a focus and talking about the most important things, checking in with client(s) regularly, interrupting respectfully as needed to help clients get what they want, making time your friend, sharing your thoughts openly with clients, preparing to end well (reaching closure if not solution or resolution), leaving the door open and listening to client voices (following up, seeking feedback and utilising it). Families are viewed as resourceful and resilient. The therapist's role is to actively support family members in achieving their desired outcomes for the session. Put simply, each aspect of the approach is guided by the question, "What will be most helpful for the family today?"

Locating WIT within the Telehealth Literature

The COVID-19 pandemic saw unprecedented restrictions in Australia and elsewhere on people's movement and ability to gather. Along with many other organisations, The Bouverie Centre was suddenly required to deliver its services online. Acceptance of online therapeutic services grew for both clients and practitioners (Aafjes-van Doorn et al., 2021; McLean et al., 2021). Online delivery opened the way for communities previously precluded by distance and cost to access support (Anderson et al., 2017; McLean et al., 2021).

Therapeutic services delivered online are often referred to as 'telehealth'. We have adopted this term due to its applicability to "all forms of ICT[2]-enabled health care (across) all health care professions" (Doraiswamy et al., 2020, p. 2). Other terms such as ehealth, telemental health, or digital health video therapy could also be applied.

Despite emerging evidence for the efficacy of telehealth services (McLean et al., 2021), they do not in themselves address overwhelming demand. WIT combines the advantages of telehealth to increase access to family therapy services with those of single-session thinking and a walk-in delivery model to reduce waiting times and length of service.

The WIT Service Delivery Model

People contacting The Bouverie Centre seeking family therapy are offered WIT in addition to, or instead of, a scheduled Intake appointment (where the caller will be screened for the ongoing family therapy waiting list or redirected to another service). The only eligibility criteria for WIT are that two or more people attend together and at least one of them resides in the jurisdiction of the Centre's State Government funding body.

To date, the WIT pilot has operated one afternoon a week over a five- to six-hour period, providing a series of standalone 75- to 90-minute sessions of family therapy which take place online using the videoconferencing platform, Zoom. Under the model applied for the first 18 months of WIT and described in this chapter, a family member requiring therapy calls reception during WIT's operating hours, at or near the time the family is ready to be seen. The family is informed of its position in that afternoon's queue and given an approximate start time.[3]

The 'front door' to WIT is critical. Reception staff explain how the service operates and actively assist the family to prepare for the upcoming session. This may include advising on the type of devices to use, the number of people per device, supporting those unfamiliar with or anxious about the technology, helping family members download and get started on Zoom, resolving audio, camera and other technical issues and liaising with interpreters or support workers when required. About 10–15 minutes before a session is due to start, reception staff telephone family members and obtain the requisite details for registration. The videoconferencing link is then emailed to family members and the WIT session can begin.

A Walk-in Together Session

Operating on a roster system, the WIT therapy team of the day comprises three[4] family therapists trained in single-session thinking. Occasionally, an additional therapist from a partner organisation joins the team as part of a mutually beneficial, in-kind arrangement.

The therapy team enters the teleconferencing 'room' and designates two therapists to conduct the session. One of these two therapists is selected to open the session and the other takes responsibility for monitoring time. Once all participating family members have gathered in the waiting room, the team welcomes the family in, introductions are carried out, and the designated therapist outlines the suggested process for the session. The third therapist then turns their camera and microphone off and the session begins.

The third therapist plays a complex and vital role entailing:

- Maintaining a typed, electronic record of the session, called the session summary, which plays a crucial therapeutic role
- Providing to the therapists 'in the room' peer support and oversight regarding risk (relayed directly and privately between therapists via the Zoom chat function)
- Communicating with reception staff via text message about technical assistance needs of the family being seen, the number and any support needs of families in the queue, and the estimated end time of the session in progress so families in the queue can be kept informed.

About 20–30 minutes before the end of the session, the third therapist is invited to turn their camera and microphone back on. While the family observes, the team offers a brief and focused therapeutic reflection (Young & Rycroft, 1997) of their observations, rhetorical questions, ideas and suggestions. Following this, family members are invited to respond with their thoughts on what they have just heard.

In the final phase, the session summary is shared on-screen for all participants to read, or, when indicated, is read aloud by the third therapist. Edits are made in collaboration with the family to ensure the document is accurate and captures the points most salient to them. Referral options and resources are included. Each family member is then invited to share what they are taking away from the session and, while the family looks on, these are added to the summary using family's own words.

On leaving, family members are informed they are welcome to 'walk back in' at any time and encouraged to first try out the ideas raised in the session. Eligible families may also seek ongoing family therapy at The Bouverie Centre through the usual pathway. As soon as possible after the session, the session summary is emailed to the family. Once this document is saved on the Centre's database, all tasks are complete.

Outcomes

As of December 2022, 147 WIT sessions had taken place. Of those, 129 (88%) families attended once, while 18 (12%) were with families returning for a second, or in one case, third, session. Families attending WIT presented with similar issues to those accessing ongoing therapy at The Bouverie Centre, including a serious mental health issue of a family member (eating disorders, schizophrenia, major depressive disorder, personality disorders, bipolar affective disorders), self-harm, suicidal thoughts, and trauma. WIT families also presented with issues related to grief, neurodiversity, parenting, gender identity, cross-cultural inter-generational issues, and conflict and/or family violence.

A proof-of-concept study was undertaken after the first six months (Hartley et al., 2023) to investigate the acceptability and short-term effectiveness of WIT. Twenty-two families shared their experiences pre-session, post-session and at a six-week follow-up. The WIT therapists also completed a qualitative interview to understand their experience of working within the WIT framework. The findings were largely consistent with existing evidence regarding the value of walk-in models of service delivery (Slive & Bobele, 2019). Specifically, it found most family members (85%) reported their WIT session provided effective support for their presenting challenge. Half of adult participants were more optimistic about their future as a family after their WIT session. At the six-week follow-up, benefits continued to be reported: 88% of family members continued to feel confident about what to do next. All therapists experienced the model as offering a timely, beneficial and flexible service that is effective for a range of presentations and constellations of families.

These preliminary results suggest WIT provides families effective, accessible support at the time it is needed. The proof-of-concept study has opened the door to further research into and development of WIT services at The Bouverie Centre, and work is underway to develop a research protocol and methods of data collection that can be seamlessly incorporated into WIT's clinical processes.

Key Considerations

In this section, we share ideas for those thinking about establishing a walk-in telehealth family therapy service. Rather than reiterating themes already well covered in the literature, our focus will be on the more novel features of WIT, namely its online and co-therapy aspects. We have gained these insights from direct experience, reflecting on our successes, mistakes, and missteps, and from ideas articulated and interrogated in our monthly group supervision.

Fostering Accessibility and Inclusivity Online

Ironically, the same communication technology that makes WIT more accessible to many can be a barrier for others. We will never know how many potential clients have not attempted to access WIT. Of those who do, some are unfamiliar with telehealth technology or must manage with poor internet connection. This adds an element of stress to the anxiety commonly experienced by families coming to therapy for the first time:

> By the time Clara, 54, enters the virtual therapy room she is sobbing. She has had numerous unsuccessful attempts to enter the Zoom room with her camera and audio functioning. Through her tears, she shares her belief that this is just another example of her failure as a person, as nothing in her life ever works. Her presence in the session, however, suggests otherwise to the team. Team members validate her experience and set out to understand what else is 'not working' in Clara's life that has led to this response. This has a calming effect and opens the way for the team to begin exploring with Clara and her mother, Dorothea, what they would like from their session. As the conversation unfolds, Clara and Dorothea can see the role that the trauma from past family violence plays in their relationship and in Clara's feelings of incompetence. At the end of the session, despite initial concerns that telehealth might not suit this family, Clara states that it has been the best session of therapy she has ever had. This positive outcome was made possible by the hospitality, technological skill and support offered by reception staff.

WIT starting times can be pre-arranged to support access for families needing interpreters or to allow for a First Nations therapist to be present for First Nations families.

Providing Containment and Flexibility Online

Thank you very much for the session yesterday; it was great (my 7yo) felt so comfortable. It will mean other opportunities to talk to people won't be so scary. Thank you for the case notes. Lots of reading and digesting going forward.

Family therapy traditionally takes place in an environment largely controlled by the therapist. The combined walk-in and telehealth aspects of WIT reduce this control. Family members may attend together or from different locations. It is not known to the team how safe or private those spaces are. From the outset, the team attunes to each person's environment while engaging the family. The family might need support to adjust their surroundings (move to another room, go outside, close a door). It is requested that all family members can be seen and heard, with their cameras switched on.

In keeping with single-session principles, flexibility and choice are essential components of a respectful, ethical and safe online therapeutic environment. Examples of flexibility shown by the team include the in-the-moment reallocation of roles, the use of breakout rooms to see family members separately, doing reflections differently, and not sharing the session summary when this is not the most helpful use of time. Flexibility is shown when determining which family members attend and how they participate. Children and young people, for example, can step in and out as needed, and creative solutions can be found to meet specific client needs:

Mia, 16, is brought to WIT by her parents, Leo and Tanya, along with Mia's younger sister, Maddie. Leo and Tanya want to talk about how they can better support Mia, who has in recent years developed anxiety, begun to self-harm and sometimes has suicidal thoughts. Maddie wants to restore the close relationship she once had with Mia. Mia, with her camera turned off, uses the zoom chat function to share that she does not want anything from the session. The team gently explores the possibility of Mia switching her camera on, explaining why it is helpful. Mia types that she does not want her camera on. The team asks Mia how she will let them know if she is becoming upset or uncomfortable during the session, given that they will not be able to see or hear her. Mia types that she will let them know through the chat. One of the two co-therapists volunteers to keep a close eye on the chat box for input from Mia and the session continues. Using chat, Mia makes some detailed and deeply poignant contributions that provide vital information to her family that she has never shared before.

Picking up on Non-verbal Cues Online

In a physical room, family members' whole bodies and faces are in full view, when via telehealth, it is often only their heads and shoulders.

Multiple family members sharing one device need to sit further back to be captured by the camera. In these conditions, their images are small, especially when the device is a phone. Discerning facial expressions and shifts in posture can be difficult. Sound quality varies. Therapists' ability to pick up on cues that would usually prompt a response is reduced. To offset this, reception staff coach families to use multiple devices where possible. In the session itself, WIT therapists check in regularly with the family about how the session is going and how they are feeling and ask directly about any non-verbal cues that are detected:

> John and Mary attend WIT with their four children, Alex (3), Brent (6) Krystal (10) and Kevin (12) following the sudden loss of the children's grandparents six months earlier. Brent is playing with the device settings and tools and moving on and off camera. This begins to frustrate his parents, who are concerned he is wasting everyone's time. The team wonders out loud if this behaviour is telling us something about how Brent is feeling. Is Brent, rather than being difficult, in fact anxious about talking about his loss? When Brent is asked directly if this is so, he becomes much calmer and less distracted. He then tells his parents he does not want to talk about it now and is allowed to go to his bedroom, allowing his older siblings and parents to continue the session.

Working with Trauma Online

The session was just what we needed then and put a floor under what felt like the bottom was about to fall out of everything. Not out of the woods by a long way but feeling like there's a way out which is what we needed. Thanks again.

The Bouverie Centre is funded to provide therapy to families where a member has a diagnosis of a serious mental illness or has experienced significant trauma. Establishing WIT raised questions about the safety of this service for families facing complex issues. Could it provide safety and containment without physical proximity? Would one unplanned session via telehealth be enough?

> Jenny, 26, attends with her mother, Sophia. Jenny wants to know more about her father, Marc, Sophia's husband, who died by suicide when Jenny was young. Jenny and Sophia have never been able to talk about Marc together before. Jenny tells the team she has PTSD and has been in individual therapy for some time. She describes herself as 'easily triggered'. The team asks Jenny if she knows some useful strategies for managing her triggers. Jenny knows a breathing exercise that is effective, so

the team asks if she would mind teaching them this technique. Jenny steps them through the exercise, and everyone practises it together. The conversation about Jenny's father begins. The team checks in with both family members from time to time. To the team's surprise, neither becomes overly distressed despite the range of deep emotions Jenny and Sophia experience over the course of this session.

Managing Family Violence Risk Online

WIT therapists know very little about the families they will be seeing prior to meeting them in the session. Rather than relying on screening processes or tools (which may or may not detect family violence, and which may deny or delay families living with family violence from being seen), WIT therapists assume family violence and other risks to client safety may be present in every session. As in ongoing family therapy, risk that becomes known in session is managed in the moment and according to current best practice principles. These include: an understanding of the risk factors, drivers, and impact (on adults and children) of family violence, the obligation of all practitioners to identify, assess, and respond to family violence risk with the safety of victim survivors as the core priority, and the importance of creating opportunities for those using violence to be accountable for it[5] (Australia's National Research Organisation for Women's Safety, 2018; Toivonen & Backhouse, 2018).

The WIT response to family violence is guided by several factors. These include whether the person using violence is present in the session, whether the violence is known to the team or merely suspected, whether the violent behaviour is acknowledged by the family in the session and able to be safely and openly discussed, and the nature of the violence. WIT therapists are alert to 'red flags' that suggest the possibility of family violence. Where the person using violence is not present, or its victim-survivors imply a level of safety by volunteering information about the behaviour, the issue is carefully explored, risk assessed, and plans put in place to promote safety. When the person using violence is present, the priority is to avoid inadvertently increasing risk to other family members, for example, by inviting them to say something that might attract retribution after the session.

WIT therapists employ a sensitive and trauma-informed response to the person using violence while not condoning the behaviours of concern. With safety as a priority, they explore motivation for change and promote responsibility-taking by the person using violence. The WIT model is applied flexibly and guided by the informed professional judgement of the team. For example, on one occasion, the therapists were made aware prior to the session that family violence was occurring. The two attending family members also knew that the therapists had been informed. The session began with the therapist obtaining agreement with the family that the team would split and simultaneously conduct the first part of the session with each family member separately. The team then met to consider whether regrouping for the second part of the session would be safe for the partner of the person using violence.

WIT families benefit from the added layer of oversight of the WIT inbuilt 'one way screen', with the observing third therapist assuming the role of peer supervisor, able to send alerts or suggestions via the chat function directly to the co-therapists 'in the room'. Any concerns about safety become the priority for the session and, where safe to do so, appropriate referrals are made, safety plans developed, and other protective actions taken as required. After the session, WIT therapists discuss whether follow-up with family members, managers or other services is indicated. The experience of the team is that the need for next day follow-up is uncommon. No critical incidents have been reported during the life of WIT:

Jules hesitates and glances at Heath before answering the therapist's question. Heath appears fidgety and tense. While he does not live with Jules and 10-month-old Ivy, it is important to Heath to have a good relationship with his daughter. Heath has come to WIT because he and Jules are "always getting into arguments." "Could you give us an example of the kind of argument that brought you here today, Heath?" "And then what happens?" "What's the worst it's ever got?" Heath has flashes of frustration at some of the questions. His answers are mumbled; the team remains unclear about the nature of the arguments. Heath says he has done an anger management course, which taught him to walk away when he gets "really worked up". What are the signs that tell him he is getting "worked up"? The team asks what happens in Heath's body during the arguments, what it might be like for Jules and Ivy when he gets "really worked up", and what kind of relationship he'd like with his daughter. The end-of-session reflection includes, among other things, an acknowledgement of Heath's determination to be a good partner and dad. It includes a clear statement that aggression and violence are harmful to both adults and children, information about trauma and its effects, and a musing about whether some of Heaths' current difficulties could be connected to childhood experiences he has briefly alluded to. It is stated that safety is needed before relationships can heal and grow strong. Heath is encouraged to continue to work on ways to avoid "getting worked up", and relevant services are recommended. In response to a request from Jules, counselling options are suggested to help with her anxiety.

The following morning, mindful that Jules might not be alone or her emails private, a therapist from the team emails Jules asking her to call at a time that suits, as the team has further information that might help with her anxiety. During that call, when Jules can speak freely, the risk to Jules and Ivy is assessed, a safety plan devised and referrals to a family violence service made.

Attending to the Co-therapy Relationship

... the (multi-therapist) team is excellent. We've been to lots of psychologists over the years, but this has been so much more helpful. Thank you.

The co-therapy relationship is key to the success of the work. Co-therapists need to be safe and supported in that relationship to contain and support the family in theirs. Like any other relationship, co-therapy relationships can take time to evolve and grow. In the words of Jeff Young, previous Director of The Bouverie Centre and peer consultation group facilitator, "there are always issues in a co-therapy relationship, whether small or extreme. The important thing is whether they are discussed or not" (personal communication).

The co-therapeutic relationship can be attended to:

Before the session: "How would you like to work with me?" "What is your preferred style of working?" "Is there anything in particular you'd like to focus on, or like me to focus on, today?" "What will we do if things aren't going well between us, and our relationship needs attention during the session?" "How would you let me know if you felt this way?"

In session: In the spirit of improvised theatre, WIT therapists aim to make their partners look good. They support each other and give each other space, know each other's strengths and put them to good use, and check in with themselves and each other during the session. The team is mindful that if problems arise within the co-therapy relationship, it could be in parallel process with the family's relational patterns. Curious, non-blaming meta-conversations are had in front of the family, where therapists might 'talk about the talking' or share reflections with each other while the family looks on. For example, one therapist might ask the other "I don't know about you, but I'm thinking Chrissie is probably feeling pretty overwhelmed right now and that things aren't going to change any time soon. While Ben seems to be hanging on to hope. I wonder if you and I might also be feeling caught between these two understandable positions?"

Post session: Time is taken to debrief – "What did we do well? What didn't work so well?" "What were you guided by at this point in the session?" "What could we do differently next time this happens?"

Thanks ...for providing us with a safe and understanding space when we needed it to share and as a team your respective roles in listening, guiding and reflecting was all helpful to us.

The Power of the Session Summary

I am truly amazed at the quality of the service you were able to provide. The detailed notes and the referral to additional counsellors is also appreciated. We may not have solved everything during the session but the fact we were able talk and hear each other in a safe structured environment was very helpful.

The session summary (Figure 7.1) is an intervention in itself. Written for the family as a therapeutic document, it also serves as the case notes for the client file. It is not a verbatim transcript of the discussion but is carefully curated by the third therapist, emphasising salient moments using the family's own language, while introducing subtle reframes.

The session summary typically includes the following:

• New information for family members and points that resonate for them
• What has been tried so far and has not worked for the family
• Exceptions to the problem, successful strategies the family has employed and other resources
• Information that might help the family achieve their hopes for change
• Thoughts from the reflection that made an impact on the family
• The family's feedback to the therapists' reflection
• The family's agreed actions
• Referral and resource options with website links

It is unhelpful to record too much information. Lengthy session summaries take a long time for the family to read at the end of a draining session. Facts that are well known to the family and not related to the achievement of their goals are not included. Shared in real time, this document validates family members' experiences and plays an important role in them getting what they need from the session.

Potential Wider Applications

We attended the Monday walk-in program yesterday and found the session to be very helpful and a positive experience. Given that, I write to cancel the Intake appointment with you on the 25/11 as it is no longer required.

WIT has shown the capacity to deliver high-quality and effective walk-in family therapy via telehealth, offering flexibility and access to family members from any location. Clinicians appreciate the energising and mutually supportive aspects of the therapy team approach. Client-focused follow-up

LA TROBE
UNIVERSITY

the bouverie centre

Walk-In Together Session Summary
Who came:
Therapists:
Date:

What we came for:
-

What we talked about:
-

What we are taking away:
-

Figure 7.1 The WIT session summary

outside shift hours and consultation with line managers is rarely required. The benefits to clients, referring services, clinicians and managers are evident, and the model has applicability to a wide range of services.

The multi-therapist team structure also creates opportunities for clinicians from partner organisations to participate on the team. This benefits the guest therapist through direct experience, and the WIT team and family through their additional perspective and specialist knowledge. The WIT development plan includes initiating partnerships with specialist services in mutually beneficial collaborations.

Based on the positive reception to date from Aboriginal and Torres Strait Islander families attending WIT, we are currently seeking funding to develop a specialist First Nations WIT.

Conclusion

The Bouverie Centre's *Walk-In Together* pilot represents an important step in advancing the availability of accessible, brief mental health care for families in distress, offering a quality mental health intervention at the time of greatest need. While further research is required with larger samples, early indications suggest that when families know there is opportunity for further support via another WIT session and/or joining the waitlist for ongoing therapy, many find an immediately available, one-off session sufficient. There is emerging evidence that WIT helps reduce the number of families waiting for therapy, offering hope for efforts to reduce the burden on the mental health system, whilst at the same time improving client care.

The Bouverie Centre has committed to the expansion and further research of WIT, with a view to informing future service design by building a pool of data over time to illuminate the critical features of this model of walk-in family therapy by telehealth. Knowledge translation to the field and avenues for collaboration and partnership will increase the reach of walk-in support to a greater number of families and communities, providing more people with the help they need, when and where they want it.

Acknowledgements

The authors would like to acknowledge the staff and clients of The Bouverie Centre[6] for contributing to the practice wisdom upon which this chapter is based.

We would also like to acknowledge the traditional custodians of the land on which Walk-in Together operates, the Wurundjeri Woi Wurrung people of the Kulin nation.[7] We pay our respects to Elders past, present and emerging.

Notes

1 WIT is part of a planned comprehensive tiered model of service delivery comprising three components; a 24/7 self-help family mental health e-hub (in development); a virtual walk-in one-off family therapy service (the focus of this chapter) and an ongoing family therapy service inspired by single-session thinking (established; see Young, 2020).
2 ICT – Information and Communications Technology.
3 Currently, a trial is underway whereby calls are taken from earlier in the day and families are offered an allocated afternoon session time. This provides the family with certainty about when to convene and therapists and administration staff with greater predictability.
4 A two-person delivery format is now also being trialled.
5 Victorian Government Multi Agency Risk Assessment and Management framework, https://www.vic.gov.au/maram-practice-guides-foundation-knowledge-guide/principles-based-approach-practice.
6 The Bouverie Centre is an integrated practice-research-translation family therapy centre at La Trobe University, Melbourne, Australia.
7 The Wurundjeri Woi Wurrung people are one of five Clans making up the Kulin Nation, which prospered for over 60,000 years until colonised by Europeans. Today, Kulin people continue to live, practice and strengthen their culture in Melbourne and central Victoria.

References

Aafjes-van Doorn, K., Békés, V., & Prout, T. A. (2021). Grappling with our therapeutic relationship and professional self-doubt during COVID-19: Will we use video therapy again? *Counselling Psychology Quarterly, 34*(3–4), 473–484. https://doi.org/10.1080/09515.070.2020.1773404

Anderson, K. E., Byrne, C. E., Crosby, R. D., & Le Grange, D. (2017). Utilizing telehealth to deliver family-based treatment for adolescent anorexia nervosa. *International Journal of Eating Disorders, 50*, 1235–1238. https://doi.org/10.1002/eat.22759

Australian Bureau of Statistics. (2015) Mental Health Statistics – Cat. no. 4330.0. Available from: https://www.abs.gov.au/ausstats/abs@.nsf/second+level+view?ReadForm&prodno=4330.0&viewtitle=Mental%20Health%20Statistics~2015~Latest~31/03/2015&&tabname=Related%20Products&prodno=4330.0&issue=2015&num=&view=& [Accessed 25 May 2022].

Australian Institute of Health and Welfare. (2021). *Mental Health Expenditure.* https://www.aihw.gov.au/mental-health/topic-areas/expenditure#Overview

Australia's National Research Organisation for Women's Safety. (2018). *Culturally and linguistically diverse project with action research initiative: Cultural safety principles and guidelines.* ANROWS.

Bloom, B. L. (1981). Focused single-session therapy: Initial development and evaluation. In S. H. Budman (Ed.), *Forms of brief therapy* (pp. 167–216). Guilford Press.

Bloom, K., & Tam, J. A. (2015). Walk-in services for child and family mental health. *Journal of Systemic Therapies, 34*(1), 61–77.

Boyhan, P. (1996). Clients' perceptions of single session consultations as an option to waiting for family therapy. *Australian and New Zealand Journal of Family Therapy, 17*(2), 85–96.

Campbell, A. (2012). Single-session approaches to therapy: Time to review. *Australian and New Zealand Journal of Family Therapy, 33*(1), 15–26.

Doraiswamy, S., Abraham, A., Mamtani, R., & Cheema, S. (2020). Use of telehealth during the COVID-19 pandemic: Scoping review. *Journal of Medical Internet Research, 22*(12), e24087.

Harper-Jacques, S., & Foucault, D. (2014). Walk-in single session therapy: Client satisfactions and outcomes. *Journal of Systemic Therapies, 33*(3), 29–49.

Hartley, E., Moore, L., Knuckey, A., von Doussa, H., Painter, F., Story, K., Barrington, N., Young, J., & McIntosh, J. (2023). Walk-in together: A pilot study of a walk-in online family therapy intervention. *Australian and New Zealand Journal of Family Therapy.* https://doi.org/10.1002/anzf.1534

Horton, S., Stalker, C. A., Cait, C. A., & Josling, L. (2012). Sustaining walk-in counselling services: An economic assessment from a pilot study. *Healthcare Quarterly (Toronto, Ont.), 15*(3), 44–49.

Hoyt, M. F., Bobele, M., Slive, S., Young, J., & Talmon, M. (Eds.), (2018). *Single-session therapy by walk-in or appointment: Clinical, supervisory, and administrative aspects of one-at-a-time services.* Routledge.

Hoyt, M. F., Young, J., & Rycroft, P. (Eds.), (2021). *Single session thinking and practice in global, cultural, and familial contexts: Expanding applications.* Routledge.

Hymmen, P., Stalker, C. A., & Cait, C. -A. (2013). The case for single-session therapy: Does the empirical evidence support the increased prevalence of this service delivery model? *Journal of Mental Health, 22*(1), 60–71.

Josling, L., & Cait, C.-A. (2018). The walk-in counselling model: Research and advocacy. In M. F. Hoyt, M. Bobele, A. Slive, J. Young & M. Talmon (Eds.), *Single-session therapy by walk-in or appointment: Administrative, clinical, and supervisory aspects of one-at-a-time services* (pp. 91–103). Routledge.

Lamsal, R., Stalker, C. A., Cait, C.-A., Reimer, M., & Horton, S. (2018). Cost effectiveness analysis of single-session walk-in counselling. *Journal of Mental Health, 27*(6), 560–566. https://doi.org:10.1080/09638237.2017.1340619

Levin, S. B., Gil-Wilkerson, A, & Rapin De Yatim, S. (2018). Single-session walk-ins as a collaborative learning community at the Houston Galveston Institute. In M. F. Hoyt, M. Bobele, A. Slive, J. Young & M. Talmon (Eds.), *Single-session therapy by walk-in or MHMB appointment: Administrative, clinical, and supervisory aspects of one-at-a-time services* (pp. 72–90). Routledge.

McElheran, N., Harper-Jacques, S., & Lawson, A. (2020). Introduction to the special section: Walk-in single-session and booked single-session therapy in Canada. *Journal of Systemic Therapies, 39*(3), 15–20.

McLean, S. A., Booth, A. T., Schnabel, A., Wright, B. J., Painter, F. L., & McIntosh, J. E. (2021). Exploring the efficacy of telehealth for family therapy through systematic, meta-analytic, and qualitative evidence. *Clinical Child and Family Psychology Review, 24*, 244–266.

Miller, J. K. (2008). Walk-in single session team therapy: A study of client satisfaction. *Journal of Systemic Therapies, 27*(3), 78–94.

Miller, J. K., & Slive, A. (2004). Breaking down the barriers to clinical service delivery: Walk-in family therapy. *Journal of Marital and Family Therapy, 30*(1), 95–103.

Rycroft, P., & Young, J. (2021). Translating single session thinking into practice. In M. F. Hoyt, J. Young & P. Rycroft (Eds.), *Single-session thinking and practice in global, cultural, and familial contexts: Expanding applications* (pp.42–53). Routledge.

Senate Select Committee on Mental Health and Suicide. (2021). *Final Report.* Commonwealth of Australia.

Slade, T., Johnston, A., Teesson, M., Whiteford, H., Burgess, P., Pirkis, J. (2009). *The mental health of Australians 2. Report on the 2007 National Survey of Mental Health and Wellbeing.* Department of Health and Ageing.

Slive, A., & Bobele, M. (Eds.), (2011). *When one hour is all you have: Effective therapy for walk-in clients.* Tucker & Theisen.

Slive, A., & Bobele, M. (2019). Ideas for addressing doubts about walk-in/single session therapy. *Journal of Systemic Therapies, 38*(4), 17–30.

Slive, A., MacLaurin, B., Oakander, M., & Amundson, J. (1995). Walk-in single sessions: A new paradigm in clinical service delivery. *Journal of Systemic Therapies, 14*(1), 3–11.

Stalker, C. A., Horton, S., & Cait, C. A. (2012). Single-session therapy in a walk-in counseling clinic: A pilot study. *Journal of Systemic Therapies, 31*(1), 38–52.

Stalker, C. A., Riemer, M., Cait, C. A., Horton, S., Booton, J., Joslig, L., Bedgood, J., & Zaczek, M. (2015). A comparison of walk-in counselling and the wait-list model for delivering counselling services. *Journal of Mental Health.* https://doi.org/10.3109/09638237.2015.1101417.

Stewart, J., McElheran, N., Park, H., Oakander, M., MacLaurin, B., Fang, C.J., & Robinson, A. (2018). Twenty-five years of walk-in single-sessions at the eastside family centre: Clinical and research dimensions. In M. Hoyt, M. Bobele, A. Slive, J. Young & M. Talmon (Eds.), *Single-session therapy by walk-in or appointment: Administrative, clinical, and supervisory aspects of one-at-a-time services* (pp. 72–90). Routledge.

Talmon, M. (1990). *Single-session therapy: Maximizing the effect of the first (and often only) therapeutic encounter.* Jossey-Bass.

Toivonen, C., & Backhouse, C. (2018). *National risk assessment principles for domestic and family violence: Quick reference guide for practitioners (ANROWS Insights 10/2018).* ANROWS.

Young, J. (2020). Putting single session thinking to work: Conceptual, practical, training, and implementation ideas. *Australian and New Zealand Journal of Family Therapy, 41*(3), 231–248. https://doi.org/10.1002/anzf.1426

Young, J., & Rycroft, P. (1997). Single session therapy: Capturing the moment. *Psychotherapy in Australia, 4*(1), 18–23.

Young, J., & Rycroft, P. (2019). *Single session thinking: Going global one step at a time,* Third international single session and walkin services symposium. Melbourne, Australia.

Young, J., Rycroft, P., & Hoyt, M. F. (2020). Guest editorial special issue: Expanding applications of single session thinking and practice. *Australian and New Zealand Journal of Family Therapy*, 41(3), 215–217. https://doi.org/10.1002/anzf.1425

Young, K. (2018). Change in the winds: The growth of walk-in therapy clinics in Ontario, Canada. In M. F. Hoyt, M. Bobele, A. Slive, J. Young & M. Talmon (Eds.), *Single-session therapy by walk-in or appointment: Administrative, clinical, and supervisory aspects of one-at-a-time services* (pp. 59–71). Routledge.

Young, K., & Jebreen, J. (2019). Recognizing single-session therapy as psychotherapy. *Journal of Systemic Therapies, 38*(4), 31–44.

Chapter 8

Applying Walk-In/ Single-Session Therapy in Indigenous Mexican Communities

Saúl Cruz Valdivieso and Montana M. Holmes

Introduction

The psychotherapy literature needs more research informing practitioners on delivering meaningful, practical, and culturally relevant therapeutic services to indigenous populations in Mexico. Rarely do randomized controlled trials represent individuals from indigenous communities like San Cristóbal Chichicaxtepec, La Capellanía Guadalupe Etla, Aguaje El Zapote de Santa María Huatulco, San Isidro Apango, or Santa María Pápalo, Mexico. Nonetheless, psychotherapists such as I (Saúl) have been invited into these communities to offer services for various concerns. My relationship with indigenous villages such as San Isidro Apango, Bahías de San Agustín, Santa Ana Zegache, Santa Cruz Xoxocotlán, Santa María Temaxcalapa, and Santa Cruz Llano Crucero Tepuxtepec requires trust, sensitivity, and respectful non-intervention on behalf of the villages' cultural traditions and norms. For many years, my family cultivated and nurtured relationships with indigenous villages in Oaxaca, Mexico, and have been trusted to invite outsiders to provide medical services including psychotherapy, in what have been called "Medical Clinics." However, the socially dominant Westernized delivery of psychotherapy has not adequately captured the needs of indigenous people nor the practicality of delivering therapeutic services in such spaces. The transient nature of the Medical Clinics in indigenous villages requires brief and sustainable services. Because of these needs, single-session therapy (SST), or one-at-a-time therapy (OAAT), has positively informed my delivery of psychotherapy in indigenous communities. With the scholarly support of American psychologist Dr. Monte Bobele, I have applied and witnessed the success of walk-in/single-session therapy (WI/SST) with indigenous people and their unique problems. The following chapter includes an overview of my family's philanthropic relationship with indigenous villages in Oaxaca, Mexico, and professional psychotherapy work. Throughout this chapter, co-author (Montana) offers reflections and descriptions of WI/SST in indigenous

DOI: 10.4324/9781003351375-8

communities. We hope that this chapter highlights the applicability of WI/ SST with communities in the global majority.

Organización Armonía

In the late 1980s, my parents, Saúl Cruz Ramos, and María del Pilar Valdivieso López, went into impoverished communities such as the Jalalpa Tepito slums of Mexico City, Mexico, to offer religious, medical, psychological, and a host of other services in the hope to uplift communities. After some success, Cruz Ramos and Validivieso López founded Organización Armonía, known now as "Armonía," to serve these communities. Armonía is a non-governmental organization and Christian ministry that aims to walk alongside people in poverty to help facilitate change. Armonía's successful presence in indigenous villages is significantly due to Cruz Ramos' and Valdivieso López's strong partnerships with leaders of Oaxacan communities. Through such fellowships, Armonía has played a role in the transformation of many impoverished communities by introducing services that otherwise would not have been accessible.

As a result of recognizing the inaccessibility to primary medical care in impoverished and indigenous communities, Cruz Ramos, and Valdivieso López developed an integrated health service called "Medical Clinics." Armonía's Medical Clinics aims, over a few days, to provide annual pediatric medicine, general medicine, gastrointestinal, ophthalmology, optometry, dental, pharmaceutical, and mental health services to indigenous communities. Services are free of charge and open to anyone willing to receive health services. This comprehensive delivery of medical services was made possible through a partnership Cruz Ramos and Valdivieso López established with Orangewood Church in Maitland, Florida, USA, in the late 1980s. Since then, the congregation of Orangewood Church has volunteered time, resources, and expertise to multiple slums and indigenous villages in Mexico City, Taxco, and Oaxaca. Volunteers of Medical Clinics come from Mexico, the United States, and the United Kingdom.

In the 1990s, Armonía began to accept formal invitations from authority figures in Oaxacan indigenous villages to bring Medical Clinics to their people. Villagers began to celebrate the arrival of volunteers with song and dance performances, beverages made with cocoa, corn, and molasses called Pozontle, and other unique foods. We interpreted these celebrations as an expression of their gratitude for the health services we provided. The medicines, vitamins, medical supplies, and other goods such as toys and candy that volunteers bring to share with the community are greatly appreciated. Toward the end of each Medical Clinic's visit, it has become customary for village leaders to provide a written document thanking Armonía for our services. The document includes an invitation for Armonía and its volunteers to return the following year.

In 2007, Armonía started the Armonía Indigenous Mexican Scholars (AIMS) program, which provides services to high school students in the village of Villa Hidalgo Yalálag. Armonía's mission to improve indigenous high school students' living conditions, educational systems, and physical and mental well-being has been made possible through donations from religious organizations from the United States, the United Kingdom, and Germany. AIMS's services address a wide range of physiological, emotional, and spiritual needs. Students enrolled in AIMS can access room and board and clothing. Additionally, students participate in religious activities to support their spiritual development, receive health services that attend to physical needs and may meet with psychotherapists to address mental health concerns. The AIMS program provides remedial academic services and supplies students with computers, printers, stationery products, and all the necessary educational tools. The AIMS program is currently based in the village of La Capellanía Guadalupe Etla in the outskirts of Oaxaca City, Mexico.

Introducing Mental Health to the Medical Clinics

The first Medical Clinic occurred in the Jalalpa Tepito slums of Mexico City when I (Saúl) was only six years old. From an early age, I observed people living in extreme poverty experiencing significant health and mental health issues. One of my earliest memories is of a woman experiencing schizophrenia who lived in the same *vecindad* (neighborhood) as my family. I remember feeling frightened by the woman's disheveled appearance and wondered why she did not dress and behave like the adults in my life. My father, the psychologist, spoke with the woman often about her concerns and I witnessed his compassion and understanding of her experiences. The memory of my father's way of interacting with her continues to influence my work in different ways and reminds me of the importance of serving impoverished communities and individuals with mental health concerns.

Shaped by these experiences and my parent's dedication to providing accessible medical and psychological services to indigenous communities, I pursued a master's degree in clinical psychology from the Universidad de las Americas in Mexico City, Mexico. My training was in traditional psychotherapy that prepared me to see clients on a scheduled, reoccurring basis. I operated on the premise that once an individual attended their first session, they would require more meetings in the future. Although this method of psychotherapy works in some settings, such as private practices, I noticed that it was limiting access to therapeutic services in the Medical

Clinics in remote Oaxacan communities. I was meeting with only a select few individuals for three to five intensive sessions once every year. The traditional delivery of psychotherapy was not meeting the community's demands, and something needed to change.

While earning my master's degree, a UDLA professor, Dr. Helen Selicoff, invited Dr. Monte Bobele to provide a weekend workshop in Querétaro, México, on walk-in/single-session therapy in 2012. This atheoretical service delivery model provided solutions to many of the issues I experienced during the Medical Clinics. I hoped that the application of WI/SST, paired with my knowledge of Solution-Focused Brief Therapy, would be more effective when providing time-limited services. When I implemented the change from by-appointment to WI/SST, I noticed a marked increase in the utilization of services. Feedback from clients was remarkable. They reported that the ability to decide "right then and there" to talk to a professional about their problem encouraged them to try the service. Additionally, they noted that meeting with the medical doctors instilled courage and confidence to try something new.

Since 2010, I have built trusting and authentic professional relationships with indigenous villages. My indigenous roots from both Zapotec from Istmo de Tehuantepec and Zapotec from Sierra Juárez privileged certain access into indigenous communities. Nonetheless, I was still a man from the city, educated in traditional western-style psychotherapy, and influenced by larger systems. The SST mindset provided me with tools to build a strong therapeutic alliance in the hour I shared with clients, a typical finding in SST/OAAT research (Young & Bhanot-Malhotra, 2014). As a result, I noticed clients' increased satisfaction after the sessions and at follow-up visits. It has been my experience that trust established at both the community level and individual level is required to deliver helpful therapeutic services in indigenous villages. Transparency and honesty about your personal and professional motives to enter one of these communities is paramount. It is important to be clear when sharing your intentions and respect that it is the community's choice to welcome or turn you away. Client satisfaction following a successful single-session of therapy engenders trust, and that trust leads to a continued relationship between therapist and community/client.

When I integrated WI/SST into my work, I noticed that clients were often satisfied with one meeting, a finding that is consistently reported in SST literature (Bloom, 2001; Hubble, Duncan, & Miller, 1999; Talmon, 1990) and I was able to engage in many more therapeutic conversations during the yearly Medical Clinics. Inspired by the effectiveness of WI/SST, I eventually invited Dr. Bobele and a team of psychology graduate students from Our Lady of the Lake University in San Antonio, Texas, USA, to join the Medical Clinic in Oaxaca de Juárez. Over the following years, we have provided WI/SST services to indigenous people in villages such as Villa de Etla, Totontepec Villa de Morelos, Santa Ana Zegache, Valles Centrales, San Cristóbal Chichicaxtepec, and the Sierra Norte of Oaxaca.

Oaxacan Indigenous Communities

According to the *Instituto Nacional de Estadística y Geografía* (INEGI) (Mexico's Statistic and Geography Institute), the state of Oaxaca represents 4.8% of Mexico's territory and consists of 570 municipalities. Oaxaca has 4,132,148 inhabitants, representing 3.3% of Mexico's population. Communities vary in degree of isolation from mild to extreme (INEGI). Most indigenous communities have their own way of electing their local authorities, called *usos y costumbres,* which come from colonial times and are still used today (De la Garza Tavalera, 2012).

Oaxaca's population comprises 49% urban areas and 51% rural landscapes. During my work in Oaxaca, I have noticed how privilege is bestowed upon individuals depending on their geographical location. Indigenous communities are primarily located in Oaxaca's mountainous regions, and villagers are often viewed elsewhere as second-class citizens. In contrast, individuals living in the valley of Oaxaca City are granted a higher status in society.

In Oaxaca, 35% of the population speaks an indigenous language (INEGI, 2020). Indigenous communities include Mazatec, Zapotec (from Istmo, Valles Centrales, and Sierra Norte), Mixtec, Triqui, Huave, Chontal, Ixcatec, Chocholtec, Tacuatec, Chatin, Cuicatec, Mixe, and Chinantec. In my experience working in indigenous villages, I have come to consider any individual who was born, or whose parents were born, in an indigenous community as an indigenous person. The census conducted in 2020 showed that there are 1,193,229 people aged five and over who speak some indigenous language in the state of Oaxaca (INEGI, 2020). It has become more common for a language that was once shared between villages to be borderline incomprehensible by villagers in the same geographical area.

Someone who speaks Loxicha Zapotec would have trouble understanding a neighbor who speaks Temaxcalapa Zapotec. Languages and dialects have varied, and community members have often served as interpreters for us to facilitate therapeutic conversations. Once, I was helped by an indigenous man from the village of Chichicaxtepec who served as a translator for a mother and her son. The mother was distressed because her son was experiencing hallucinations and needed help. The man translated my Spanish to Zapotec to help explain that the mother could find what she needed for her son in Oaxaca City. I explained that psychotherapy would not be helpful at that moment due to the son's active psychosis; however, psychiatric services might help address the son's current state with medication. The mother understood and agreed that she would be willing to take her son into the city, and with Armonía's resources, the mother and her son were transported to the hospital in Oaxaca City. Single-session therapy, in this case, encouraged us to optimize every moment we have with a client. Such moments may not look like a traditional 50-minute psychotherapy session, but they can help individuals connect with resources that otherwise were unknown. Moreover, the single-session mindset emboldens therapists to utilize resources available to them at the moment, such as the impromptu translator and the transportation services offered by Organización Armonía.

An Example of SST in Indigenous Contexts

To illustrate single-session therapy within an indigenous context, we provide the following example of Saúl's therapeutic work. Certain details about "Juan" have been changed or altered in some way to protect his identity. I (Saúl) met with a young man named Juan, whom a medical professional had seen in Villa de Etla after experiencing a panic attack. Juan had been attending the high school in his village of Santa María Pápalo where he lived with his parents and younger sister. Santa María Pápalo is about five hours away from Oaxaca City by car. Juan had both a younger and an older brother in his family system; however, his older brother lived in a neighboring village. Juan belonged to the *Cuicatec* community and spoke their native language. Juan hoped to receive an education that would better prepare him for college, so he joined Organización Armonía Student Residence and was offered a full scholarship that would help him complete a degree.

My first therapeutic encounter with Juan was on November 16, 2022. Juan was 17 years old, in his final year of high school, earning an associate degree in computer support. Juan explained that he felt "stress" and was "missing family." Juan asserted that he had never experienced a "panic attack" in the past. The following is a portion of dialogue shared between us in the first minutes of the session:

Saúl: Can you tell me what happened?
Juan: It took place about fifteen days after I arrived at the Armonía student residence in September. What happened was that I got too stressed about school and family problems.
Saúl: Could you tell me more about those things?
Juan: Well, being away from my family affected me. And then, little by little stress built up that caused me to feel unwell and

overthink things. Every time overthought things, my breathing increased and... I couldn't deal with back pain anymore because I would bend over, and it hurt. Then my heart would race, and I couldn't breathe well anymore. So, the only thing I did was to lie down, but lying down I couldn't breathe; I felt like I couldn't breathe. Then, Chucho (Armonía's Student Residence Coordinator) came and helped me and then took me to a clinic.

Saúl: Did they tell you what had happened to you?

Juan: Yes, a panic attack.

Saúl: Ok. What did they do at the clinic?

Juan: They gave me naproxen pills and said I had to take them. If I remember correctly, they said I had to take one every 24 hours. They didn't help me calm down.

Saúl: I think it would be a good idea to check with another doctor what the ingredients in naproxen are and what it is used for. I'm not a doctor or a pharmacist, but I've never heard of it being used for panic attacks before. Does checking that sound like a good idea to you?

Juan: Yes.

Saúl: What else did they do? Did they check your blood pressure?

Juan: Yes. They told me that this had happened to me because I got too stressed. It was stress... it was too much! They told me to relax. That's all.

Saúl: Okay. You mentioned overthinking things. What things did you overthink before you had the panic attack?

Juan: My grades at school: I didn't want to get less than 10 (the highest grade is 10; equivalent to 100%).

Saúl: I think your grades are excellent and that if you don't get straight 10s, no one would be upset with you, so there's no reason to be upset with yourself. Does that make sense?

Juan: Yes, it is not necessary to get all 10s all the time. I also overthink family problems.

Saúl: What kind of family problems?

Juan: Well, that I haven't been able to talk to my dad as much as I would have liked about my life.

We proceeded to talk about how he could begin conversations with his father. This led to another topic concerning the desire to fix his relationship with his friends at school. Juan confided that he had two previous anxiety events that almost caused him to have a panic attack. I explored the factors contributing to the anxiousness Juan was experiencing, and they included being away from home, family issues, and his friendships deteriorating at school. After examining each factor and the role they played in the anxiety, I transitioned into asking SFBT questions about the panic attacks to uncover exceptions and opportunities for solutions-building.

Saúl: What did you do on those two occasions to feel less distressed?
Juan: Walking and exercising. Those things helped.
Saúl: That's great! I think you should keep walking and exercising. If you ever feel that you're going to have a panic attack, you can call my number, which I will give to you.
Juan: Yes, that's all right.

Once we identified walking and exercising as successful behaviors that decreased Juan's stress, I recommended that he do more of them. Throughout the conversation, Juan brought up thoughts about "ansiedad (*anxiety*)." "Ansiedad" was the word Juan used to describe his feelings before the panic attack. We spent a few minutes reviewing the thoughts related to the anxiety, ensuring that Juan felt heard and validated. I was interested in how Juan overcame the anxiety-producing thoughts and used scaling questions to "open up the possibility for a dialogue around differences" in the anxiety (de Shazer, p. 61, 2012). Juan felt relieved when he thought about his positive experiences with decreased anxiety, and I emphasized Juan's strengths. I offered to teach Juan breathing exercises that he could use nightly, and we practiced them together in the session. Additionally, I reminded Juan to visit a medical doctor to rule out any potential health issues. As the session ended, I assigned Juan homework to do more of what was working: weekly walking, exercising, and thinking of the positives in his life.

Six months later, I had a follow-up session with Juan and was delighted to hear him report on the progress he experienced in different areas of his life. Juan's six-month follow-up session was atypical for my work. Follow-up sessions usually occur one or two years after the single session since I do not return to the same village every year. Since Juan lived in the student residence, I was able to follow-up with him on one my trips to Oaxaca City. Juan had attended his appointment with the medical doctor and was relieved to hear that nothing was medically wrong with him. He would continue to be under the care of this new medical doctor who believed that Juan should continue to work on managing his stress and finding ways to relax:

Saúl: Juan, what was your experience like with walking, exercising, and breathing exercises, as well as thinking positive thoughts before falling asleep?
Juan: Mostly, I calmed myself with those. I did those things at times, and they did help me!

Saúl:	They did help you?
Juan:	Yes. They helped me control myself. So, they really worked even though I just did the exercises thrice!
Saúl:	Good! You also mentioned that you had some problems with your friends. What has been taking place in that regard since we had our first session?
Juan:	Over time, I noticed that they would exclude me from the group. That had an impact on me. So, it felt bad. I then began to reflect on that and decided to distance myself from them. It's hard for me to make new friends. There are other kids that talk to me in school but it's hard for me to make new friends.
Saúl:	Would you like to keep talking to those kids and see where that leads? - No expectations, no stress, just keep the conversations going.
Juan:	Yes, I'd like to do that. I used to talk to people a lot.
Saúl:	So, you used to talk a lot and get friends that way? Would you like to try to do that again to make new friends?
Juan:	Yes, I'd like to try that.
Saúl:	You also mentioned that your parents argued with each other and that you hadn't been able to talk to your dad as much as you'd like. What's been going on in those areas?
Juan:	I understand that my dad doesn't talk much to me because his childhood was hard, he went through hardship in childhood, and I understand that.
Saúl:	I think that is a very mature way of seeing your father! I think you're a good son. Maybe in the future your dad will feel like opening up about his life with you seeing that you understand him on a deep level.

The follow-up session revealed what Juan found helpful in the first session and what changes had developed since we met. On a scale of 1 to 10, where (1) meant no help and (10) meant very helpful, Juan rated the previous session a 10. Juan excitedly reported that the exercises had worked for him on the three occasions he needed to calm himself. In each conversation, I was guided by the belief that Juan was the expert in his life and possessed the internal and external resources to overcome the anxiety/panic attacks. By going slow in the therapeutic conversation, I discovered details about Juan's interpersonal and social relationships that played a significant role in Juan feeling whole. I honored Juan's family values, beliefs about friendships, and past successes like walking and exercising, adding simple breathing exercises and positive thinking to Juan's toolbox.

From the Classroom to Practice

I (Montana) was a team member on the 2019 Medical Clinic to San Cristóbal Chichicaxtepec and was newly graduated from the marriage and family therapy master's program at Our Lady of the Lake University. I was excited and ready to use my postmodernist stance, anticolonial practices, strengths-based theories, and culturally humble approach to therapy in Oaxaca. I attempted to culturally tune my beliefs, biases, and values to what I might hear, see, and talk about with the indigenous people of Oaxaca. Aware of my Westernized training, I tried to prepare myself for the worldview of others. Still, it was not until the real-life interactions that the meaningful evaluation of my multicultural competencies occurred. In conversation with Saúl, we reflected on interactions with indigenous Oaxacan clients that stood out for one reason or another. We noticed that when we started our reflections with "I wish I did this" or "I wish I said that" it was often the belief that therapy had to look and sound a certain way to be done correctly. We deconstructed this belief and found that it lies in more Westernized and Eurocentric prescriptions of psychotherapy that we were taught in institutionalized settings. Doing so offered insight into several adaptations that can be made to meet clients where they are in the moment. For instance, I consulted with a colleague at the Medical Clinic who met with a young man experiencing "shakiness." According to the young man, the "shakiness" began randomly; only later did he share that he had recently been robbed at gunpoint in Mexico City – but asserted that the event did not influence him and had nothing to do with the reported shakiness. My colleague and I very quickly identified the robbery at gunpoint as a traumatic event – even though he did not. Between us, we discussed the possibility of post-traumatic stress disorder (PTSD) and what treatment options would be effective given the short period of time we would be there. Pomerville, Burrage, and Gone (2016) write, "the absence of controlled outcome trials in the empirical psychotherapy literature with indigenous populations is a serious gap that renders evidence-based recommendations for specific treatments impossible […]." My colleague referred the young man to counseling or "platicas" as we called them at the Medical Clinic, and he attended a single-session of therapy. Ultimately, we took into consideration Dryden's (2020) "pluralistic perspective on psychology [that] encourages SST/OAAT practitioners to take very seriously clients' view about their problems and possible solutions." We decided it was more important for western psychotherapists to adopt indigenous ways of knowing rather than imposing our traditional beliefs about psychotherapy and etiology – hoping that one day we achieve a both/and approach.

Psychotherapy Challenges in Indigenous Communities

We have discussed the unexpected challenges we encountered when providing mental health services to indigenous communities in Oaxaca. In different ways but similarly, there was an assumption that access to the language and bits of knowledge of Mexican traditions and norms would make this work easier. It brought to our attention the transformation of culture that occurs depending on geographical location. Additionally, how one's own expression of culture changes with time, training, and experiences. We agreed that there is an ongoing need to evaluate values, belief systems, and preconceived ideas, to privilege the cultural ideology of indigenous Oaxacan villages while holding your own.

Challenge #1 – What Is Therapy?

In some extremely rural indigenous communities in Oaxaca, there is little or no concept of psychotherapy practices. When individuals have an important matter to discuss, they typically visit with their local priest/pastor and/or brujo (*witch doctor*). Visits with priests/pastors center around spiritual advice, whereas a visit with a brujo might entail learning a new incantation. In other words, visits happened when individuals needed them most, like SST. Therefore, we have explained psychotherapy in a framework customary to the indigenous communities, and what we noticed was that it began to make sense. On the other hand, in some impoverished urban and indigenous communities where access to television and television shows is more common, it has been challenging to rescript the existing perception of a psychotherapist portrayed by the media. In these communities, psychotherapists are believed to be "mind doctors" who can mysteriously resolve mental and emotional problems through conversations on a couch. As magical as those sound, it has felt like a personal and professional responsibility for me (Saúl) to describe the scope of my practice and the practice of professional psychotherapy in general. Despite efforts to describe therapeutic work in simple and general terms, indigenous peoples consistently call me a mind doctor.

Challenge # 2 – Language

As described in an earlier section of this chapter, language and dialect can vary widely between villages and even between generations. I (Saúl) often had to undergo a matching of language dialects to conduct sessions. Frequently, younger members of indigenous communities who speak their native dialect and mainstream Spanish serve as translators for outsiders. During the 2019 Medical Clinic, I (Montana) worked with a very young woman who was a Mixe translator. The young woman translated my Spanish to Mixe and the client's Mixe to Spanish, and we ended up having a successful single-session of therapy. It is now routine to include Spanish, Mixe, and Zapotec translators in Medical Clinics to increase accessibility to individuals receiving medical and therapeutic services.

Challenge # 3 – The Origin of Problems

When I (Saúl) began to offer mental health services to indigenous communities, I approached it as an opportunity to examine my "city ideas" and urban values. I attempted to prepare myself professionally for the problem stories unique to rural areas. Nonetheless, the first interactions with individuals in primarily rural villages of Oaxaca came as a shock. Remembering back to an early therapeutic exchange during a Medical Clinic, an indigenous woman was encouraged by a volunteer medical doctor to have visits with me after they diagnosed her with vitiligo. In Western medicine, vitiligo is understood to be an autoimmune disorder that causes areas of the skin to lose pigment or color (National Institute of Arthritis and Musculoskeletal and Skin Diseases, 2022). She was dissatisfied with the medical doctor's diagnosis and firmly believed that the condition was caused by her encounter with an armadillo when she was younger. One of the main features of the SST mindset is keeping on track (Dryden, 2020). Therefore, when I met with the woman, I did not challenge her ancient medicine; I instead operated within the narrative of her condition and was able to help her prepare for life with vitiligo.

Applications and Conclusions

One of our goals as therapists who understand SST both as a service delivery model and a mindset is to demonstrate how it has been successfully utilized in a variety of contexts. SST has been applied in settings such as community mental health clinics, university counseling centers, hospitals, private practices, and remote counseling services. It has been superimposed on theoretical orientations like Solution-Focused Brief Therapy, Narrative Therapy, Cognitive-Behavioral Therapy, Rational Emotive Behavior Therapy, and Acceptance and Commitment Therapy. We hope this chapter contributes to a better understanding of how SST has been applied in a non-western setting and that our readers feel inspired to incorporate SST into their work with culturally different individuals.

The extreme rurality of some indigenous Oaxacan villages has made it very difficult to access education, basic healthcare, and mental health services. Organización Armonía and its volunteers provide aid when possible; however, their continuity of services is still limited to once yearly. For that reason, SST has not only provided a framework to deliver therapeutic services that fit with the pacing of Medical Clinics, but it has prepared therapists to maximize positive change in one encounter. The brief and purposeful style of SST resembles the process individuals from indigenous communities in Oaxaca follow when they meet with a spiritual leader or healer. When we visit communities and offer SST, it is viewed as an additional resource for solving problems, just like their priest, pastor, curandera (*medicine woman*), or brujo (*witch doctor*).

In the process of writing this chapter and sharing our experiences with one another, there were several recommendations we hoped to pass down to our readers. Based on our reflexive observations about our SST work in indigenous Oaxacan communities, we settled on the following:

Build Trust

Trust can be found in almost every aspect of our work with indigenous Oaxacan communities. At the "usos y costumbres" level, we cultivated strong relationships with village leaders, so much so that outside volunteers were trusted by extension. Many villages are survivors of colonialism and are hesitant to accept care from outsiders despite the need. Therefore, familiarizing yourself with village power structures, customs, traditions, and historical context through trusted community members will help when offering services. Features of SST, such as joining, emphasizing strengths and resources, acknowledging the client as the expert of their own life, and promoting hope-filled conversations, have helped us develop strong working alliances with clients that support a continued trusting therapeutic relationship.

Expect the Unfamiliar

If you have been conducting your therapeutic work in an office setting, with electricity, running water, and access to technology, then your work environment, it looks very different from the work carried out in the slums or indigenous villages of Mexico. Our specific geographical location and the walls or lack thereof that frame our sessions significantly impact our therapeutic work. Most days, I (Montana) find myself in a private, well-lit, air-conditioned, fully equipped office setting where client confidentiality and comfort are paramount. This is a stark contrast to the session I had with a woman in Chichicaxtepec on two folding chairs in an open room with no door overlooking the town square. It was important that I set aside my professional discomfort with the idea of breaching confidentiality to uphold the village's access to trusting conversations. Additionally, I encountered many unfamiliar problems during my time in the community. I met with a woman who felt "coraje" (anger/frustration) because she could no longer journey up the mountain that separated her from the group of women with whom she embroidered. I can say that problems have felt like mountains in the US, but the presenting problem had never actually been a real mountain. In SST practice, "we collaborate with each client to establish specific behavioral goals that efficiently directs the therapy and structures the session to work toward those goals" (Bobele & Slive, 2014). Unfamiliar problems produce unfamiliar solutions, and the SST agenda lends a sense of security, knowing that our sessions are client-led and therapist-guided.

Find a Mentor

It is crucial to find a trusted adviser in the community that can provide guidance on the customs, traditions, and process of establishing a safe professional relationship with an indigenous community. It is equally important to find a mentor in the field of psychotherapy to review your work. I (Saúl) have found mentorship from psychologists in Mexico City and the United States to evaluate my work within indigenous contexts. I have found that mentoring/supervisory relationships provide some structure to an unstructured line of work.

Work with a Team

The work in indigenous communities can be heart-wrenching, especially in areas affected by violence, drugs, and corruption. I (Saúl) have witnessed the effects of compassion fatigue, burn-out, and symptoms of vicarious trauma on volunteers during Medical Clinics. If possible, gathering a team of mental health professionals who work together to deliver therapeutic services can provide comfort, support, and reassurance in the course of this work. When Dr. Monte Bobele's team accompanied me during the 2019 Medical Clinic in Chichicaxtepec, they created a space to debrief heavy stories and even shared their ways of conducting co-therapy.

References

Bobele, M., & Slive, A. (2014). Walk-in single-sessions: When you have a whole hour. In Hoyt, M. F., & Talmon, M. (Eds.). *Capturing the moment: Single-session therapy and walk-in services.* Crown House Publishing.

Bloom, B. L. (2001). Focused single-session psychotherapy: A review of the clinical and research literature. *Brief Treatment and Crisis Intervention, 1*(1), 75–86.

de la Garza Talavera, R. (2012). *Usos y costumbres y participación política en México.* Tribunal Electoral del Poder Judicial de la Federación.

de Shazer, S., Doloan, Y., Korman, H., Trepper, T., McCollum, E., & Berg, I. K. (2012). *More than miracles: The state of the art of solution-focused brief therapy*. Routledge.

Dryden, W. (2020). Single-session one-at-a-time therapy: A personal approach. *Australian and New Zealand Journal of Family Therapy, 41*, 283–301.

Hubble, M. A., Duncan, B. L., & Miller, S. D. (Eds.). (1999). *The heart and soul of change: What works in therapy*. American Psychological Association.

National Institute of Statistics and Geography (INEGI). (2020). *Demography and society*. https://en.www.inegi.org.mx/temas/estructura/

National Institute of Arthritis and Musculoskeletal and Skin Diseases. (2022, October). *Overview of vitiligo*. https://www.niams.nih.gov/health-topics/vitiligo

Pomerville, A., Burrage, L. R., & Gone, P. G. (2016). Empirical findings from psychotherapy research with indigenous populations: A systematic review. *Journal of Consulting and Clinical Psychology, 84*(12), 1023–1038.

Talmon, M. (1990). *Single session therapy: Maximizing the effect of the first (and often only) therapeutic encounter*. Jossey-Bass.

Young, K., & Bhanot-Malhotra, S. (2014). *Getting services right: An Ontario multi-agency evaluation study*. https://irp.cdn-website.com/b3809351/files/uploaded/Brief%20Services%20Evaluation%20Final%20Report%20pdf_uLjOCr4Sf6UgiafBfYjg..pdf.

Chapter 9

A Visit to Our Home

A Brief Journey through the History of the Community Care Center at Casa Tonalá[1]

Marina González

The Main Entrance: Encountering Single-Session Therapy[2]

The idea for the Centro de Atención Comunitaria de Casa Tonalá (CACT) emerged from the support I provided to the community at the Domus Autism Institute from 2011 to 2015, which primarily consisted of therapy services provided to the families and individuals who worked there. During that experience, I found there was a need to provide brief, supportive, and gender-sensitive therapeutic services. Despite this high demand for a fair listening space, those who came to the Domus Autism Institute did so sporadically, indicating an inability or unwillingness to engage in traditional therapeutic processes.

Based on that experience, we sought a form of psychotherapy services assistance that would meet these needs and be both fair and ethical. During this search, our colleague and friend Monica Sesma recommended *Cuando sólo tienes una hora: Terapia efectiva para clientes de Atención Inmediata* (Slive & Bobele, 2013), which had recently been translated into Spanish. This book introduced us to the idea of walk-in single-session therapy (SST), arguing that it is possible to offer complete therapy that promotes significant changes, even in long-standing issues, in just one hour. This opened the door to consideration of how we could contribute to this field. Months later, I met Monte Bobele during a visit to Casa Tonalá by marcela polanco and her group from Our Lady of the Lake University of San Antonio and the possibility of exploring the creation of a space offering SST psychotherapy services without an appointment at Casa Tonalá emerged.

The project itself was born from the friendship between Andrea Cabriales and me to contribute to a space that was economically accessible, inclusive, comfortable, and gender-conscious. Such a space would align with the general values of Casa Tonalá that addressed the inequality experienced in Mexico City, where therapeutic support services are costly and, therefore, unsustainable for a large part of the population (Cruz, 2021).

DOI: 10.4324/9781003351375-9

Single-session therapy without the need for an appointment became a way to respond to this inequality since, in other contexts, it has been found that it offers ethical support at low cost for populations with diverse social, economic, and cultural characteristics (Bloom, 1992; Clements et al., 2011; Crow, 2016; Hoyt et al., 2018; Bobele & Payne, 2022).

Through conversations with Monte, who generously guided the establishment of the CACT, I realized that creating a program to train professionals interested in providing SST was also necessary. Thus, in 2016,[3] the Single-Session Therapy Diploma at Casa Tonalá, which we continue to offer yearly, was born. This course provides training in SST with an added focus on narrative therapy (White, 1993, 2002, 2016), which is the central axis of our clinical and educational efforts and would eventually allow for our clinic to have a team trained not only in narrative therapy but also in SST, a service that continues to this day. It was the inauguration of this program along with its production of our first team of therapists working in this modality that marked the beginning of the CACT at Casa Tonalá. Thus, SST from a narrative therapy perspective has characterized the CACT since its inception. There we have also honored, questioned, and reflected upon the knowledge of all those who participate as volunteers to clarify the ethical standpoint from which our team operates and recognize the knowledge that adds to our work.

The Main Room: Our Way of Working

Our OA/SST based workflow has evolved over time as it has been enriched by the knowledge of all those who have worked with us in the CACT. We, as a team, have constructed a shared space that challenges dominant stories that impose upon and neutralize people's lives by basing ourselves on everyday experiences to focus on building shared and disobedient hopes and dreams – dreams that are counter-cultural and in opposition to the norm. We aim to witness people's stories, seeking plurality in the particularity of experiences without generalizing people's lives. We seek to create spaces where we can activate and enhance Narrative Therapy. Our primary guide is a political stance that invites us to look at the context in which people live and how those we talk with relate to it, enabling us to encourage practices that favor an understanding that an individual's problems are contextually mediated and created (White, 1993, 2002, 2016). Single-session therapy based on narrative therapy also promotes deep and meaningful conversations that are rich in meaning (Young, 2013, 2018), thus enabling people who come for an SST to contact their preferred identities and take action based on the personal agency that is proposed in re-authorship conversations.

It has also been essential to adopt a "good treatment"[4] approach to ethical care (White, 2011) as a collective practice to sustain hope. We have found that the language of the body, metaphorical thinking (Lizcano, 2006), poetic imagery (Bachelard, 2000) – all that which cannot be evaluated as a product of reason but must instead be seen as born of intuition – is a way to honor and expand people's stories, both shared and individual, to characterize both their situation, context, sensation, or problem, as well as their knowledge in relation to it: to create images when words fall short. In other words, we believe that good treatment implies the understanding that images or metaphors have greater staying power and are more easily remembered than traditional textual descriptions.

We also adopt the session structure[5] proposed by Slive and Bobele (2013), which itself consists of the structure invented by the Milan associates. We incorporate ideas from Brief Solution-Focused Therapy by Hoyt (2009) and Beyebach (2014) to recognize and highlight some of the strategies and skills with which people have already faced life situations.

Single Sessions can be conducted with just one therapist; however, we prefer a Reflecting Team approach for most of our sessions[6] (Andersen, 1994). Typically, a Team consists of three to four therapists, although there is flexibility regarding the number of team members that participate. The session can be conducted by one therapist, without a Reflecting Team, or a lead therapist and another therapist who acts as a Reflecting Team, or by one therapist and a Reflecting Team plus someone documenting the session in writing. Sometimes, it can be two therapists doing co-therapy with a Reflecting Team and someone in charge of documentation.

The CACT started by offering in-person, Walk-in/SST sessions[7] but, due to demand and post-2020 cultural shifts, changes have been made to how sessions are managed. We have now adopted an Open-Access/SST model. It used to be that people would walk up and literally ring the doorbell to ask for a session, but now they call or communicate via WhatsApp to ensure there is an available, same day, time slot before coming to the CACT. Moreover, during Mexico's 2020 lockdown in response to the COVID-19 pandemic, we moved from in-person sessions to fully virtual services, which we will also describe alongside the traditional in-person format in the following segment of this document.

Single-Session Therapy, In-Person Format (2016–2022)

The original CACT was located within Casa Tonalá[8] in the Roma Norte neighborhood of Mexico City. This space, an early 20th-century house, is the main headquarters of Casa Tonalá. It is welcoming, with spacious and aesthetically pleasing areas, and intentionally designed to make people feel at home, ensure their safety, and invite them to explore freely.

The Welcome

We intend to make people feel welcome from the moment of first contact. Thus, the person scheduling the appointment and explaining the method is crucial in the process. What, at first, might seem like administrative work was transformed into a role of relational responsibility; it was understood from the beginning how important it was to welcome visitors, represent the team's values, and transparently share how we work. It is vital to explain to clients the uniqueness of narrative practices and to emphasize that it is a respectful form of therapy that aims to bring people closer to their preferred stories. All of this is done over the phone when scheduling the appointment. Upon arrival, individuals are received as if they are visiting someone's home; they are directed to the waiting room and are given a pre-session questionnaire. The receptionist then waits for them to finish filling out the questionnaire, explaining and addressing any questions about the consultation's specifics, such as the presence of a Reflecting Team in the office and its role.

The Appointment

Ideally, the pre-session questionnaire is given to the Reflecting Team responsible for the session to be read before the client enters the therapy space. The Team, usually consisting of a therapist leading the therapeutic conversation and a three-person Reflecting Team, share ideas after reading the questionnaire. The client is then received and sits across from the therapist for the interview while the Team sits in a circle within the office, facing away from the client. Then, the therapist invites the Reflecting Team to introduce themselves informally, stating their names and whether they are narrative therapists, clinical psychologists, or some other distinction to help the client feel comfortable in the space.

The following case example illustrates our approach because of its richness in local wisdom. Cassandra was a 50-year-old single mother who contacted us because she was worried about her children. She completed the pre-session questionnaire shortly before she met with the therapy team in April 2022. She also indicated on the questionnaire that she was a teacher. She wrote that the most important thing she wanted to talk about was "How worried I am about my adult children" and that these worries were at an 8 out of 10 in her life. She indicated that she felt very comfortable discussing these things with the team. She wrote what people who know her admire most about her: "companionship, enthusiasm, and sympathy." She wrote that if the conversation were to make a difference in her life she would "be calmer and more confident in what my children can do." When all was ready, Lucy,[9] the therapist, began the session.

The Session, Part One: Conversation between the Therapist and the Client

The conversation may begin by referencing the questionnaire, focusing on the present: "What would you like to talk about today?" Attention is given to focusing on the topic and understanding how this session can be helpful to the person consulting us. Questions such as: "What would let us know this session was useful for you?" and "What would need to happen for this conversation to be successful?" are asked. The therapeutic conversation lasts approximately 30–45 minutes. The therapist then says it's time to listen to the Team, and both client and therapist become witnesses to the Team's conversation:

Lucy: Welcome. What brings you here today?
Casandra: Well, I'm worried about my kids, it's not a clear worry but it has me trapped, thinking I'm not seeing something or that there's something I'm not getting. I think I'll find something useful in telling it.
Lucy: How is it useful to *tell* something problematic? What happens in the telling? In being heard.
Casandra: That maybe I'll understand my worry more.
Lucy: Where does this worry come from?
Casandra: It comes from doubt, I want to see my children happy, but what if I adopt a different attitude? Seeing successful and happy children, but on the other hand they have their own lives and I'm not responsible for where they're headed or where and how they are successful. In contrast to accompanying them in their processes. What if I'm wrong?
Lucy: Have you been wrong before?
Casandra: Of course, many times, but there are many instances in which I am trapped by worry. As if there's something I can't see. What if I don't see something I'm supposed to be seeing?
Lucy: What aren't you seeing?
Casandra: I see that they're having a tough time, but I don't know if it's because of something I should be seeing.
Lucy: What do you see that makes you think they're having a rough time?
Casandra: I see them worry about their future, or unsure about where to go. I see other moms who still heavily intervene in their kids' lives.

Lucy: Would you like to intervene in their lives? Because I think I hear a little bit of opposition to that idea.

Casandra: Of course! I don't know if I agree with that. I feel like they feel if their kids aren't doing well it's because they didn't do something they should have.

Lucy: And why don't you agree with that?

Casandra: Because their lives are their own. I see them as complete things.

Lucy: Do you think moms are responsible for everything that happens to their kids?

Casandra: No, I don't have to be responsible for everything. There's things that are beyond me. I'm reading an incredible book that talks about the forest and a thing I love about it is the way it describes how trees take care of each other, especially large trees caring for younger trees, in community and letting them grow integrally with the forest. In contrast, it seems like us mothers, fathers, families in general focus more on just directing, like we think in terms of intervention strategies. Instead of observing and caring for them and letting them grow.

Lucy: So you don't want to intervene. What would you like to do instead, then?

Casandra: Hmmmm [she thinks for a moment] I just want to accompany them. Accompany them in their processes. I don't want them to be a copy of their father or of me. I don't want that; I want them to live whatever they want to live.

Lucy: What do you see in them that makes you want them to live their own lives?

Casandra: [she answers, moved] They have so much to offer.

Lucy: What moved you emotionally?

Casandra: I see them as wonders. I see them. If I danced like Anel, if I cooked like Fernando, and if I were rebellious like Brenda, I'd be so happy, and I tell them all the time.

Lucy: [Reading from their notes, Lucy repeats what Cassandra said, using her words exactly, and then gives her a moment to hear herself and asks:] A few minutes ago you said you wanted to accompany, how did you learn to do that?

Casandra: I've always rebelled against control and have prioritized ways of being close as a family. Trying to be democratic. Because there can be oppression within a family, although sometimes I lose myself listening to other moms and their strict norms. I know control is an illusion.

Lucy: What have you learned about life that makes you think control is an illusion?

Casandra: [she laughs] Because they're stubborn, they defend themselves. And they've chosen to live particular lives. I don't want them to be copies, and that makes me think that I also don't want to live my life wrong...

Lucy: Hey I'd like to make a pause here, would you like to listen to the team?

Casandra: Of course!

Lucy: I want to remind you to let anything that doesn't apply to you slide, if you hear questions you don't have to answer them, they're questions for you to take home, I'll be taking notes on a document you can take with you.

The Session, Part Two: Team Participation

The Reflecting Team participates from a non-pathologizing perspective, without being critical of the client or giving advice, and with respect, resonance, and reflections based on their own experiences that could be useful to the client. Suggestions are made tentatively and based only on what was heard, using the same language the client used. While listening to the Team, the therapist takes notes for documentation, which the client can take home after the session (more on documentation in the final section about the Team):

Ramona: While listening to Cassandra I was thinking: Of course nobody wants to live the wrong life! But how can one know? Maybe the fact that we know that we enjoy our children tells us that our life is going well and makes us separate our worries. And it gives them space to ask whether or not they're living the life they want. And I kept thinking about this question: when you ask yourself if you're wrong, what have you done on other occasions when that doubt arises? What have you seen or heard be done? On the other hand, what happens if something that might not turn out all right is shared with you? And maybe sharing in worry can open the possibility of knowing that in life we can always make mistakes, and that it's probable for us to have access to other stories.

Diego: While listening, the image of a four-leaf clover came to mind and what would happen if this were the clover for not being trapped, for making mistakes and for accompanying. I think about it in the context of being a dad. Worry traps me and silences me. I resonate with Cassandra when she says, "I want to accompany them in their lives," and it would seem that as mothers and fathers, the only thing we can do is accompany them because they know how they're going to do things. Sometimes making mistakes accompanies us all the time and accompanying changes everyone in the family.

Jimena: While listening to her I resonate with what she says, and the image of the forest stayed with me. One has to let them grow and there's no point in just taking care of the branches, you have to care for the whole forest. Accompanying versus being solely in charge of caring for the kids. Like forests, we are in relationship with a wide variety of plants. And our contribution is just one more. You and all of your community are responsible for the care and growth of your children. I wonder if what you've learned to do is respecting, being close as a way of caring and challenging many ideas about being a mother and maybe you've found a way of being a mother, doubts and all.

The Session, Part Three: Second Conversation between the Therapist and the Client

The therapist and client then discuss what they have heard, seen, felt, or thought about the Team's comments: "What was it like for you listening to the Team?" Emphasis is placed on the client's ability to hold onto the comments that resonated with them and let go of those that didn't; they have the final say:

Thank you, team.

[Lucy asked Cassandra: how was listening to the team?]

Casandra: Very interesting and moving, I could see context I hadn't noticed before.

Lucy: Was there something that caught your attention?

Casandra: Yes, I felt something that made me feel good. There's no correct way of being a mom and it's clear to me that there's no way to control the situation and that they will do what they wish as best as they can.

Lucy: If that were to accompany you in the future, be that the next few days or weeks, what would you do differently?

Casandra: Enjoy my kids instead of feeling like I'm doing something wrong as a mother. And I'll keep fighting like Brenda fights, I'll keep enjoying the love of food like Fernando and I'll keep learning how to express myself with my body like Anel.

Lucy: Ok, Casandra, if you're okay with it we can end the conversation here, and you can come back whenever you wish.

Casandra: Thank you so much to the whole team for listening to me.

End of session

The therapist concludes the session by making it clear that, while the client may return whenever they decide, the session itself will be treated as a unique and singular event, and how, in the event of their return, it is highly likely they will work with a different therapist and Reflecting Team. Before she left the office, Cassandra was given the document Lucy generated while listening to the Team so that Casandra would have their central points at hand and keep them in mind. She was invited to return in the future when she thought another session would be helpful.

Single-Session Therapy: Virtual Format

The CACT, which had predominantly provided in-person services for a long time, transitioned to a virtual modality during the COVID-19 pandemic in 2020. This change allowed us to serve more people from different locations within Mexico and abroad. The core structure remained the same, with some essential modifications:

- The questionnaire is completed virtually.
- Sessions are conducted through Zoom, a teleconference platform.
- Before the session begins, the client's contact information is shared with the Team members and the therapist so that if there are connection issues, communication may continue via mobile phone.
- During the welcome, everyone has their camera and microphone on. At the start of the conversation, everyone but the client and therapist turn them off.
- During the second part, the Reflecting Team members turn their cameras and microphones back on and talk among themselves. Meanwhile, the therapist and client turn theirs off and focus on listening.
- In the third part, the Team members turn off their cameras and microphones again, and the session concludes.

Framework

The CACT is an inclusive space that opens its doors to all individuals and considers how our stories and identities are diverse. Everyone contributes and resonates with the stories of those who consult with us in a unique and meaningful way. We also understand that our experiences are informed by different structural oppressions (sexual orientation, gender expression, racialized individuals, marginalized communities, and disability, among other cultural factors). This is part of our political stance and works based on narrative therapy at Casa Tonalá. We invite everyone to contribute to making this space comfortable and safe for those who inhabit it, being aware of our privileges and avoiding reproducing oppressive systems within the therapeutic space.

The Heart of the House: The Volunteer Team

Why Do We Use the Reflecting Team at the Community Care Center?

Casa Tonalá's entire multidisciplinary staff has reported that using the Reflecting Team is irreplaceable in operating the CACT, given its value for therapists and the resulting positive client outcomes. Moreover, 90% of our clients have provided feedback on the benefits of having a Reflecting Team in the same space, reporting that the effect on them is rich regarding their vision and meta-reflection on the session. The following themes were identified from discussions with our therapists about their observations of the values Reflecting Teams promote in the CACT's service to clients.

It's An Act of Care for Therapists

- The Team generates horizontality, decentering the therapist's voice, and nurturing its own reflection by discussing shared topics during the session.
- We promote care and attention among ourselves, emphasizing relational kindness in its social dimension, where constructing the ordinary is a priority.
- We change hierarchical relationships into relationships of equality, respecting differences and developing skills of solidarity and negotiation.
- The therapist has weight in the conversation, and there are things that should not be suggested to avoid being centered and overly influential.
- The remote listening/participation of the Reflecting Team, on the other hand, creates a different, more horizontal, perception of what is being said.

It's a Tool for Learning

- Single sessions become a horizontally (as opposed to hierarchically) supervised and horizontally formative practice where we all learn from each other's styles while also generating spontaneous supervision among colleagues. Together, we explore topics and do the inevitable personal work that is sharing resonances with the community, representing a non-normative therapeutic practice.
- By using the structure of the Team, we can question the ways of life valued by the dominant culture in an in-depth way.

- We take a stance that allows the inclusion of other ways of seeing and understanding life based on local knowledge.
- The Team can dedicate its listening to deconstructing negative conclusions associated with stories saturated by the problem at hand. That is to say; it allows the reframing of stories to be less problem-centric; it better understands the multiplicity of stories within consultants and the fact that they are not dominated or defined by the problems they face.

It Generates a Transformative Effect on the Clients

- Participating therapists act based on the assumption that people have local knowledge and can reflect on their own lives in a particular and knowledgeable manner in addition to developing their own skills.
- The Team can consider and reflect the skills clients have, the knowledge they can draw on, and the networks that can help them to deal with their problems.
- The multiplicity of voices contributes to a deeper understanding by the client of their own thoughts, knowledge, and new meanings found in the session.
- The Team's participation is like a prism: everything the team is listening to passes through their minds and bodies and comes back refracted in a different light, which is an interesting and useful way for the client to see and understand their own situation, knowledge, and what they might take away from the session.

We Have Common Goals and Teamwork

- Both the team and the therapist's role is to ensure that they serve the person consulting.
- Shared work increases the weaving of knowledge and propels us all.
- Our responsibility is to contribute to the construction of safe therapeutic spaces where people can be heard in different ways.
- The therapist can lean on the Team's participation if they feel the need to do so, taking a break and asking: "I would like to know if you have any questions about where we can take this conversation."
- We have been trained with a gender perspective, and therefore, we talk about feminist practice as a way of giving space to the practices that accompany us in creating a new world, both within sessions and among ourselves in spaces of knowledge co-construction.
- The Team operates on a different rhythm than the therapist. It gives them time to be actively listening, with a peripheral yet distant look, not thinking about the next question or how to lead the session, as is the case with the interviewer. They are not thinking about their

own performance. Instead, they are simply observing, witnessing, and taking notes so that they can build a better understanding of what they witnessed in the conversation that will take place later in the session.

We create mutual trust and a posture of not knowing and co-responsibility.

- The team favors the posture of not knowing by generating dialogue and a shared possibility space.
- We say "our neighborhood stands by us" because we share responsibility and the Team in each session can be composed by any combination of us.
- We challenge the understandings of competition that exist in relation to work among colleagues and contradict the dominant idea that learning can only be vertical and must be led by the person with the greatest knowledge. On the contrary, we trust that in interaction, in the exchange within the session, the intercession, and in the spaces, we use to reflect on our work, we actively contribute to the construction of an internal knowledge base within every consultation or session.

The Experiences of CACT Volunteers[10]

For CACT Volunteers, the experience of working within a Single-Session system provided a host of interesting experiences and reflections. Firstly, volunteers noted the value of the collaborative nature of working with a Reflecting Team. It is, generally, a novel experience to create meaning in a collaborative space; to work in such a way that no one voice dominates over others or can take total credit. This novelty, combined with the power of what was created, collectively served to inspire and challenge the volunteer team.

The experience of collaborative work was not exclusive to the therapists involved in the session but instead included the consultant. The consultants' reflections, experiences and what they share during the session is a vital part of the horizontal collaboration that happens during SST. Working in this way promoted horizontal relationships within the therapeutic space and worked to demystify the therapist as an expert figure. This, specifically, was something the volunteers found enriching; the experience of challenging the notion of authoritative expertise in the therapeutic space was both enlightening and challenging for the volunteers and their own practice and, as the volunteers see it, for the consultants. This newfound horizontality, along with narrative therapy practices, allows clients to realize that they themselves hold the knowledge and power to face and resolve the problems they come into sessions with.

The hybridization of methodologies was another point the volunteers highlighted. It was enriching to do work that combined various schools of thought into a method that managed to cover and address different biases, points of views, and manners of working. Specifically, how this method managed to meld a social and contextual view of situations (understanding that individuals are moved and affected by social and material forces beyond their control) with a subject-centric view of the world that highlights individual lived experiences, the generation of personal narratives and the belief that everyone has the tools for growth and problem resolution within themselves already.

Furthermore, volunteers noted the value of single-session therapy in terms of the degree of impact it has on clients. In other words, the volunteers were inspired by the fact that a single session could leave a lasting and profound impact on the people who came to the CACT. Another point the volunteers noted was the accessibility, the Open-Access/SST, as it is applied in Casa Tonalá. An OA/SST service is a more affordable alternative to traditional therapeutic processes, and it is also much easier to schedule and generally open to people who do not have the time or money to invest in a long process. As such, OA/SST helps to make therapy and its benefits much more accessible to a demographic that is, in the eyes of Tonalá and the volunteers, chronically underserved. This dovetailed with a shared interest in social justice and therapy as political action expressed in the team; the accessibility and political possibility of OA/SST synergizes very easily and constructively with Casa Tonalá's own interest in building an inclusive and radical therapeutic space. In short, the entirety of the volunteer team believes that the addition of an OA/SST space to Casa Tonalá has been a great boon to the effectiveness, variety, and value of our services.

Documentation as Another Team Member

For us, it is of the utmost importance to reclaim, care for, and treasure the understanding that individuals have in the therapeutic space we are providing. Thus, we can learn about the new discoveries they made in the session or the movement that was generated, which guided them toward a new place of knowledge about the issues in their lives. We are aware that when they leave the CACT, they will return to facing their everyday life, experiencing both good and bad moments depending on the context where they live, relate, or work. Understanding this, we provide them with the document generated during the session, enabling them to consult it in the future whenever necessary. In this document, the voices of the therapists from the team have been included, providing feedback on the wisdom, questions, skills, and knowledge that the client shared with the team during the session. For this document to be helpful, the historical version of the problem is not documented; instead, only the alternative or exceptional history of the problem generated during the session is recorded for future use. It also becomes part of a definitional ceremony (White, 2016) containing information that attests to the team's perspective. It creates an audience that validates other stories in the person's life, such as their preferred identity. Moreover, aesthetics and words are politically relevant to us; therefore, we like to document phrases that the client shared, as we believe they hold intrinsic power. In addition to recovering the client's own wisdom, these phrases contribute to everyday yet profound poetics that speak to the values of individuals. Our responsibility also involves developing an aesthetic commitment to how this knowledge is presented to clients.

The Evolution and Challenges of the Model at CACT: Inclusivity, Social Justice, and Narrative Therapy

As of today, our service at CACT is centered on a hybrid model of open access and appointment-based sessions due to the high demand. Since 2023, we have opened a branch in the south of Mexico City to expand our capacity to serve people at two locations, facilitating face-to-face sessions in two different regions of the city. Additionally, we continue to provide online services, which began during the COVID-19 pandemic and have allowed us to extend our reach, offering support to broader populations. This adaptability has reinforced our commitment to inclusivity, ensuring access to our services for diverse communities.

Our clinic still faces challenges, especially as we strive to deliver a consistent service. Our volunteers, who have been with CACT since the beginning, work to prepare new volunteers while upholding our therapeutic approach, which integrates open-access/single-session therapy (OA/SST) with narrative therapy (NT). This method challenges traditional therapy norms by creating a space that is economically accessible and culturally sensitive, addressing systemic inequalities in mental health care. The collaborative nature of our Reflecting Team further enriches this process, fostering non-hierarchical, contextually aware conversations that empower clients to re-author their narratives.

Our meetings also promote the ethics of care among ourselves and the community surrounding Casa Tonalá. We hope that this project will continue to contribute to our city's broader community care network, remaining a beacon of innovation and social justice as it evolves to meet the mental health needs of our diverse populations.

Notes

1 This document is composed of multiple voices from the team at the CACT.
2 In collaboration with Andrea Cabriales, Abril Cruz, and Mauricio Duarte.

3 The first program was in collaboration with Irma Rodriguez from Grupo Campos Elíseos in México City.
4 Good treatment: a form of expression of the respect and love that we deserve and that we can manifest in our environment, a desire to live in peace, in harmony and balance, to develop healthily, in a state of well-being and enjoyment.
5 It consists of a joining, the session, an intercession, and a closing.
6 We now strive for 99% of our sessions to involve a Reflecting Team.
7 When the walk-in clinic was first opened, it was advertised by handing out flyers to the people at Casa Tonalá and by hanging a poster inviting people to access immediate psychological services (see annex) outside the house. The population attending Casa Tonala's walk-in clinic is composed mainly of women (63.4%), followed by men (31.3%), then couples (4.7%), and finally, people with other requests, such as family therapy (1.2%). The reasons cited for consultation were emotion management (30.9%), family relationships (27.2%), relationships with couples (20%), decisions about the future (9.1%), work-related issues (6.4%), and finally, grief and issues related to the 2017 Mexico City earthquake (6.4%) (Cruz, 2021).
8 Casa Tonalá was established in 2012 as a community-based counseling agency in Mexico City. Its mission has been to promote the principles of narrative practices and to provide dignified spaces for psychological work for individuals, families, couples, and others. A critical perspective on gender issues perspective is central, acknowledging the intersections of power, gender, ethnicity, class, sexual preference, and diverse capacities. Initially situated in the Roma Norte neighborhood due to its centrality and easy accessibility via Mexico City's public transport network. Despite being considered a privileged area, Casa Tonalá recognized the neighborhood's diverse population. The accessibility of Roma Norte and the constant foot traffic near the house allowed for a diverse presence, welcoming individuals from various walks of life. Due to demand and the sheer size of Mexico City, we have decided to open a branch in one of Mexico City's southern districts, on #1 Febo Street.
9 All of the names used in this case example are pseudonyms added to make reading clearer.
10 This is a brief summary of reflections given by the following volunteers: Emilia, Yazmin, Ivan, Andrea, Pilar, Carminia, Debora, Mónica, Héctor, Mauricio, Abril, Maite, Ismael, and Cecilia.

References

Andersen, T. (1994) *El Equipo Reflexivo. Diálogos y diálogos sobre los diálogos.* [The reflecting team: Dialogues and dialogues about the dialogues.] Gedisa (Original work published in 1991).

Bachelard, G. (2000) *La poética del espacio.* [The poetics of space.] Fondo de Cultura Económica (Original work published in 1958).

Beyebach, M. (2014) *La terapia familiar breve centrada en soluciones.* [Brief Solution- *Focused Family Therapy.*] (At A. Moreno Fernández, Ed.) *Systemic therapy manual. Intervention principles and tools.* Desclée de Brouwer.

Bloom, B. L. (1992) Bloom's focused single-session therapy. In *Planned short-term psychotherapy: A clinical handbook.*

Bobele, M., & Payne, D. (2022). Once upon a walk-in (érase una vez sin cita). Journal of Systemic Therapies, 41(1), 1–12.

Clements, R., McElberan, N., Hackney, L. y. Park, H. (2011) *Eastside Family Centre: Veinte* años de terapia de sesión única de atención inmediata. Dónde estamos y hacia dónde vamos. en: *Cuando solo tienes una hora.* [Twenty years of walk-in single-sessions at the Eastside Family Centre. Where are we and where are we going]. Routledge.

Crow, N. J. (2016) T*he usefulness of a walk-in therapy session: A qualitative phenomenological case study.* Doctoral thesis in psychological counseling. Faculty of the Department of Psychology. Our Lady of the Lake University, United States.

Cruz, B. (2021) *Terapia de Sesión Única desde la experiencia de las consultantes en México* [Tesis de licenciatura]. Instituto Politécnico Nacional. (Single Session Therapy from the experience of the Consultants in Mexico) [Grade Final Work].

Hoyt, M. (2009) Single-Session Therapy: When the first session may be the last. Recovered from: https://www.brieftherapyconference.com/download/handouts/HOYT.pdf

Hoyt, M., Bobele, M., Slive, A., Young, J. y., Talmon, M. (Eds.) (2018) *Single Session therapy by walk-in or appointment: Administrative, clinical, and supervisory aspects of one-at-a-time services.* Routledge.

Lizcano, E. (2006) *Metáforas que nos piensan. Sobre ciencia, democracia y otras poderosas ficciones. (Metaphors that think of us. About science, democracy and other powerful fictions.).* Traficantes de Sueños.

Slive, A., & Bobele, M. (2013) *Cuando solo tienes una hora. Terapia efectiva para clientes de Atención Inmediata. [When one hour is all you have: Effective therapy for walk-in- clients.]* Ediciones Culturales Paidós.

White, M. y., Epston, D. (1993) *Medios narrativos con fines terapéuticos.* [Narrative means to therapeutic ends.] Editorial Paidós (Original work published in 1990).

White, M. (2011) *Práctica Narrativa. La conversación continua.* [Narrative practice: Continung the conversation.] (Marina González Gutiérrez, translator.) Pranas Chile Ediciones.

White, M. (2016) *Mapas de la Práctica Narrativa.* [Maps of narrative practice.] (Marcela Estrada Vega, Ítalo Latorre-Gentoso, Carolina Letelier, translators) Pranas Chile Ediciones (Original work published in 2007).

Young, K. (2013) When all the time you have is Now: Narrative practice at a walk-in therapy clinic. Narrative approaches. https://www.narrativeapproaches.com/when-all-the-time-you-have-is-now-narrative-practice-at-a-walk-in-therapy-clinic/

Young, K. (2018) Change in the winds: The growth of walk-in therapy clinics in Ontario, Canada. In. M. F. Hoyt, M. Bobele, A. Slive, J. Young y M. Talmon (Eds.) *Single-session therapy by walk-in or appointment.*

Chapter 10

Single-Session Therapy for Survivors of Acid Attack Violence in Cambodia

John K. Miller, Jason J. Platt and Sokhon Marn

Introduction

Since 2006, the lead authors (John and Jason) have been traveling annually to Cambodia to conduct scholarly exchanges between Western psychology, family therapy, counseling, and social work students and their counterparts in the *Royal University of Phnom Penh* (RUPP)'s psychology department, one of the country's top psychology programs. We originally began working with the psychology program at the invitation of the faculty and administration to rebuild the department, given the historical decimation of the university system during the Khmer Rouge regime and the country's history of civil war from 1975 to 1979.

During each annual exchange, our delegation of Western graduate students and faculty would offer lectures at the RUPP and would listen to lectures by Khmer (Cambodian) students and faculty. In this way, we tried to cultivate a bilateral exchange of ideas between the two groups and foster collaborative relationships that would hopefully lead to further connections in the future. To date, these efforts have paid off, leading to a number of joint research and scholarly projects between the faculty and students from both cultures (Miller, Platt & Conroy, 2018; Miller, Platt & Nhong, 2019).

In addition to the educational exchange of ideas at the university, we also worked to conduct community and human services projects during our annual visits that would hopefully provide both a valuable service to the community and an opportunity for the RUPP and Western students and faculty to work together. We anticipated that these projects would provide a chance to train the students from both groups to conduct fieldwork. Over the years, we have led many of these community projects, including working with HIV-positive children in an orphanage, conducting mental health evaluations and interventions with individuals and families in rural settings using a mobile mental health unit, organizing training and support services for survivors of domestic violence, and leading training

DOI: 10.4324/9781003351375-10

for community leaders about various group psychotherapy methods and techniques. Over the past three decades, both lead authors have had extensive experience utilizing single-session therapy (SST) methods in international settings, including Canada, the United States, Mexico, Cambodia, and China (Miller, 2011, 2014, 2011a; Platt & Mondellini, 2014).

In this chapter, we will describe how we conducted a community service project in Phnom Penh, Cambodia, in collaboration with our Khmer and Western students and faculty using SST methods. Our project was designed to train our students to provide a unique SST service for the survivors of acid burn violence. At the conclusion of the project, we explored the challenges and resources of survivors of acid attacks through structured interviews we conducted with consenting acid burn survivors. Interviews were carried out and recorded by the researchers, then translated, transcribed, and analyzed through thematic analysis. Our aim was to elucidate the problems and coping strategies of survivors in order to better inform efforts to develop resources for current and future survivors. A second aim of the project was to help mental health clinicians understand the phenomenon of acid attacks in Cambodia in order to develop useful clinical approaches for treating this population. The phenomenon of acid attacks in Cambodia takes place in the context of the country's history of war and genocide (Brinkley, 2011).

Acid Burn Violence in the Cambodian Context

In Cambodia, from 1975 to 1979, during the reign of the Khmer Rouge, about one-fourth of the population of Cambodia lost their lives. Many people died through starvation, execution, or disease (Chandler, 1999). Mental health counseling, in the form of psychiatric services established in Cambodia prior to 1975, was completely destroyed by the Khmer Rouge. All universities were closed, and many faculty, scholars, and intellectuals were executed (Chandler, 1999).

In Cambodia, mental health issues receive little attention, predominantly due to stigma, and a general lack of knowledge. Over the last two decades, various mental health services have begun to be rebuilt, often in response to the high prevalence of post-traumatic stress disorders and other psychosocial problems (van de Put & van der Veer, 2005). Yet even now, most who would benefit from mental health services never receive treatment. Through the years, the authors have worked with the Khmer faculty and students to create services to overcome these barriers, including various single-session therapy projects (Miller et al., 2018).

The violence and terror experienced during the Khmer Rouge period continues to make a significant impact on the culture and contemporary values of Cambodia (Brinkley, 2011; Gellately & Kiernan, 2003; Hsu,

Davies, & Hansen, 2004). One particularly vicious act of violence that is historically common in Cambodia is acid attacks, which are often inherently relational in origin (Cambodian Center for Human Rights, 2010; Golloglya, Vatha, & Malmberg, 2008). Perpetrators of these attacks throw liquid acid at their victims (usually on the head and face), burning the skin tissue and permanently scarring them, sometimes even dissolving the bones (Golloglya et al., 2008). The rate of acid violence in Cambodia has been historically among the highest in the world due to the availability of cheap industrial acid and the impunity for acid attack perpetrators (Cambodian Center for Human Rights, 2010; Kalantry, Sital & Getgen, 2011). In Cambodia, acid attacks are often motivated by jealousy between spouses and/or lovers, anger, revenge, and as a means to settle interpersonal family and business disputes (Cambodian Center for Human Rights, 2010; Kalantry et al., 2011). Yet sadly, many victims of acid attacks are simply mistaken targets who were in the wrong place at the wrong time. There is limited information in the professional literature on acid attacks and the implications for mental health, counseling, and family relationships. Our SST project with the survivors of acid attacks was designed to both provide a quality SST service and attempt to shed light on the problems and needed resources of the survivors.

The Development of Single-Session Therapy (SST) Services for the Survivors of Acid Burn in Cambodia

Over the years, John and Jason have endeavored to create collaborative relationships with the various non-governmental organizations (NGOs) in Cambodia that provide the most services for the Khmer people, usually in collaboration with foreign experts. One NGO, we worked with was the *Cambodia Acid Survivors Charity* (CASC), an NGO in Phnom Penh that works to provide a variety of essential services for the victims of acid burn and their families. Many of RUPP's psychology department students and graduates complete internships or post-graduate work at the CASC, including offering some limited counseling. The CASC requested that we work with our delegation of Western students/faculty and RUPP students/faculty to provide a single-session therapy service for a group of acid burn survivors who receive other services from CASC. The CASC staff told us that one of the main problems they felt impacted the survivors was the social isolation that occurred after the attack because of the disfigurement and social stigma. The CASC staff felt that these profoundly isolated survivors would benefit from an opportunity to connect with counselors via a single-session therapy format.

John and Jason worked in collaboration with Sokhon Marn (third author) to develop a one-day SST service at one of the sites operated by

CASC. Mr. Sokhon Marn studied in the psychology program at RUPP and also had experience with translations and working with the staff at CASC. The site was a compound on the outskirts of Phnom Penh where the CASC staff would hold meetings, training, and other services for survivors. We decided to provide the SST service during one of the CASC events, which was a day-long jamboree occasion, bringing together the survivors to enjoy a lovely meal, play games, and generally connect with each other and the CASC staff. The SST service was described to the survivors before the jamboree, and anyone who wanted to attend the service was welcome to participate. The CASC staff provided several meeting spaces for our therapists to conduct one-hour SST sessions with those who signed up. We paired one Western therapist with a Khmer RUPP therapist to provide the SST session. We also provided a translator for each therapy team. All the translators were graduates of RUPP's psychology program. Before the actual event, the two lead authors provided a day-long training to the therapy teams about how to conduct an SST session utilizing the methods we developed over the years. The CASC staff were unsure how many of the acid burn survivors would participate but were hopeful, given their feeling that the survivors would be eager for a chance to connect with others. At the conclusion of the project, 15 out of 25 total participants chose to attend an SST session.

Single-Session Therapy Procedures for Acid Burn Survivors

Our basic outline for conducting the single-session consultations with the acid burn survivors was developed based on our previous SST work internationally (China, Cambodia, Canada, the United States, and Mexico) and in national disaster settings (Miller et al., 2018; Miller, 2011, 2014). Each therapist in the project was qualified to conduct regular counseling sessions, and we encouraged them to use their fundamental counseling skills while also holding the following theoretical points in mind while conducting the SST sessions. The two lead authors served as clinical supervisors for the therapy teams, conducted live observations during all sessions, and consulted directly with the people in the session when requested.

One fundamental difference in working with the acid burn survivors compared to other international groups we have worked with was that it was not necessarily a "problem-solving" oriented session; rather, it was largely an opportunity for the participants to tell their stories. Giving them this opportunity helped make sense of their experience storytelling which is important to individual development and healing (Mair, 1988). When the CASC staff initially approached us about the service, they shared their belief that simply connecting, witnessing, and providing a space for the participants to review their life situations would be the most valuable part of the sessions. The following were our fundamental theoretical principles and procedures for conducting single-session consultations with acid burn survivors.

Making the Most of Time

As is typical in most SST treatments, the therapist strives to make the most of time. We held this concept in mind when working with acid burn survivors by streamlining the typical intake procedures. Therapists began meetings by politely introducing everyone involved and explaining the fundamental purpose of the session. This introduction included an explanation of the necessary elements of any counseling session, such as informed consent, the importance of confidentiality, and its limits. Yet, we thought carefully about how to trim this process to make the most of the time we had. It was clear to all from the onset of the meeting that this one conversation would be our sole interaction. This is in stark contrast to more traditional therapy situations where there is an expectation that there will be future meetings. We believe this basic fact has a tremendous influence on the structure and nature of the meeting and the performance of the therapist and the client. We endeavored to tailor the service to fit this dynamic.

Since the inception of SST services, therapists have experimented with various "first question" prompts, and successive follow-up questions (Miller & Slive, 2004; Miller, 2008, 2011, 2011a, 2018). The following questions, common in brief and solution-focused approaches, have proven to be useful in that they orient the client toward a clear direction to proceed.

Can You Tell Us about Yourself, and a Concern You Would Like to Talk about Today?

Most sessions began with some variation of this question. Yet we noticed that almost invariably, the clients would respond with the story of their acid attack and the effects that it had on their lives. Many talked about the difficulties they had since the attack, including social isolation, discrimination, difficulty earning money, family disruptions, and continuing medical concerns. Others talked about their sense of injustice in the situation, as they felt their attackers had faced few, or no repercussions for their actions. Some talked about the judgment they felt from others in the community. They told us that some people asked a lot of questions about what they had done before the attack as if to imply they had done something wrong to deserve what they got.

In each session, it was clear to us that the participants were eager to make use of this opportunity to tell their stories. Many prepared for the meeting by bringing pictures of themselves before the acid attacks and showing and telling the story of their lives before. Many would hold the pictures on their chest as they talked as a way of communicating, "This is me in the picture, not the way I look now." The stories they told were powerful and often very emotional. We had the feeling that there was a tremendous pent-up demand for the clients to make the most of this opportunity to show us who they were, who they are now, have some cathartic experience, and tell us their stories of struggle and survival.

A few of the participants requested specific resources or other services. These included requests for job opportunities or vocational training. Others talked about financial struggles, especially those involving ongoing medical expenses. Based on our previous experiences with similar SST situations, we knew it would be important to predict some of these needs and be able to connect the participants with additional resources. With this in mind, we prepared lists of resources by category and other NGOs that we could call upon for assistance. For example, the Cambodian League for the Promotion and Defense of Human Rights (LICADHO) offers training aimed at increasing employment opportunities. One function of our SST meetings was simply to connect the participants with existing resources that were available but unknown to the clients. With several participants, we were able to end the meeting with clear recommendations for resources that they could call upon in the future.

What Things Have You Tried to Improve the Situation?

This is a typical question in brief therapy, but it takes on new significance in this SST setting. We have the assumption that many people have dealt with trauma or loss in their lives and have learned a few things about their unique personal and interpersonal resources. Perhaps they have already begun the process of putting their lives back together, but simply need encouragement to continue in the efforts they have begun. This question can help orient everyone to existing strengths and resources in the client's life. Another purpose of the question is to cultivate a sense of hope for the client, which we believe is often the first step in healing. Finally, we find it is important to find out what the client has already done so that we can avoid recommending something they have already tried. For example, some participants shared how after the attacks they would cover themselves with scarves and avoid going out in public. The CASC staff had encouraged them to stop doing this and to interact more in society, and this had been helpful. The SST highlighted this change and encouraged the participant to continue doing what has been working for them.

What Inner Strengths Would It Be Useful for Us to Know About?

We have found that this question is useful in that it orients the clients to focus on something positive, in a situation that typically invites a negative, deficit, and problem-oriented discussion. We believe that in the human experience there are many factors the therapist can focus on the cultivate a greater sense of "resilience" (Walsh, 2006). The resilience resources we tried to focus on included cultivating a sense of hope, promoting a feeling of personal control, encouraging creativity and creative outlets, and even the ability to utilize humor. While it may seem difficult to find any humor in this situation, we found that there was joy and fun experienced by the participants through the communal and game-playing activities of the CASC staff during the event. In fact, we observed that many of the participants greatly enjoyed the singing, dancing, game-playing, and creative activities organized by the CASC. Finally, many participants readily discussed their spiritual life as a main resource. If there was any silver lining they discussed, it usually involved their greater sense of their spiritual selves.

What Will Be the Smallest Change to Show You That Things Are Heading in the Right Direction?

In our previous SST work, we have found that many people stay stuck in a problematic situation partially because they find it difficult to get started. They become overwhelmed by the enormity of the problem and essentially freeze. Many models of psychotherapy (cognitive behavioral therapy, strategic therapy, solution-focused therapy, etc.) focus on helping clients to identify the smallest steps that could be taken, not the bigger steps. We find identifying the next small step that the client can actually accomplish helps accentuate the clients sense control, in what often feels like a powerless situation. As the popular quote by Confucius goes, "the journey of a thousand miles begins with a single step." In our SST work, we believe that figuring out what this first step will be might be the most important step of all.

Pragmatics Versus a Specific Model of Intervention

Inevitably each of the therapists that participated had their own unique models of therapy and special skills and techniques in their practice. This is natural, and we believe that this does not interfere with the provision of a quality outcome in SST treatment. As Virginia Satir once said (paraphrasing) *we have two therapists with two very different approaches, yet we find that each one can produce a good outcome using very different methods.*

We find this idea is encapsulated in the systemic concept of **equifinality**, where there may be many different approaches a therapist can take to achieve a desirable outcome. With this in mind, we do not tend to focus on training SST therapists to all operate one way but to embrace the idea that no matter how they achieve it, the goal is to produce a pragmatic outcome for the client at the end of the session. This is in contrast to traditional outpatient treatments that focus on promoting change over many sessions. Instead of focusing on the potentially differing ways the therapist may go about promoting pragmatic outcomes, we embrace the idea that each therapist may intervene very differently and still achieve a positive and pragmatic outcome at the end of the session. Yet, we are always mindful that a small step in the right direction is often the most important intervention of all.

More Is Not Better – Better Is Better

Our work in Cambodia and other developing cultures has taught us many things about meaningful intervention and the hazards of intervening more than is needed or requested. While it may seem obvious that more intervention in especially desperate situations would be better, we have found that this is not always the case. The hazard we have found as Western experts applying interventions in the developing world is that we can unintentionally create a dependence on our interventions versus empowering people to solve the dilemmas they face on their own (i.e., teaching them to fish versus giving them a fish). Also, we have found that if we always try to provide the services and interventions ourselves as the "foreign experts," we can unintentionally enfeeble those on the ground who will actually be the ones dealing with the situation long-term after we leave. With this in mind, in all our international SST projects, we have focused on training the indigenous therapists to provide the services, versus providing it for them. As Henry David Thoreau said, "*It is not enough to be busy. So are the ants. The question is: What are we busy about?*" (Thoreau, 1854). We detail three principles we keep in mind when applying SST and other clinical interventions internationally.

The Universal, Essential, and Imperialistic: Three Concepts to Keep in Mind When Working Internationally

Social science scholars have long debated the dilemmas of our increasingly global situation (see Gray, 2005; Yunong & Xiong, 2008). The application of Western models of therapy in non-Western contexts is becoming more important in a global sense. In our SST work, we have tried to maintain a sensitivity about how to operate in useful ways, without over-imposing, or ignoring the already existing and culturally congruent methods of intervention.

Yet, we also want to keep in mind the *universal* aspects of our work that may be applicable in almost all cultural situations. What methods and interventions can be transmitted without any special modification or adaptation? Secondly, what are the various aspects of the cultures that we are dealing with that are *essential* to the culture, and if we ignore them in our endeavor, we lose something valuable? Finally, what part of our work may be *imperialistic*, and therefore, even our best intentions to intervene meaningfully may be oppressive or even harmful to the culture we are interacting with? These are three questions we hold in mind as Western SST therapists working in non-Western contexts. A valuable aid in answering these questions has always involved a humble position on our part as we enter each new culture, always collaborating with and seeking out the advice and direction of the indigenous experts.

In this project, we began by asking the indigenous experts at RUPP and the CASC what they thought would be most meaningful about our SST work. They told us that one special dilemma of the acid burn survivors was that they were usually shunned by society after the attack, and they struggled to have their voices heard. Also, the CASC reported that they needed more information about the challenges and additional services that could be provided to the acid burn survivors in the future. With this in mind, we developed a small exploratory research project as part of our intervention in an effort to address the unique situation at hand.

Honoring the Voices of Acid Burn Survivors through Research

The final aim of this SST project was to collect information about the unique dilemmas and needs of the acid burn survivors. The CASC staff believed that this would be helpful both for the survivors and the CASC staff as they worked to provide better services. The authors developed a semi-structured interview protocol to be carried out with any survivors who consented to participate. An institutional review board (IRB) protocol for the protection of human subjects was developed and approved by a university IRB board before the research began. The semi-structured interview protocol asked open-ended questions about what the survivors believed their main dilemmas were and what other services or resources they would like to see. Interviews were carried out by the third author. Each interview was audio recorded, transcribed, and translated. A total of eight interviews were collected and analyzed by the authors.

Three main challenges and four main requests emerged from the analysis. The main challenges included emotional and physical difficulties, financial struggles, and social discrimination and isolation.

Three Main Challenges Reported by Acid Burn Survivors

Emotional and Physical Challenges

The respondents reported that they faced significant emotional and physical challenges as a result of the attack. They often experience feelings of isolation, depression, and low self-esteem due to societal discrimination and stigma. The respondents also reported that the immediate pain and trauma from the attack, the long healing process, and the scars and disfigurement all have a profound impact on their lives.

Financial Struggles

The respondents reported that they often face significant financial difficulties. Most of those who had jobs before the attack, lost their jobs as a result of the attack. As they healed, they reported that they had limited job opportunities due to their changed appearance. They felt that the limited job opportunities arose from the discrimination from potential employers because of their appearance, as discussed below. Finally, they reported that other financial difficulties arose from the medical expenses that accumulated after the attack.

Social Isolation and Discrimination

The respondents reported that they often face social isolation and discrimination in their communities. They experience pity or disgust from others, encounter difficulties in social interactions, and find it challenging to reintegrate into society. Many interviewees mentioned being treated differently or discriminated against due to their changed appearance.

Four Main Resources and Requests for Future Support

Coping Strategies

Many of the respondents mentioned various coping strategies they employ to deal with the challenges they face. These strategies include seeking emotional support from family, engaging in vocational training or employment, and turning to religion and spirituality for solace. They also reported that participating in support group meetings with fellow acid burn survivors, such as those organized by CASC, was invaluable in their efforts to cope.

Support from Family and NGOs

The respondents reported that they relied heavily on the support of their families. They felt that the encouragement, motivation to move forward, and financial assistance provided by families were a major resource. They also reported the vital role NGOs such as CASC and others have played to provide vocational training, resources for medical treatment, and emotional support as they struggle to reintegrate into the community.

The Need for Justice

Several of the respondents expressed a profound desire for justice. They reported that many perpetrators faced minimal punishments, and some faced no repercussions at all. They believed that this lack of justice made it more difficult for them to find closure and wished that the legal system would do more. Some reported that more should be done to have the perpetrators pay for the medical expenses of the survivors. They felt that a greater sense of justice would go a long way to curb the possibility of future attacks.

Desire for Greater Awareness

Some of the respondents stressed the importance of raising awareness about the problem of acid burn attacks in the community as well as the challenges faced by the survivors. They expressed appreciation for the support they had received from NGOs, governmental organizations, and the wider community. Yet they also felt there was more to be done. They called for future initiatives to educate the community about the problem of acid attacks, challenge social biases that contribute to social stigma, and advocate for social and legal changes in order to prevent future attacks.

Conclusion

Our SST intervention with the survivors of acid burn violence was a powerful and meaningful experience for both the therapists and participants. Many of the participants who attended the SST sessions waited for the therapists at the gate of the compound at the end of the day so they would have a chance to thank the therapists and express their appreciation for their efforts to witness their stories and help when possible. One of the participants took the hands of each of the therapists one at a time and, with tears in her eyes, expressed her deep appreciation for caring about the acid burn survivors and giving them a chance to share. During our SST project, our team conducted 15 SST consultations and 8 interviews with participants about challenges and needed resources. The CASC staff utilized the information gathered to inform future efforts to address the challenges and needs of the acid burn survivors.

One fortunate outcome of the efforts of the CASC staff has been alerting governmental officials about the need to regulate the sale of the industrial-strength acid used to carry out the attacks. These efforts have been successful over time, and the incidence of acid burn violence in Cambodia has been curbed substantially. For us, this highlighted the importance of being aware that sometimes our most powerful therapeutic interventions are at the larger systems levels and sometimes involve educating society about various needs, and advocating for regulation and safeguards. For us, this is in keeping with the ideas of Ignacio Martín-Baró, who worked internationally in developing countries in an endeavor he termed *liberation psychology* (Martín-Baró, 1994). In his way of thinking, the therapist cannot sit and wait for those in need to come to us, but we need to create services that overcome the unavoidable barriers to service. We will not be able to do this from our well-appointed offices, but only by bringing our efforts to the people. We hope that our SST intervention with acid burn survivors in Cambodia served as one small step in the right direction.

References

Brinkley, J. (2011). *Cambodian curse: Modern history of a troubled land*. New York: Perseus Books.

Cambodian Center for Human Rights (May, 2010). Breaking the silence: Addressing acid attacks in Cambodia. Retrieved February 20, 2011, from https://cchrcambodia.org/storage/posts/1546/2010-05-21-reports-eng-breaking-the-silence-addressing-acid-attacks-in-cambodia.pdf

Chandler, D. (1999). *Brother number one: A political biography of Pol Pot*. Boulder, Colorado: Westview Press.

Gellately, R., & Kiernan, B. (2003). *The specter of genocide: Mass murder in historical perspective*. New York: Cambridge University Press.

Golloglya, J., Vatha, S., & Malmberg, A. (2008). Acid attacks in Cambodia: Serious reminders of personal conflicts. *Asian Biomedicine*, 2(4), 329–334.

Gray, M. (2005). Dilemmas of international social work: paradoxical processes in indigenisation, universalism and imperialism. *International Journal of Social Welfare*, 14, 231–238.

Hsu, E., Davies, C., & Hansen, D. (2004). Understanding mental health needs of Southeast Asian refugees: Historical, cultural, and contextual challenges. *Clinical Psychology Review*, 24, 193–213.

Kalantry, S., Sital, & Getgen, J. (2011) Combating Acid Violence in Bangladesh, India and Cambodia. Cornell Legal Studies Research Paper No. 11–24. Available at SSRN: https://ssrn.com/abstract=1861218.

Mair, M. (1988). Psychology as storytelling. *International Journal of Personal Construct Psychology*, 1, 125–138.

Martín-Baró, I. (1994). *Writings for a liberation psychology*. Cambridge, MA: Harvard University Press.

Miller, J. K. (2008). Walk-in single-session team therapy: A study of client satisfaction. *Journal of Systemic Therapies*, 27(3), 78–94.

Miller, J. K. (2011). Single-session intervention in the wake of Hurricane Katrina: Strategies for disaster mental health counseling. In A. Slive & M. Bobele (Eds.), *When One Hour is All You Have: Effective Therapy for Walk-In Clients* (pp. 185–202). Phoenix, AZ: Zeig, Tucker, & Theisen.

Miller, J. K. (2011a). Single-session intervention in the wake of Hurricane Katrina: Strategies for disaster mental health counseling. In A. Slive & M. Bobele (Eds.), *When One Hour is All You Have: Effective Therapy for Walk-in Clients* (pp. 185–202). Phoenix, AZ: Zeig, Tucker, & Theisen.

Miller, J. K. (2014). Single session therapy in China. In M. F. Hoyt & M. Talmon (Eds.), *Capturing the Moment: Single Session Therapy and Walk-In Services* (pp. 195–214). Bethel, CT: Crown House Publishing.

Miller, J. K. (2018). Single session social work in China. In Z. Fang (Ed.), *Fudan University Social Work Teaching Case Collection* (Vol. 1, pp. 129–148). Fudan: Fudan University Publishing House.

Miller, J. K., Platt, J., & Hmong, H. (2019). Perceptions of family issues and challenges in post-genocide Cambodia: A survey of the next generation of Cambodian mental health workers. *Journal of Family Psychotherapy*.

Miller, J. K., Platt, J. J., & Conroy, K. M. (2018). Single-session therapy in the majority world: Addressing the challenge of service delivery in Cambodia and the implications for other global contexts. In M. F. Hoyt, M. Bobele, A. Slive, J. Young & M. Talmon (Eds.), *Single-Session Therapy by Walk-In or Appointment: Administrative, Clinical, and Supervisory Aspects of One-at-a-Time Services* (pp. 116–134). New York: Routledge.

Miller, J. K., Platt, J., & Nhong, H. (2019). Psychological needs in post-genocide Cambodia: The call for family therapy services and the implications for the "majority world" populations. *Journal of Family Psychotherapy*, 30(2), 153–167. https://doi.org/10.1080/08975353.2019.1613610

Miller, J. K., & Slive, A. (2004). Breaking down the barriers to clinical service delivery: Walk-in family therapy. *Journal of Marital and Family Therapy*, 30(1), 95–103.

Platt, J. J., & Mondellini, D. (2014). Single-session walk-in therapy for street robbery victims in Mexico City. In M. F. Hoyt & M. Talmon (Eds.), *Capturing the Moment: Single Session Therapy and Walk-in Services* (pp. 215–231). Bethel, CT: Crown House Publishing.

Thoreau, H. D. (1854). *Walden*. Chicago: University of Illinois.

van de Put, W., & van der Veer, G. (2005). Counselling in Cambodia: Cultural competence and contextual costs. *Intervention*, 3(2), 87–96.

Walsh, F. (2006). *Strengthening family resilience* (2nd ed.). New York: The Guilford Press.

Yunong, H., & Xiong, Z. (2008). A reflection on the indigenization discourse in social work. *International Social Work*, 51(5), 611–622.

Chapter 11

Everyone Matters. The One Session Center in Italy

Vanessa Pergher and Flavio Cannistrà

Introduction – The Model Models You

The workshop is over. Colleagues are standing in the middle of the room, chatting and exchanging thoughts, happy. Someone runs because they have to catch a train. Music plays in the background. We're wrapping up the PC cables and gathering our notes, when Lorenza approaches and shakes our hands.

"Thank you." she tells us. Her eyes sparkle, "It was exactly what I needed."

This exchange took place in Rome, at the end of our fourth workshop on single-session therapy (SST). We were astonished: what did she mean, "It was exactly what I needed"? SST, did she mean? Because of her tone, her expression, and the desire to thank us that shone so intensely through her words, from her very presence, we had the feeling that she wasn't referring to that. Not only that, at least.

"The model models you," we once heard Giorgio Nardone say one day. He meant that the psychotherapeutic model you adhere to ends up shaping the way you see things. We add that the word "model" also represents the person who is there to teach you and, as Alan Watts (1948) might say in his personal reading of Buddhism, something of him will remain with you forever. This is his reincarnation.

The Italian Center for Single Session Therapy (ICSST) arose from Flavio Cannistrà and Federico Piccirilli's desire to study and disseminate single-session therapy, as well as training therapists interested in this method. Today, it has become the beating heart of the ICNOS Institute (from the Greek *Ichnos*, meaning footprint), the center for study, research, and training in systemic-strategic brief therapies (a restrictive but necessary label within which we include approaches, such as SST, Solution-Focused Brief Therapy and MRI Strategic Therapy).

We believe that Brief Therapies still have a lot to contribute (Cannistrà & Hoyt, 2025) because of the considerations they enable

DOI: 10.4324/9781003351375-11

about the role of psychotherapy, the psychotherapist and the client, and mental health systems and services. We do not believe that one model can fit all: we adopt a pragmatic view in which theories and related psychotherapeutic practices are no more than conceptual tools whose main purpose is to help the person achieve a desired and co-constructed goal within the psychotherapeutic setting (for a general overview of Pragmatism, see Bernstein, 2010).

But our work cannot avoid the need to reflect on the impact that, first and foremost, affects our students and trainees. To the best of our ability, we cultivate a horizontal climate, where the experience of those who teach is not a substitute for the personal development of those who learn; on the contrary, we keep that development in mind as essential feedback for questioning the professional and moral growth of our Institute.

It is with this mindset that we created the "One Session" Center (OSC), an online single-session therapy service capable of reaching hundreds of people in Italy, which we will go on to describe later in this chapter.

Pandemic

2020. Pandemic. Lockdown. Our lives are paused. The streets of Rome, Milan, and Naples are deserted. There is a surreal silence in every city, broken only by fire trucks: "It is absolutely necessary to stay in your homes," says the metallic voice on loudspeakers. Certainties come to a halt. "Everything will be fine" is the slogan that appears on the balconies of houses, on store fronts, in the windows of schools. Who knows if we really believe it, that everything will be fine?

The level of fear is high. The internet is teeming with articles and information telling us "How to maintain good mental health during the lockdown," because right now, mental health is indeed at risk.

A review in *The Lancet* (Brooks et al., 2020) considered findings from 24 studies on the psychological effects of lockdown, highlighting the emergence of depressive symptoms, stress, irritability, insomnia, low mood, anger and post-traumatic symptoms.

The mental health of Italians (and the world generally) is under strain.

At the Italian Center for Single Session Therapy, work does not stop; we study and get informed. We create tailor-made training for our students and trainees to meet the urgent emerging needs. We believe in the people we train and, most importantly, we know that single-session therapy can be a tool perfectly suited to the current situation (see the chapter by D'Alia, Giannetti, and Bonadies in Cannistrà & Piccirilli, 2021): people need immediate answers.

After studying the many successful cases of single-session walk-ins (Hoyt & Talmon, 2014; Slive & Bobele, 2011), meeting international therapists who have been practicing for a long time, and teaching psychologists about the benefits of this type of service, we decided to get involved ourselves. A few months earlier we had already opened a walk-in center in the small town of Monterotondo. Moving to its online version became, at this point, almost a given.

And so, the One Session Center Online was born.

One Session Center in Action

As mentioned above, OSC was created with two purposes:

1 To provide citizens with an accessible mental health service in a time of emergency.
2 To give students of the ICNOS Institute the opportunity to put into practice what they have learned in the classroom, using a learning-by-doing approach with constant support and supervision.

Participation in the service as therapists is on a voluntary basis and involves about 15 student-therapists, coordinated by a student and team member of the Italian Center for Single-Session Therapy (Vanessa Pergher), who oversees the organizational aspects and publicizes the service through management of the social media pages and the website. It is not uncommon for students and trainees to be involved in the Italian Center's projects, even to the point of becoming full members. The horizontal relationship created by the Italian Center facilitates professional exchange and personal relationships, empowering many students to feel free and welcomed in their proposals, and the Italian Center to quickly grasp the personal resources they can bring to bear.

The One Session Center service was originally designed to run every Tuesday, from 6:00 p.m. to 8:00 p.m., engaging three different therapists each week. Users can access it in two ways: without appointment, by directly contacting the dedicated Facebook page during the time slot when One Session Center is active, or by making an appointment. While writing this chapter, we decided to extend the booking option to other days as well. In our experience, in fact, the online psychological walk-in service still has a relatively low access rate in Italy, while we found that many people wish to book a day that suits them, a modality facilitated by the high number of volunteers present. In this chapter, however, we will focus on the walk-in service.

Before the Session

There is a lot of "behind the scenes" with OSC. For people to access the service, they need to know about it. Facebook, Instagram, and a website with a constantly updated blog are the main channels for spreading the word about the service. We tell potential users how one session can change their situation; we debunk myths about the need for long courses of therapy in order to get better; we make ourselves known. For most people, the idea that one session with a psychologist can be enough is a strange new narrative, perhaps even to be regarded with suspicion. "What else are they trying to sell me?" some people think.

Students are also at the forefront when it comes to writing and publicizing content. Vanessa creates and constantly updates an editorial calendar. Students who participate in the service are responsible for writing informative articles which aim to explain how a single session can help with various issues and difficulties, e.g. insomnia, anxiety, and couple communication. The same articles are then used to create informational graphics which are posted on the Facebook and Instagram pages kept updated by Vanessa, assisted by the Italian Center Social Media Manager Beatrice. Although this activity requires a considerable amount of work, we believe that the more channels we use to publicize our valuable service, the wider the audience we will reach.

Behind the scenes is not only about publicizing the service but also about constant communication between therapists. Vanessa manages it all. To do this, she needs: a Google Drive spreadsheet, shared and accepted by all, where she keeps track of the various therapists' shifts and the list of any booked sessions; a WhatsApp group of which all therapists are members, so that they can communicate efficiently; constant monitoring of incoming messages on the Facebook page; and a dedicated email address for the service.

At the start of each week there is a reminder of who will be on call. "Tomorrow it's Sharon, Linda and Rosita's turn, do you confirm?" "Yes!"

The three therapists are assigned as moderators of the One Session Facebook page so that during their shift they can read incoming messages. This is the channel to which people interested in the service are directed in order to access the session.

During the Session

Tuesday, 6:08 p.m., a notification on Antonella's browser tells her there is a message on the One Session Facebook page. It's from a client who wishes to access a free session. The first step for her is to view and accept the informed consent form. "Before we begin our session, I'm going to send you two links. This is the first one: it's the informed consent and you need to accept it by entering your email." By clicking on the link, the person opens a Google form where the functioning of the service and the processing of his or her data according to privacy laws is explained in detail.

This step is essential and mandatory in order to access the service. "Okay, done," the client writes. "Well, on this second link you'll find a questionnaire, designed to assess your state of well-being before the interview takes place." This is part of a research project on the effectiveness of single-session therapy, from pre-treatment to follow-up 12 months later, which we are conducting with the scientific director of the ICNOS Institute, Giada Pietrabissa, using OQ-45 and VAS (0–10) as measurement tools.

Once the questionnaire is filled out, the client can proceed to his or her free 30-minute single-session Therapy interview, which will take place via WhatsApp or Skype video call.

After the Session

At the end of the session, we want to make sure that the consultation was effective and actually helpful for the client: we then make sure that the work we did together was useful and that the person benefited from it.

Should the person feel the need for a further conversation, they can safely contact our service again; however, it will be pointed out that they will not be guaranteed to find the same therapist. For both client and therapist, this means that the One Session will not be seen as the beginning of a multi-session psychotherapy process, but will be experienced in its entirety according to the mindset (see below) of single-session therapy.

At the end of the video call, the person will be sent an additional questionnaire to measure post-interview well-being at 1-, 3-, 6-, 9-, and 12-month intervals.

Supervision

When Flavio enters the virtual room, Vanessa is already there. Three more windows open soon after, and then five more, showing the faces of therapists. Soon, the virtual space is filled with a dozen participants:

"Is everyone here?" Flavio asks.

"Yes," Vanessa replies.

"Perfect. Vane, will you update us on the latest data before we start the supervision?"

One Session is a volunteer service, so students do not receive remuneration for their work. But if we were to identify a form of recompense for the service, it would definitely be supervision.

Flavio Cannistrà, co-director of the ICNOS Institute and a Brief Therapist with decades of experience, provides a supervision session each month free of charge for One Session therapists regarding access to the service. This time is extremely valuable and eagerly anticipated by all participants: it is an opportunity to review One Session therapy and to learn communicative and therapeutic maneuvers in particular situations. The occasion is also an opportunity to update everyone on how One Session is progressing, how many sessions have been done in the past month, how the communication and promotion of the service are working and the progress of research, as well as how One Session itself is functioning. Everyone is invited to bring ideas and input to improve the service in both contextual aspects (such as how to improve promotion or adapt communication) and structural ones. Rather than dropping ideas from the top on how the service should work, we strongly believe that the most experienced people to propose such ideas are primarily the therapists who work there. To put it even more clearly, it would not make sense for Flavio – despite being a co-director of the institute and the company headed by One Session – to decide how this should work. Therapists are invited to talk about their experience of using the service, to make suggestions and give feedback, possibly even to participate in an initial design phase of the project, so that it can be aligned as closely as possible with the needs and desires of the people who actually use it and are in contact with the end users.

Why Is OSC a Free Service?

How can a machine with as many components as One Session offer a free service?

First of all, because this clinical center is not the core business of the Italian Center for Single Session Therapy: the main mission of ICSST is to train colleagues in single-session therapy and brief therapies, through its workshops and the ICNOS Institute.

Secondly, because the costs of maintaining the service are low: Vanessa, a member of ICSST, is paid by ICSST for the hours she spends organizing and creating content to publicize the service, while the therapists volunteer their time. This service is often seen by students as an initial testing ground for their freelance practice: when they begin their training with us, many of them have not yet received patients and do not feel ready to jump in as independent professionals, preferring a service like OSC where, thanks to the supervision offered by Flavio, they can take their first steps as professionals in a safe and supported way.

Finally, because at the Italian Center for Single Session Therapy, we want to train excellent professionals, and we believe that this can only happen through what is our mantra: practice, practice, practice.

Our students see OSC as a training ground where they can practice before stepping into the ring: thanks to the clinical center, they gain an understanding of the areas they need to train more or differently in, they test themselves in a protected environment, and they can decide whether to step up their participation or, conversely, slow down.

However, we do not rule out the possibility that in the near future OSC may become fee-for-service; a single session service with capped prices to maintain our purpose of making psychotherapy accessible to all.

The Method of the Italian Center for Single-Session Therapy

At this point, it may be useful to give an idea of the SST method provided by the Italian Center for Single-Session Therapy, taught to all One Session therapists in three specific training weekends followed by a series of further days of supervision, review and practice. In fact, therapists can only participate in the One Session Center project three months after the school's first training weekend, which corresponds to the first TSS workshop. This gives us a chance to get to know the student, form an initial idea of their skills, follow them through an initial training process, and also give them an opportunity, whenever possible, to practice SST on their own and to bring any cases to supervision with the class (or at least to listen to others' supervision).

The Italian Center's method has already been extensively explained in Cannistrà and Piccirilli's book *Single-Session Therapy:* Principles and Practices (2021), to which we refer for an in-depth discussion. Here we will limit ourselves to its essential points. Although we strongly and gladly apply solution-focused approaches, this is primarily a problem-oriented method whose aim is the identification and definition by the client of a problem and a related goal to be achieved. This decision is probably in large part influenced by our educational background. Indeed, in our Institute, we teach and practice theoretical and methodological pluralism (Cooper & McLeod, 2007), which leads us to use different approaches and methods (specifically SST, Solution-Focused Brief Therapy, and MRI Strategic Therapy) with the idea that a single approach simply cannot cater for people's many differences. However, at the time of our initial SST studies, all the founders of the Italian Center came from a background in Strategic Therapy (Watzlawick et al., 1974), and this certainly guided our decisions. To this day, we also experiment with other ways of conducting SST, although the following remains our preferred one.

Firstly, we consider the mindset adopted by the therapist to be fundamental (Cannistrà, 2022). Without a single-session mindset, no technique or method can produce the desired results. In fact, the mindset will orient the therapist toward some fundamental points, such as: conducting the session knowing that it may be enough (and thus avoiding embarking on concepts or interventions that would intrinsically require more than one meeting); believing that what makes the difference is primarily the client, their resources and their definition of what is not working, what they need to achieve and how they can achieve it (thus avoiding giving or imposing definitions of the problem, goal or tools for change that, however valid, would risk slowing down the process because they are at odds with the client's belief systems); remaining open to the possibility of using multiple methods, in line with the person's preferences, the problem presented, or the specific moment in which they find themselves (and thus avoid a Procrustean bed that is too narrow or too wide for their needs). Elsewhere we have discussed 14 principles of the single-session mindset, drawn from a review of the literature (Cannistrà, 2022).

Starting from a single-session mindset, interventions used during the session are designed, thought out, and applied with the idea that they help maximize its effectiveness. As is well known, in fact, adopting certain mindsets and practices does not "create" the possibility of a single session (an eventuality that may occur in any case), but strongly increases the likelihood of it (by more than twice as much – see the chapter by Cannistrà and Pietrabissa in Cannistrà & Piccirilli, 2021).

Picking up on the work of Hoyt (2009), we find it useful for teaching purposes to divide the session into three phases.

In the initial phase, which usually occupies the first ten to 15 minutes, our main focus is defining the problem, setting the goal, and asking for constant feedback. The One Session Center therapist, first of all, tries to guide the person toward an operational definition of their problem in terms of the actions and interactions that make up the problem. In addition to implementing an important initial restructuring, as it helps the person move from "I have this" to "I do this," this also allows the client and the therapist to identify points on which change could or should be focused and support structures which can be leveraged. Next, the conversation is about identifying the goal of therapy and, more importantly, the goal of the session. The latter is crucial because, in our opinion, it allows the person to gain a sense of competence and self-efficacy that may motivate them to continue on their own: while it is true that at the end of a single meeting, most problems may not have been solved, it is equally true that many may have been re-signified as less problematic or, in other words, the person may come to discover that they have more resources or possibilities for action than they initially thought, thus receiving the motivation needed to continue on their own. In this sense, the request for constant feedback, punctuated by paraphrasing and small-scale reformulations of what the client says to the therapist, becomes an excellent tool for expanding the meanings that emerge as we go along. Although didactically, it is useful to mention this here, the request for feedback runs throughout the entire session.

Next, we enter the core of the session, the central phase. Here, the task is primarily to identify the person's resources on the one hand and dysfunctional behaviors on the other, with the idea of giving feedback aimed at reinforcing the former and modifying the latter. The search for resources is more generally a process of identifying what can be useful in solving the person's problem: in fact, we agree with that strand of research that believes that the main variance in the therapeutic process is determined by factors internal and external to the client, rather than by techniques used by the therapist (Asay & Lambert, 1999). The One Session therapist is already trained to notice, during problem definition and goal setting, resources that might be amplified and dysfunctional behaviors to be blocked, but at this stage, in addition to deepening the inquiry, he or she also begins to explore with the client what it might be helpful for them to do or not do in order to achieve the goal. The process is guided by the concept of the Client's Theory of Change as expounded by Duncan and Miller (2000), which can be summarized in the idea of asking the client what they think might be helpful to achieve the goal of the session (or even just to begin taking the first small steps). Our starting position is that we consider the client to be the expert in their own life: for us this means that in order to achieve their goals, it is much more effective to draw on a behavioral and meaning repertoire illustrated by the client, rather than suggested by us. In other words, before proposing techniques or prescribing behaviors and before suggesting new frames within which certain facts are read, we find it more useful for the client themselves to provide possible ways forward. While the therapist remains the expert in terms of method, i.e. the processes that can help people achieve goals, the client is the expert in content, i.e. the particular way in which they can achieve their specific goal. Following the Client's Theory of Change usually has three outcomes:

The person proposes ideas that the therapist agrees are appropriate for achieving their goal: "appropriate" not in terms of content (i.e. an evaluation of values, morals, and ethics), but in terms of the process of change. Our therapists choose for themselves whether to take more directive or strongly non-directive approaches, but even in the latter case, it is possible to pursue the idea that if something does not work, do something else (de Shazer et al., 2007).

1 The person suggests ideas, and the therapist feels that some adjustments could make them even more useful for the purpose they want to achieve.
2 The person comes up with ideas about which the therapist has reservations: again, not in terms of content or judgment of the person's actions and meanings, but in terms of usefulness to the process of change.

All three of these situations must be embedded in a process of co-construction. Even if he or she believes that the client's ideas may lead to dysfunctional outcomes, the therapist proposes, not imposes, and delivers feedback in a transparent sharing perspective, aimed at exploring possibilities. The choice of how to do this (e.g. through the use of metaphors or considerations, with open-ended questions or with a more maieutic approach, involving the client in role-plays, or proposing other active techniques) remains a decision that the therapist makes based on what he or she feels is most appropriate for that client.[1]

This central phase finds its heart and its conclusion in this process of exploring possible ways to help the person, meant both in terms of behaviors (things to be done) and by reframing previous facts and meanings. The idea is to achieve the goal set or to arrive at a new narrative that will enable this to happen, if not quite to different meanings of the problem and/or goal which the person brings to the session. And yet even these "in-session" changes are not always necessary: we believe that the process itself, which puts the person and their resources at the center, may be able to convey the idea that they are themselves the primary agent of change, and this may frequently be enough to keep them from deeming further sessions necessary.

The final phase generally includes the possible proposal of a task, co-constructed in the previous phase or its direct consequence, and/or a summary of what emerged, as well as the administration of paperwork (e.g. instructions for completing the post-session questionnaire). Fundamental, however, is closure. Therapist and client assess together whether the session may be sufficient or whether more sessions are needed, bearing in mind that in any case it is the client who is better able to give an adequate response (generally, except in risky situations, our therapists tend to agree with the client's decision, but do not hesitate to offer their own views). Of crucial importance is the clarification that the door remains open. In the case of One Session, this means that the person can freely decide whether to have further sessions with the therapist, contacting him or her privately in that case, or whether to access the service again, most likely with a different therapist (due to the rota system). In this case, we keep track of any returns: lest we ourselves become a dysfunctional attempted solution, we avoid having a person who has accessed the service three times continue working on the same problem with three different therapists, suggesting that they seek other services such as ongoing therapy.[2]

Of course, as we know, SST can't do everything. Being a way to deliver therapy (Young, 2018), it is important that the therapist offers the option to have more than one session when necessary. It is also important to consider those situations in which there is a risk for the client or another person involved. For example, we suggest that all OS therapists are cautious and prefer "one more session" (or invite the client to access other services) if they think that they or others are at risk – such as a client considered to be at risk of suicide or to threaten the life of a family member. A lot can be done in one session, but not everything. And when facing a risky situation, we prefer to be over-cautious and ask, for example, for another session, rather than underestimate the risk.

Clinical Case

This case and its report are by Dr. Valeria Campinoti, who was a student at our Institute at the time and is now a member of the team at the Italian Center for Single Session Therapy.

Introduction

The cell phone emits a soft "ding!". Valeria's on duty: she opens the Facebook page and checks the mail. It's Viola, a young woman who looks less than 20, with long black hair, as her profile picture shows:

Viola writes: "Is anyone there?"
Valeria: "Hello Viola, this is Valeria. How can I help you?"
Viola: "I read that you do therapy, is that correct? I need to talk to someone."
Valeria: "Sure! I need to ask for a few minutes of your time to get some information, after which we could start the counseling right away."

So begins another day at One Session, the walk-in online volunteer service of the Italian Center for Single-Session Therapy:

Valeria: "Good evening Viola! Nice to meet you. Before we start our session, I'd like to explain a little bit about how the One Session service works. One Session is a Single Session Therapy Service, a method of maximizing the effectiveness of each individual session. So today we're going to try and make sure that this meeting is useful to you and you can benefit from it. At the end of the session we'll evaluate together whether this one meeting may have been enough for you. Would you like to tell me why you contacted us?"
Viola: "So, I've finished all my exams, I have a very high average, now all that's missing is the obstacle of the dissertation, but every time I think about starting to write it I feel bad."
Valeria: "What do you mean when you say you feel bad?" (requesting more details to define the problem in operational terms)
Viola: "That I get anxious, I start thinking I don't know where to start, then I get tachycardia… and I try hard not to think about

it, delaying the commitment to write it until the next day. I've been stuck like this for two months!"

Valeria: "Can you tell me more about what happens when you try to write the dissertation?"

Viola: "I usually take my laptop and books to my usual place, in my room, where I have my desk. The minute I pick up my stuff I start thinking about the previous time when I did the same thing. So, when I sit down and open my laptop, I'm already thinking "You're not going to be able to write this," and when I open Word and see that blank page... I get paralyzed."

Valeria: "And then what happens?"

Viola: "Then I force myself to wait. But the waiting is getting shorter and shorter. Yesterday after five minutes I slammed my laptop shut and burst into tears. Not being able to do this thing makes me sick."

Valeria: "I guess... Viola, look, what needs to happen here today so that we can say goodbye feeling that it was a useful meeting for you?" (defining the goal of the session)

Viola: "I want to get unstuck, start writing. I know the problem is all in the beginning, in my inability to start: I don't know why, but I know that if I start then the rest is all downhill."

Valeria: "Okay! So, in today's meeting we need to focus on getting you started on writing your dissertation, right?" (feedback and agreement on the goal)

Viola: "That's absolutely the thing I want most!"

Valeria: "Well, what have you tried to do, Viola, to unblock this situation?" (exploration of attempted solutions prior to the meeting)

Viola: "Well... I've tried everything, Valeria. I started going to the library: I went a couple of times, but to no effect. Then I got my classmates involved, asking if we could meet and write our dissertations together, since we should theoretically graduate in the same session. A few times I searched online for articles, maybe even on student blogs or forums to see if others had the same problem as me and if they had overcome it somehow. But I only did that two or three times in these months. Then it confused me even more and I let it go."

Valeria: "Yes, I agree about dropping this solution. Sometimes we use the internet a bit like an answer book, but not all answers fit all situations and all people. And I can also tell you that we often enact behaviors in an attempt to solve a problem, but these not only don't solve it, but they also actually make it worse! Do you think the things you were telling me about just now have been good solutions for you?" (therapist's response to the solutions attempted by the client)

Viola:	"I would say no, in fact: as you were saying, they made me freeze even more, so much so that all I can do is sit still. And the thing that makes me most frustrated, really, is the waste of time!"
Valeria:	"It really sounds like wasting time is a big worry for you. The more you're aware of the value of time, the more you regret losing it. Has this situation happened to you before? I guess you also wrote a dissertation for your three-year degree. How did it go on that occasion?"
Viola:	"In the three-year degree it was a different story. I wrote that dissertation quickly, no hitches! Just think, one day I forgot to save the file and ten pages were erased. Ten very long pages of work. I cried, but then I rolled up my sleeves and rewrote them. Maybe even better than before, you know."
Valeria:	"How did you manage to write that dissertation fluently, smoothly?" (investigation of resources and exceptions to the problem in such a situation)
Viola:	"Well you know, I didn't do anything in particular. I used to go to the library and get the books, read them, underline and then process the information."
Valeria:	"So it sounds like you know how to write a dissertation!" (smiling)
Viola:	"Well yes... Do you know that in these past two months I've never thought about the fact that I wrote a dissertation for my three-year degree? It reminds me that for that dissertation I used to give myself set times during the day. In those days I was a waitress, so the whole week was punctuated by my shifts and everything had to fit together."
Valeria:	"How is your day organized now?"
Viola:	"Now I wake up, go for a walk, then come home and start thinking that I should spend at least four or five hours on my dissertation: at least the whole morning or the whole afternoon. But in fact this thought kills me, because I know I won't do anything. I sit down, I pick up my books and I waste time, I get lost in thought. I think I'll fail, I think I'll do a mediocre job, and I keep catastrophizing. And the day passes like that, between attempts to write and a thousand other distractions."
Valeria:	"So Viola, do you think if you organized your day into slots to devote to the dissertation that might help you?" (exploring solutions during the session)
Viola:	"That's actually something I haven't experimented with in the last few months, I should try it."
Valeria:	"Great, it seems to me that you've identified a way forward. To make this solution work even better, we can add

another little piece. So I suggest that you establish a regular appointment with your books every day at the same time, in the same place, along with everything you need to write your dissertation. Clear your desk of unnecessary things and anything that might distract you, such as your phone or other items. Set a timer for forty-five minutes - so, for example if you decide that your start time is 10:00 a.m., you set the alarm for 10:45. What you have to do in those forty-five minutes is not write the dissertation. So, I want you to stay there, sitting in front of your computer, your books and your notes, but you are absolutely forbidden to write the dissertation. In those forty-five minutes, I don't ask you to do anything else except not write it."

Viola:	"Hmm…it's all very strange, but I'm curious. I'll give it a try…"
Valeria:	"Well Viola! It seems to me that quite a lot of things have emerged during our meeting, haven't they? And it seems to me that you really have a lot of resources."
Viola:	"I want to start implementing this new strategy from tomorrow, see if it works, and so I would stop here for now."

After three weeks Viola writes to us again on our Facebook page: "I wanted to thank Valeria for our session! I wrote my dissertation!"

Valeria accesses One Session's Facebook mail to congratulate her and asks how those weeks had been. Viola says that for the first three days the exercise was a real torture: she sat down with her books and, although the first moments were spent thinking and ruminating about the dissertation, afterward, she got nervous because she felt she was wasting time. She admits that she lasted three days, and by the third day she had opened one of the books to read the table of contents and circle the paragraphs useful for the dissertation. By the fourth day, she states: "I couldn't do it any longer! Those 45 minutes seemed like the worst thing that could happen to me, and rather than sit there doing nothing, I started writing." She reports that she initially wrote down a preliminary table of contents for the dissertation, along with the introduction, and spent the rest of the time trying to sort out the material she had. From the fifth day: "I exploded, in a good way: I started writing and never stopped until the timer went off!"

Valeria compliments Viola on the great job she managed to do in such a short time and inquires about the next steps. Viola says she has completed the whole of the first chapter and is waiting for revision by her supervisor. She also feels much better in terms of mood. The negative thoughts are gone, and she has also returned to studying with her colleagues, either in the library or elsewhere. She is very happy that she will be able to graduate in the session she had intended and has, in addition, started looking around for companies for her internship once she graduates.

Everyone Matters

Everyone matters. From this perspective, the One Session service was born.

Everyone matters. Through this viewpoint, it has proven to be a successful service.

One of the problems in mental health care services in Italy, Europe, and probably most of the world is the difficulty of addressing increasing demand. This is a problem: "Whereas the right to physical and mental health is a fundamental human right and whereas every human being is entitled to the highest attainable standard of health" as the European Parliament states (2022). The same body regrets

> the fact that mental health has not been treated as a priority in the same way as physical health, has been deprived of funding and has been short of qualified staff across the Member States, despite the intrinsic benefits associated with improved health and well-being and the substantial economic productivity gains and higher levels of participation in work deriving from public investment in mental health.

People who need effective answers quickly, matter. Their stories matter, even when they cannot afford the luxury (because that is often what it is) of private therapy and have to forgo it; their resources matter, which are focused on during the session by leveraging them to achieve change.

ICNOS Institute students and the training provided to them matter. This is why they are involved in projects from the very beginning, allowing them to put their learning into practice. This is also a way to compensate for the lack of practice during their time at university. Many newly licensed Italian psychologists have very high-level knowledge of psychology, but they often start a specialization course in psychotherapy with zero hours of practice with clients. OS is an opportunity to apply what they have learned and practiced during their first year in our school, with supervision by a senior therapist, and to give their ideas and contributions, both advancing the service and gaining practical experience that will help them to become better therapists. In fact the relationships that are built and constantly cultivated in this sphere also matter, from the perspective of horizontality, where every idea, proposal, criticism, and observation is carefully listened to and analyzed.

And lastly, the team of the Italian Center for Single Session Therapy matters: a heterogeneous team composed of people who work with commitment, respect, and pleasure, and try to leave traces that remain beyond the end of the workshop.

Acknowledgments

We would like to thank our great friends and colleagues Beatrice Pavoni, Federico Piccirilli, Valeria Campinoti, Pier Paolo D'Alia, Angelica Giannetti, Francesca Moccia, and Elisabeth Cinti, with whom we make up the Italian Center for Single Session Therapy team.

Notes

1 In our Institute we teach a multi-theoretical approach (Hoyt, 2009), based on learning Single-Session Therapy, Solution Focused Brief Therapy, MRI Model Strategic Therapy and Strategic Family Therapy. We believe that no one model fits all people and that an integrated model is no more than another model. A multi-theoretical model, on the other hand, allows one to change models as needed, like a change of clothes made according to the specific event.
2 For a comprehensive description of our method, we refer to our book *Single Session Therapy. Principles and Practices* (Cannistrà & Piccirilli, 2021).

References

Asay, T. P., & Lambert, M. J. (1999). The empirical case for the common factors in therapy: Quantitative findings. In M. A. Hubble, B. L. Duncan, & S. D. Miller (Eds.), *The heart and soul of change: What works in therapy* (pp. 23–55). American Psychological Association. https://doi.org/10.1037/11132-001

Bernstein, R. J. (2010). *The Pragmatic Turn*. Polity Press.

Brooks, S. K., Webster, R. K., Smith, L. E., Woodland, L., Wessely, S., Greenberg, N., & Rubin, G. J. (2020). The psychological impact of quarantine and how to reduce it: Rapid review of the evidence. *The Lancet*, 395(10227), 912–920. https://doi.org/10.1016/s0140-6736(20)30460-8

Cannistrà, F. (2022). The single session therapy mindset fourteen principles gained through an analysis of the literature. *International Journal of Brief Therapy and Family Science*, 12(1), 1–26. https://www.jstage.jst.go.jp/article/ijbf/12/1/12_1/_article

Cannistrà, F., & Hoyt, M. F. (Eds.). (2025). *Single-Session Therapies: Why and How One-At-A-Time Mindsets are Effective*. Routledge.

Cannistrà, F., & Piccirilli, F. (2021). *Single Session Therapy: Principles and Practices*. Giunti.

Cooper, M., & McLeod, J. (2007). A pluralistic framework for counselling and psychotherapy: Implications for research. *Counselling and Psychotherapy Research*, 7(3), 135–143. https://onlinelibrary.wiley.com/doi/10.1080/14733140701566282

de Shazer, S., Dolan, Y., Korman, H., Trepper, T., McCollum, E., & Berg, I. K. (2007). *More Than Miracles: The State of the Art of Solution-focused Brief Therapy*. Routledge.

Duncan, B. L., & Miller, S. D. (2000). The client's theory of change: Consulting the client in the integrative process. *Journal of Psychotherapy Integration*, 10(2), 169–187. https://doi.org/10.1023/A:1009448200244

European Parliament (2022). *European Parliament resolution of 5 July 2022 on mental health in the digital world of work.* https://www.europarl.europa.eu/doceo/document/TA-9-2022-0279_EN.html

Hoyt, M. F. (2009). *Brief Psychotherapies. Principles and Practices.* Zeig, Tucker & Theisen.

Hoyt, M. F., & Talmon, M. (2014). *Capturing the Moment: Single-Session Therapy and Walk-in Services.* Crown House Publishing Limited.

Slive, A., & Bobele, M. (2011). *When One Hour is All You Have: Effective Therapy for Walk-in Clients.* Zeig, Tucker & Theisen.

Watts, A. (1948). *Zen.* James Ladd Delkin.

Watzlawick, P., Weakland, J., & Fisch, R. (1974). *Change Principles of Problem Formation and Problem Resolution.* Norton & Co.

Young, J. (2018). Single-session therapy: The misunderstood gift that keeps on giving. In M. F. Hoyt, M. Bobele, A. Slive, J. Young, & M. Talmon (Eds.), *Single-session therapy by walk-in or appointment administrative, clinical, and supervisory aspects of one-at-a-time services,* (pp. 40-58). Routledge.

Chapter 12

Miracle on Ice and Snow—How Walk-In Therapy Caught on in Finland

Tuomas Perkiö and Mikko Mäkelä

All of us like stories where the underdog wins. One of our favorites in this category is how the United States won the 1980 Olympic hockey gold medal in Lake Placid. A team of amateur players managed to surprise everyone by taking the brightest medals by sensationally defeating the great and powerful Russian Red Machine. In our story, we are challenged by a serious mental health crisis among young Finns. It will take amateur and professional teams alike to overcome it.

In the world's happiest nation, an estimated 20–25% (THL, 2022) of young people between 13 and 29 years of age suffer from mental health challenges during their adolescence. If happiness surveys were to include children and young people under the age of 18, Finland's ranking in happiness surveys would drop considerably. (Rees et al., 2020). At the same time, our society has too few resources to help people with mental health challenges. This leaves many professionals working with young people with only the option of writing referrals to specialist care while trying their best to help the young person. This is a problem we wanted to address, and one of the answers we found was single-session therapy and walk-in sessions. Our story is still short, and the end is still open, but here is what has happened so far.

As in many Western countries, the decline in mental well-being among young people has been a visible trend in Finland for a long time (Kaltiala, 2022). Mental health problems are the most common cause of disability among young people under 30. The pressure on mental health services has been massive for years. At the same time, the service structure has become such that help for mental health problems is available almost only in specialized health care (Ranta, 2018). Basic preventive and early intervention services have not been developed at the speed required by demand. Klaus Ranta, Senior Consultant in Adolescent Psychiatry at Helsinki University Hospital, has compared the situation in the service system to a patient with a wound to the leg being referred to a surgeon. In many cases, the treatment would consist simply of cleaning and dressing the wound.

DOI: 10.4324/9781003351375-12

Surgery would not be necessary. The concentration of mental health care in specialist care inevitably leads to long waiting lists and prolonged and even worsening suffering.

At the same time, societal changes treat young people with a heavy hand, demanding more and more from them. The reform of university applications in Finland makes the consequences of the wrong choice more difficult for young people to remedy. This reform emphasizes the importance of the high school report card instead of application tests, so high school students need to know what they want their future to look like at the age of 16. Formerly they had the opportunity to get familiar with different subjects at high school and form their plans for adulthood in the last year of high school at the age of 18. Now if students want to change their plan for the future, it is hard to do because they need three years of high school studies to get good enough grades on the report card to get accepted in the university. Thus, the consequences of making a wrong choice have increased considerably. Young people's own increased responsibility for themselves and their future are being driven both by school curricula that demand self-direction and by society's rules. A child as young as 12 can forbid his or her parents from seeing their medical records and their doctor from contacting their parents. Of course, the doctor must assess whether the 12-year-old can decide on his or her own treatment. The question is, "Is any 12-year-old really mature enough to make decisions that could have far-reaching implications for the future?"

We work within the Evangelical Lutheran Church of Finland. At the end of 2022, 65.1% (Evangelical Church of Finland, 2023) of Finns were members of our church. One of the church's most socially influential activities is confirmation school. In 2021, 75% of all Finns over 15 attended confirmation school (Evangelical Church of Finland, 2023). This activity is quite a window into the lives of young Finns. For years now, we have seen the deterioration of mental well-being not only in confessional schools but also in other forms of youth work. So far, all we have been able to do is try to do something to help young people who are waiting in line for services. SST has given us the opportunity to do more. That is what we have wanted for a long time. As youth work professionals, one of our important tasks is to live as adults in the world of young people. It is from this vantage point that we have for years observed young people's struggles with mental well-being challenges. We have tried to help them access appropriate services, supported them during the months they must queue for services, encouraged them to stay in services, and celebrated with them the progress they have made. In other words, we've been working with young people with mental health challenges all along, previously just without the right tools. The Solution-Focused Brief Therapy training provided one more opportunity to acquire the tools to do a little more and to try something new.

We heard about walk-in/single-session therapy when Monte Bobele gave a lecture to the Finnish Solution-Focused Brief Therapy training group in spring 2021. Mikko, who attended the lecture and got an idea of walk-in therapy in Finland. Mäkelä called Tuomas after the lecture and we talked on the phone for about an hour (Mäkelä, 2022). We decided that we would try walk-in/single-session and to recruit two of my colleagues, Riikka Peltola and Teemu Salminen, from Tampere to start planning the experiment. We studied the lecture material, read the source material (Slive & Bobele, 2012; Slive & Bobele,2018), and made the practical arrangements. In autumn 2021, we started the first walk-in therapy location in the Old Church in the middle of Tampere. The practice was new to us, and we decided to move forward in the spirit of experimental culture, constantly developing and learning from mistakes.

We chose young people and young adults under the age of 29 as our target group, according to the definition of youth in the Finnish Youth Act. We wanted the lowest possible entry threshold for our practice, so we decided to enable anonymity. We also do not keep records of the meetings. Sessions are free of charge for the client. In practice, the session starts as soon as the person walks through the door; they are greeted, offered coffee and tea, and asked to fill in a short form. If there is more than one therapist available, the client can choose who they want to work with. Most first-time clients choose the therapist who greeted them first and offered them coffee. A small proportion of first-time clients choose a therapist based on gender. Whenever possible, a second-time client always chooses the therapist with whom they have previously worked.

The following two examples illustrate what we thought we were going to encounter and what we also learned that we would encounter when engaging in walk-in therapy. The first story is a good example of what Pertti Virta (2023) means when he talks about "the need for help not turning into the need for treatment."

One of the first clients was a 25-year-old man who expressed a desire to discuss the end of his relationship. He hoped that through the session, he could clarify his thoughts. He mentioned that the breakup had been anticipated for a while, but it had now started to feel real. As he spoke, he paused and seemed to hold back tears. Validating his emotionally difficult situation and acknowledging that crying is a natural response in such circumstances provided initial relief. The client was a recovering alcoholic and had been sober for over a year. He recognized that the breakup was stirring up emotions and thoughts he had previously dealt with through alcohol. He stated that this time, he was determined to do everything possible not to resort to drinking in difficult situations. A strong motivation for him was the desire to be a good father to his 3-year-old daughter. He had decided to use all means to prevent the old pattern from recurring.

The particularly strong motivation to stay sober and deal with difficult emotions differently seemed to help the client find a way forward. It felt like he had made a decision and was preparing to follow through with it. We discussed how he had managed to become sober and stay sober. His understanding of his own ability to tackle difficult things became clearer. We also talked a lot about how he experienced quality time with his daughter. The idea of himself as a father doing everything to make life with his daughter as good as possible began to overshadow the image of a problematic alcoholic. The feeling of relief grew further.

The client felt that his self-awareness and toolkit for coping with difficult emotions had significantly improved as a result of his sobriety process. However, he mentioned that situations where feelings of anxiety suddenly arise are challenging. He was very adept at recognizing early physical and mental reactions as signs of emerging anxiety. We practiced a simple grounding technique to use in such situations. In the closing summary, he mentioned that practicing had increased his confidence in facing suddenly arising feelings of anxiety.

This second example again tells us what we learned in our work. Some of our clients are already in treatment, yet they still feel the need for help from walk-in therapy.

In the early stages of our operation, on a Monday, a 24-year-old woman walked into our office. She felt it was important to talk about her thinking that she didn't believe she would make it until Friday, when she had her next session with her own psychotherapist. She wanted hope from the walk-in session; she had written HOPE as an answer to question "What do you hope that we accomplish in this session?". She began to talk about her situation, revealing that she suffers from severe depression and has had OCD. The therapist immediately addressed the past tense and asked how she had managed to leave her OCD behind. This sparked a conversation about living one's life according to one's own values. Previously, she had been afraid to go out in public places and had succeeded in overcoming her fear by thinking about the kind of life she wanted to live. This life included meeting friends and being active with them. Despite all her successes, the client had a perception of herself as a fearful person. We managed to reframe this thought by discussing what courage is and how people can be courageous only when we are afraid.

We continued by discussing all the ways in which she had already progressed while working with her regular psychotherapist. Receiving recognition for all this progress seemed to strengthen her belief that she could survive difficult phases. We talked about what actions she could take to improve her well-being and bring some positive things into her daily life during the week before her session with her regular therapist. It seemed that discussing concrete and small actions made the difficult week feel more manageable. The first and smallest step she planned to take as soon as she got home was to pet her cat.

The startup was slow, and there were few clients, but they did come. Those who did walk in gave positive feedback, so we were encouraged and kept learning more and more. Soon other workers in the church heard about our experiment and many became interested. We held webinars and answered questions. Our colleagues from all over Finland started deciding to set up their own walk-in therapy clinics. There was a great desire to help young people and to act ourselves. Different solutions, adapted to local conditions, started to emerge. In some places, it was easy to get started. Some of the workers were already trained as solution-focused brief therapists, psychotherapists, couple's therapists or family therapists. In such cases, the decision was simply taken to start their own walk-in therapy and start advertising it. For others, it was not so straightforward. In a few places, the church decided to send their employees to study to become, for example, a solution-focused brief therapist. A third way of starting walk-in therapy was to recruit volunteer therapists. There is a long tradition of volunteer work in the church, and in some places walk-in therapy became a new activity for becoming a volunteer.

The church contacted local therapists and presented the idea to them, asking them to give their time and skills to help the young people. Many therapists and trainee therapists responded positively. During 2022, 14 new walk-in therapy locations were created in 12 localities. In 2023, number of locations increased to 20, and those locations served 1,238 clients during the year. We, who had set out two years earlier just to see what we could achieve, have been surprised throughout this process. We are used to the idea that things happen slowly in Finnish society and even more slowly in the church. We were pleasantly surprised by the amount of interest and the speed at which new points were created. The concern for young people's mental health is shared, and so is the desire to act.

As we write this, we have promoted opportunities for further training. Our idea is that youth work professionals will become good walk-in therapists for adolescents and young adults. We aim to tap into the knowledge that youth work counselors have about meeting young people, as well as the understandings that they have developed through their work with the different realities of different young people. We found teaching therapeutic methods to youth work professionals is the equivalent of replacing a handsaw and hammer on a construction site with a circular saw and a nail gun. The result is much greater. Making this possible has required new and courageous decisions from many organizational leaders. Private foundation-based funding has also played an important role.

Many people have contributed to the development of the conditions for action. They have advised and taught us, spoken up for basic services in various forums, spread awareness of our work, educated us about the SST way of working in health care, and communicated these ideas to politicians. At the time of writing, in the summer of 2023 a new government has been formed in Finland, and its program includes a clause on promoting walk-in work together with the church and non-profit organizations. We are still at the very beginning of our own journey with walk-in therapy. Our activities are still very small. If all the resources of all our practices were combined in one physical location, we would have one practice open six days a week, with four therapists working full time. Typical walk-in point-of-operation is open three to five hours on one day in the week, usually in the afternoon and early evening. There are one to four therapists working at the same time. Each of us will see our clients alone without a team. The number of clients we see per day usually varies from 0 to 10, depending on the location of the point of operation. Points in bigger cities usually have more clients, but not by default.

The record number of clients seen in one day was 24 at our first point in Helsinki. This was made possible through a Facebook sharing of a news story published by famous Finnish rap-artist Paleface. Sadly, it was a one-time thing. Our way of working is very network-based. It allows us to spread out over a wide geographical area, so that in as many places as possible, young people have a place to go at least once a week, where they can get help just by walking in. The advantage of a network approach is that many brains are working on the same problem. We insist on sharing our insights and helping each other develop solutions to local problems. We've also learned that when you give a professional new tool, new things emerge. New skills combine with old ones. Comments from trained youth workers have been encouraging; they are enthusiastic, feel their work is more meaningful, and note that new skills are being used in familiar old jobs. Here are few citations from youth workers who have been trained with solution-focused brief therapy methods:

"It changed my mindset. Solution-focused methods plays a crucial role in my work approach today. I grew and developed as a professional tremendously."

"So many skills to utilize, a refreshing addition to my previous toolkit. A new direction in work, helping to endure stressful aspects of work."

"I've never been in training that has been this useful and directly applicable to what I need in my work. The learnings were pure concreteness and easy to implement straight away."

As our work is based on anonymity, we have no client records and no follow-up. The information in this section is based on therapists' observations and a short feedback questionnaire that we ask clients to complete each time after a session. What we have learned about our clients is that they come from very different life situations. We see students, unemployed,

employed, gap years, young people with solid support, young people who are off all services, young people with families or without, relationships, loneliness. Our clients may have multiple mental health diagnoses or may be facing their mental well-being for the first time in their lives. The topics they want to talk about include emotional issues, their own or a loved one's substance abuse, relationship issues, loneliness, behavioral problems, identity issues, life direction, acute crisis, everyday stress, coping with a mental health problem. These are the topics they want to be heard on, to gain new perspectives, to find a way forward, to get concrete ways to cope better and to find hope.

In addition to the summary discussion at the end of the session, we collect feedback from our clients through three questions. First, on a scale of 1 to 10, we ask how helpful the session was and second, how well the client thought they had been heard. Finally, we ask the client to circle the suggested mood words that best describe their emotional state after the session. In the thesis from students Annamari Tammelander and Saana Sinisalo from the Helsinki Diaconia University of Applied Sciences gave survey forms to walk-in clients in the fall of 2023 at every walk-in site in Finland. They gathered 182 competed surveys (Sinisalo & Tammelander, 2024). In that study, the average score for usefulness of the session is 8.9, and the average score for being heard is 9.4. The top 5 words describing mood are *unburdened (67%), encountered (51%), relieved (44%), thoughtful (43%), and empowered (27%).*[1]

Some clients come back with the same problem. Others come back for a new visit and want to talk about a different topic. In our practice, the most common number of visits is one; the second most common is two, and so on. We do not limit the number of visits in any way, it is up to the client. The record number of visits per client is five. As I wrote at the beginning, our story is still short, and the end is still open. In the title we use the word 'miracle' based on comments we have received about our operation's quick expansion. Truth is, that the game has just started, and although there is plenty to be excited about, there is also a lot to be done. I am happy to say that there are a lot of good things happening in the field of mental health in Finland right now. Many top professionals have stepped up to the plate and are both looking for new openings and already doing even more of their very valuable work. The opposition is also strong. The stakes are high. But there are still minutes left on the clock and a game left to play.

Note

1 We use the English word "encountered" to translate the Finnish word "kohdattu", which refers to the feeling of being seen, heard, and understood.

References

Evangelical Church of Finland, (2023). Kirkon jäsenyys on 64 Prosentilla Suomalaisista. *Evl.fi.* (2023, December 20). https://kirkontilastot.fi/viz.php?id=246

Jäsentilastoja – suomen evankelis-luterilainen kirkko. Suomen ev.lut.kirkko. (2022). https://evl.fi/tietoa-kirkosta/tilastotietoa/jasenet

Kaltiala, R. (2022). Nuoruusikä tuuliajolla – miksi hyvin- ja pahoinvointi näyttäisivät kasvavan samaan aikaan? *Eduskunta.* 6, 42-53. https://www.eduskunta.fi/FI/naineduskuntatoimii/julkaisut/Documents/TUVJ-6-22.pdf

Mäkelä, M. (2022). *Kirkko Tarjoaa walk in – LYHYTTERAPIAA Nuorten Hätään – ePressi.* LianaPress. https://www.epressi.com/tiedotteet/uskonto/kirkko-tarjoaa-walk-in-lyhytterapiaa-nuorten-hataan.html

Nuorten mielenterveyshäiriöt – THL. Terveyden ja hyvinvoinnin laitos. (2022). https://thl.fi/fi/web/mielenterveys/mielenterveyshairiot/nuorten-mielenterveys hairiot

Ranta, K. (2018, April 4). Näinkö helppoa tämä olikin? espoolaiskouluissa kuunnellaan masentuneita teinejä, olo paranee eikä erikoissairaanhoitoa välttämättä tarvita. *Yle Uutiset.* https://yle.fi/a/3-10142758

Rees, G., Savahl, S., Lee, B. J., & Casas, F. (eds.), (2020). *Children's views on their lives and well-being in 35 countries: A report on the Children's Worlds project, 2016–2019.* Children's Worlds Project (ISCWeB). https://isciweb.org/wp-content/uploads/2020/07/Childrens-Worlds-Comparative-Report-2020.pdf

Rippikoulu Sinisalo, S., & Tammelander, A. (2024). *Asiakkaiden Kokemuksia Walk in terapiakäynnistä.* Theseus. https://urn.fi/URN:NBN:fi:amk-2024051411575

Slive, A., & Bobele, M. (2012). Walk-in counselling services: Making the most of one hour. *Australian & New Zealand Journal of Family Therapy, 33*(1), 27–38. https://doi.org/10.1017/aft.2012.4

Slive, A., & Bobele, M. (2018). The three top reasons why walk-in/single-sessions make perfect sense. In M. F. Hoyt, M. Bobele, A. Slive, J. Young, & M. Talmon (Eds.), *Single-session therapy by walk-in or appointment: Administrative, clinical, and supervisory aspects of one-at-a-time services* (pp. 27–39). Routledge/Taylor & Francis Group. https://doi.org/10.4324/9781351112437-2

Virta, P. (2023). Personal communication to Perkiö, March 14, 2023.

Chapter 13

Walk-In Single-Session Therapy at a University Counselling Clinic and Clinician Experience

Cheryl-Anne Cait, Alesya Courtnage,
Cheri Bilitz, and Sean Ruby

The need for more accessible mental health services is not new (Cameron, 2007), and demand has only increased since the COVID-19 pandemic. Students at Canadian post-secondary institutions are no exception, including the University of Waterloo. Well before the global pandemic, there were expressed concerns about the availability of mental health resources on campuses. The University of Waterloo is among the largest-enrolled universities in Canada (Universities Canada, 2017). At the time of the study, 31,380 undergraduate students and 5,290 graduate students were enrolled (University of Waterloo, 2018b).

In 2018 the University assembled the President's Advisory Committee on Student Mental Health (PAC-SMH) to analyse the mental health landscape on campus and develop appropriate recommendations (University of Waterloo, 2018a). As detailed in the PAC-SMH report, while results from student self-report surveys, such as the National College Health Assessment (NCHA-II), indicated increasing rates of psychological distress among students, objective symptom measures suggested little change over the past ten years (University of Waterloo, 2018a). However, the internally generated PAC-SMH report did find that University of Waterloo students are increasingly utilising mental health services, perhaps due to the reduced stigma and the increased awareness about mental health (University of Waterloo, 2018a). To address the increasing demand for accessible mental health services, many wellness centres, including the University of Waterloo's Campus Wellness (CW), have been incorporating walk-in (WI) single-session therapy (SST) into their array of services (Hymmen et al., 2013). University of Waterloo Counselling Services offered their first WI/SST appointment on August 9, 2016. Since the launch of the service, students have attended thousands of WI/SST appointments at the Counselling Services.

At the time of this study, Counselling Services offered single sessions on both a scheduled and walk-in basis. WI SST was offered two days a week. Clients identified as being at risk for ending their life, seriously harming

DOI: 10.4324/9781003351375-13

themselves, or someone else was triaged by the Intake Specialist for a walk-in emergency appointment and not to the WI SST service and did not participate in this study. The Intake Specialist met with these students for brief appointments to refer clients to the appropriate service.

Literature Review

The World Health Organization (WHO) has identified the mental health of post-secondary students as an area of concern internationally, as mental health challenges have been correlated with poor academic achievement and reduction in educational attainment (Mojtabai et al., 2015). Campus mental health (CMH) directors and counsellors working within CMH centres consistently report not feeling able to meet the demands for CMH treatment services (Linden, 2019), and over 96% of campus counselling centre directors have reported treating more students with severe psychological problems than in previous years (Gallagher, 2012). In spite of increased concern regarding the mental health of post-secondary students, students' reported service utilisation remains unchanged over time. In the NCHA-II 2019 Canadian survey, only 22% of females and 15% of males who self-identified with mental health distress sought help from their CMH Centre. Robinson et al. (2016) reported that 74% of students were aware of mental health services, but only 8% had accessed them. In their scoping review of the CMH Centres, Dunley and Papadopolous (2019) classified student barriers to help-seeking in two distinct categories: (1) institutional and (2) student barriers. Institutional barriers included issues such as ease of access and wait times for services, while student barriers included differences in gender, race, cultural background, perceived stigma and beliefs about the effectiveness of interventions.

Some have argued that low service usage highlights the need for innovative service delivery models that reduce barriers to accessibility (Shefet, 2018, Cornish et al., 2017). Traditionally, CMH centres have operated on a "supply and demand" model, with counselling services delivered by a mental health professional in one-on-one 50-minute sessions (Cornish et al., 2017). Services were offered on a "first-come, first-serve" basis, meaning that students would only be seen when a counsellor had space in their caseload (Vallianatos et al., 2019). Sessions were seldom time-limited, and regular meetings were frequently scheduled throughout the school year. If a counsellor was not available to see the student, that student was placed on a waitlist, often resulting in wait times of weeks or months. In addition to some of the barriers already described, this model is expensive for institutions and does not reflect the busy lifestyles of post-secondary students (Cornish et al., 2017).

There is a distinct gap in peer reviewed, published literature regarding existing service delivery models in Canadian post-secondary institutions, and these studies lack consistency in operationally defining the services provided. Many post-secondary institutions offer on-site counselling (De Somma et al., 2017, Heck et al., 2014). Most universities offer "crisis counselling" as a same-day service (De Somma, et al., 2017, Jaworska et al., 2016, Heck et al., 2014); however, it is unclear what constitutes a "crisis." Heck et al., (2014) found that many post-secondary institutions do not engage in systematic programme reviews or evaluations, which may be the largest contributing factor to the lack of information regarding CMH approaches. Additionally, the authors identified the absence of any central database that collates the different mental health services offered at post-secondary institutions as being problematic.

Single-Session Therapy (SST)

Concerns around mental health accessibility have been mirrored outside of post-secondary institutions, and in recent years, there has been a strong drive to develop easily accessible, responsive and flexible services that reflect the needs of people who are seeking mental health support. Mental health walk-in clinics (MH-WICs) have emerged as the first point of contact for many people seeking quick access to services (Cait et al., 2017). At present, there are over 200 mental health agencies offering WI SST across Canada (McElheran et al., 2020).

In the research literature, there is a significant intermingling of the terms "walk-in" and "single session therapy" (Bloom & Tam, 2015). While these terms are frequently used in similar contexts, there are important distinctions between them. "Walk-in" refers to a model of service delivery where appointments are not scheduled, or required, in advance. As such, walk-in therapy provides help at a time that is most convenient or meaningful for the client (Slive & Bobele, 2011a). Not all walk-in appointments are single sessions; for example, a walk-in appointment may serve as a client's intake appointment for the beginning of a longer-term therapeutic relationship (Bloom & Tam, 2015).

SST does not require assessment, diagnosis or referral and no commitment to additional services is required. SST is meant to be considered a self-contained episode rather than an intake, assessment, or stepping-stone to other services (Slive & Bobele, 2012). SST scholars have avoided specific endorsements of therapeutic models; however, SST is often associated with post-modern approaches such as Solution Focused Brief Therapy and Narrative Therapy (Courtnage, 2020). Unlike traditional counselling that assumes that service users will return multiple times, within SST, there is a need to maximise the time available, rather than spend time on assessments or history-taking. There is an "open door" philosophy that guides

SST (Cameron, 2007), meaning that the client has autonomy over when and how often they access mental health services.

As previously stated, many post-secondary institutions report incorporating a "walk-in" or "drop-in" component to their services based on urgency (De Somma et al., 2017), suggesting that some elements of WI SST are already in place. However, it is unclear whether WI SST, in the form of a therapeutic intervention rather than an intake or triage, is taking place within these walk-in sessions.

SST remains an emerging body of literature, and these authors are unaware of any peer-reviewed article that specifically discusses the role, function, or efficacy of WI SST within a Canadian post-secondary institution. The most common reason for the introduction of WI SST in community-based agencies is to reduce barriers to service by increasing accessibility (Cornish, 2020; McElheran et al., 2020; Bloom & Tam, 2015; Ewan et al., 2018). Several studies identify the potential for increased positive clinical outcomes with WI/SST (Barwick et al., 2013; Stalker et al., 2016), with most attributing success to the walk-in clinic service delivery. In particular, capitalising on a client's "readiness to change" has been cited several times (Slive & Bobele, 2012; Stalker et al., 2012) and is based on the assumption that people are more likely to change when they receive support at the time they are most motivated.

Quantitative Research Questions and Hypotheses

The aim of this study was to evaluate the effectiveness of the WI SST service model implemented at University of Waterloo Counselling Services and to understand the experiences of clinicians who had opted to work in this model. Like previous studies of WI SST (Hymmen et al., 2013), client outcomes were examined in terms of client-reported satisfaction and improvement. Because a collaboratively developed plan between client and clinician is a key feature of Counselling Services' walk-in appointments, items regarding the plan were also included to better understand clients' commitment to their plans. The following hypotheses were made based on currently available literature: (1) clients will report high levels of satisfaction, (2) clients will report a reduction in distress from pre-session to post-session; (3) most walk-in clients will not return for subsequent walk-in appointments; and (4) the majority of walk-in clients will not have accessed resources prior to their walk-in appointment.

Qualitative Research Questions

Counselling Services clinicians offer a variety of other services including crisis appointments, ongoing counselling appointments, psychological assessments, group therapies, seminars and workshop facilitation as well as supervising interns and residents. These services are provided by a team of clinicians and interns from a variety of theoretical and educational backgrounds. The research aims were twofold. The first was to understand what motivated the clinicians to initially volunteer to participate in providing walk-in services, to understand their experiences, and to understand what kept them motivated to continue to provide counselling in the WI SST model. The second research aim was to understand the experience of clinicians using WI SST as a modality, distinctly different from the other types of services they also provided at the counselling centre.

Results – Quantitative Research

At the time of the study, students at the university accessed WI SST counselling services by first meeting with an Intake Specialist for a brief 10–15 minute appointment to triage service needs. Intake Specialist appointments were accessed on a walk-in basis. During the Winter 2018 academic term (January to April), 1323 triage appointments were booked; from these, 143 (138 unique individuals) WI SST appointments (10.8% of triaged) were booked. Of this group, 73 identified as female, 65 as male and the average age was 21.8. There were 401 (391 unique individuals) scheduled SST appointments (30.3% of triaged), of which 228 identified as female and 163 identified as male, with an average age of 21.7.

Forty-three WI SST clients (30.1% of all walk-in SST appointments) completed the anonymous version of the Single-Session/Walk-in Counselling Feedback Form after their appointment. Client Outcomes Responses to this anonymous version of the Single-Session/Walk-in Counselling Feedback form are displayed in Table 1. Respondents who accessed WI SST were highly satisfied with the walk-in service in general, with an average rating of 3.77 ($SD = 0.55$) on a four-point scale. Walk-in respondents also reported being satisfied with specific aspects of the walk-in appointment. Respondents felt heard, understood and respected ($M = 3.85$, $SD = 0.41$), believed they were able to discuss their concerns ($M = 3.94$, $SD = 0.25$) and agreed that they were able to develop a plan to address the concerns ($M = 3.79$, $SD = 0.41$). The responses to the four satisfaction-related items on anonymous feedback form varied only minimally, with respondents rarely indicating dissatisfaction. Across these four satisfaction-related items ($n = 48$ responses), walk-in clients responded with a rating of four ("Definitely Agree") 42 times (87.5% of all responses), a rating of three ("Agree") 5 times (10.4%), a rating of two ("Somewhat Agree") 1 time (2.1%) and never responded with a rating of one ("Do not Agree"). Two-tailed, independent t-tests were conducted on the four satisfaction-related items to compare the responses of walk-in and scheduled SST respondents. There were no significant differences in the responses between walk-in SST (M = 3.77, SD = 0.55, n = 48) and scheduled SST respondents (M = 3.72, SD = 0.52, n = 121) in terms of overall satisfaction, $t(168)$ = –0.55, p = 0.583. Further, there were no significant differences between the two groups in terms of their responses on the other three satisfaction-related items. Both groups similarly reported they were heard, understood and respected by the counsellor, $t(168)$ = 0.10, p = 0.921, that they were able to talk about their concerns, $t(168)$ = –1.15, p = 0.253, and that they were able to make a plan to address the concerns, $t(168)$ = 0.36, p = 0.583. Pre-session distress, post-session distress and distress improvement, as reported on the anonymous version of the Single-Session/Walk-in Counselling Feedback Form, are displayed in Table 1. On average, walk-in clients reported a pre-session distress level of 4.83(SD = 1.66) and a post-session distress level of 6.63 (SD = 1.43) on the ten-point scale provided. This translates into an average change in distress level of 1.79 (SD = 1.50). A two-tailed, paired t-test of pre-session and post-session distress found significant improvement among walk-in respondents, $t(47)$ =–8.29, p < 0.001. The vast majority of walk-in respondents indicated that their level of distress had improved (85.4%, n = 41). Five respondents (10.4%) indicated no difference in their pre-session and post-session distress levels and two respondents (4.2%) indicated their post-session distress was higher than their pre-session distress. Two-tailed, independent t-tests were conducted for the improvement-related items between walk-in SST and scheduled SST respondents. There were no significant differences in the pre-session distress levels of walk-in SST respondents compared to scheduled SST respondents, t(167) = 1.08, p = 0.280, nor was any found in their post-session distress levels, $t(167)$ = 1.09, p = 0.276. Likewise, there were no significant differences in the improvement reported by walk-in SST and scheduled SST respondents, $t(167)$ = 0.261, p = 0.794.

During the winter 2018 academic term, 143 walk-in SST appointments were booked for 138 unique individuals. Most clients (96.4%, n = 133) only attended one walk-in appointment; the remaining five clients (3.5%) attended two walk-in appointments. As clients may have attended walk-in appointments before this time period, analyses were repeated using a significantly larger time period which extended well before the inception of the walk-in service. Between January 2016 and April 2018, 881 walk-in SST appointments were booked by 789 unique individuals. Even with the updated range, most clients still only attended one walk-in appointment (93.5%, n = 585). Among the 77 unique individuals (9.8%) that did return for additional walk-in appointments in the given time period, the majority (84.4%, n = 65) only attended one additional walk-in. There was little consistency in the timing between subsequent walk-in sessions. On average, the time between walk-in appointments was found to be 95 days (SD =99.5, n = 49), ranging from as little as two days to as many as 357 days.

Among walk-in clients completing the anonymous version of the Single-Session/Walk-in Counselling Feedback Form ($n = 48$), 39 respondents (81.3%) indicated that they had not attended walk-in before, while the remainder (18.8%, $n = 9$) indicated they had. Returning clients were not significantly more or less satisfied with the walk-in service overall than those who were new to the service, $t(8.8) = 1.82$, $p = 0.103$. During the Winter 2018 academic term, 123 (84.1%) of walk-in SST appointments were attended by clients who had not booked any appointment with Counselling Services previously that term. Triage appointments, through which walk-ins must be booked, were not included with "other appointments." Between January 2016 and April 2018, 621 (65.6%) walk-ins were attended by clients who had not attended any other non-triage appointments before their walk-in SST appointment.

Clinician Experiences with Walk-In Single-Session Therapy

Single-session walk-in counselling was a shift for clinicians at Counselling Services. The skill set for SST are both similar and unique compared to different models of counselling. Clinicians at the Counselling Service were given the choice of whether to participate in WI/SST, and there was no immediate buy-in from the clinical staff, even among the clinicians who volunteered to participate in the delivery of walk-in appointments. It is for this reason that the director of the service was interested in learning about the experiences of clinicians who had agreed to work within the walk-in service delivery model.

Eleven staff and interns were interviewed by a doctoral research assistant. This was an interdisciplinary group of clinicians, from psychologists to social workers, and there was variation in education, roles and clinical experience. The interviews lasted approximately 1 hour, and all interviews were transcribed. Three people (MSW RA, Doctoral RA and Study Investigator) worked on the thematic analysis (Braun & Clarke, 2012) that included organising data into patterns and themes. Our overall impressions from the interviews were the multiple roles of clinicians at the Counselling Services, the sense of risk that the counsellors themselves felt in conducting SST and their dedication to the clients with whom they worked.

Systemic Themes: Roles and Risk

The staff and interns interviewed were involved in multiple roles at the Counselling Services such as individual counselling, group work, couple counselling, supervision of counsellors and provision of workshops. The nature of the setting in a university counselling service necessitated the balancing and negotiation of multiple roles. Staff and interns interviewed also provided services in a variety of different formats including walk-in, single session, crisis and ongoing counselling. The second theme in this area was risk: counsellors had particularly heightened 'risk' sensors with respect to students and discussed what the walk-in single-session model could mean for safety, particularly suicide risk, in a university environment. Some participants wondered whether this type of model was appropriate for crisis clients and those having experienced trauma – is there an 'appropriate client.' One participant tells us:

> I've heard this phrase a lot in our counselling service. Not from anyone specifically but just kind of floating around, you know. "Such and such may not be appropriate for walk-in" And I hear that a lot. And while I understand it I think it's not a…it's hard to make that 100% overlap. Um, I mean we know that and, uh, there are times when I will meet with a student and I will have that first thought of "oh my goodness, why was this student put for a walk-in" but then very quickly my mind flips around and realizes that, um, whatever it is, we can find that one thing that is most important in this session.

Experience in Walk-In Single-Session Therapy: Motivation and Rewards

There were two dominant themes in understanding counsellor experience in the provision of service in a WI SST model: Motivation and Rewards. Participants commented that witnessing change amongst the clients was both a motivating and rewarding factor for continuing to work in the WI SST model. One person said:

> I have seen people transform and have been blessed to be in the presence of that transformation …And when I say transformed, like you can physically see people change and become lighter and, like, you can see "Aha!" happen before you lots of times.

For some participants it was not so much being motivated by client change specifically but having a 'motivation mindset'. This meant supporting the larger system for which participants were working, being driven by a strength's-based perspective, client need and accessibility to service:

> Because there is a huge demand. I've been here long enough that I have seen a transition in demand and increase in services so I know that there is a lot of people who need a lot of help, and that this is a way that they can be seen quickly, and often they may only need one session. Right?

So, they don't know where to turn or what to do, so just understanding the demand and what they need.

Participants spoke about rewards of working in the WI SST model at Counselling Services noting the change in their overall work. Some spoke about feeling more intentional and curious in their counselling to developing new skills and diversifying some of their work. One person said:

I would say it has changed my ongoing work. It has helped me to be more intentional around coming back to goals. It helped me think more about kind of termination, and that being a, not a regular conversation sort of ongoing. So, it's, it's structured in a way so that this is not meant to be ...the language that I use is that I try to work myself out of a job with everybody I see. And so, I talk with them about that in that, I'm meant to be a temporary member, right? So, I think it's enhanced that conversation and its intentionality towards solutions.

Micro Level Themes: Challenges and Transformation

The final two themes are micro-level themes connecting on a personal level for participants:

Challenges and Transformation. Participants commented on several different challenges including that the experience of providing WI/SST was draining and required a "different type of presence, there is a lot of being there, being present and, so, it drains you. It gets you really tired." Another person spoke about the development of a plan. For some developing the plan was liked, "because it's, again a little bit more concrete and sometimes I find people want us, want to come away with a plan." Other participants commented, "You want to see that plan, you want to operationalize the plan and see how it is doing, but I can't see you operationalize the plan down the road." And another participant discussed as challenging the "work to continue to build rapport in such a brief amount of time."

Participants also discussed personal change and transformation. One person said,

it is a fundamental shift in me as a person in how I see the world in that it really filled my vessel of hope. So, it is hope and possibility that I feel is part of who I am now.

Another person stated, "I sometimes, like yeah, ask myself questions that I would ask clients in a session, and try to reintegrate those things into my life." Another participant noted a reward connected to working in the walk-in SST model that:

I feel like I feel less stress during the walk-in session that I would an ongoing session. … And so, what happens is that translates into a less stressful day …that there's a different feeling at the end of the day and I'm more relaxed and calm going home …I leave here feeling more comfortable and relaxed.

Conclusions and Implications

The first hypothesis that expected high levels of student satisfaction was supported by the results of the anonymous version of the Single-Session/Walk-in Counselling Feedback Form. Most respondents reported that they 'definitely agreed' with each of the four satisfaction-related items. Of the 48 respondents during the Winter 2018 academic term, 35 responded with the highest possible option on the scale, 'definitely agree,' to all four satisfaction-related items.

The second hypothesis, which expected a significant decrease in the distress rating reported by walk-in clients, was also supported by the responses to the anonymous feedback form. Interestingly, those who reported no change or an increase in their level of distress still rated the satisfaction-related items highly and provided positive comments in the space provided. While significant improvement was found, this finding is limited by the fact that both pre-session and post-session ratings were both asked at the same time, right after the appointment. Part of this evaluation involved administering a psychological symptom measure when a client accessed single-session therapy as well as two additional administrations at the four-week and ten-week follow-up points. Unfortunately, there were insufficient responses to answer questions about the exact nature of the distress that walk-in clients were presenting, whether or not these symptoms improved, or if any improvement in these symptoms was able to be maintained through the planned four-week and ten-week follow-up points.

The third hypothesis, which predicted that the majority of walk-in clients would not return to the service, was supported by the anonymous responses to the Single-Session/Walk-in Counselling Feedback Form as well as by the evaluation of available appointment information. Even though this hypothesis was supported, the magnitude to which it was supported was unexpected. Rates of clients returning for subsequent walk-in SST appointments vary from clinic to clinic but generally are reported to be around 30% (Clements et al., 2011, Harper-Jaques & Leahey, 2011). At Counselling Services, this rate appears to be significantly lower, with less than 10% of clients returning for additional walk-ins. This lower rate does not seem to be because walk-in clients are dissatisfied, as satisfaction was observed to be high even among returning clients. A more likely explanation could lie in important differences in the structure of services at Counselling Services compared to the walk-in clinics from which the majority of walk-in research has been produced. One difference is that clients at Counselling Services attend a triage appointment before their walk-in appointment, while this may not be the case for other walk-in clinics (Slive & Bobele, 2011a). Even though triage appointments are relatively short (10–15 minutes), this additional step may discourage clients from accessing walk-in (Slive & Bobele, 2011a). Counselling Services also offers ongoing appointments to students, so the need for clients to access walk-in repeatedly is reduced. Further, while a client may go into a triage appointment initially wanting to book a walk-in appointment specifically, the Intake Specialist may suggest an alternative service that the client may opt for instead.

The fourth hypothesis, which predicted that the majority of clients would not have accessed mental health resources prior to their walk-in session, was supported by evaluations of available appointment information. However, it is still uncertain what the particular reasons for not accessing services previously were or even whether clients had previously accessed mental health resources outside of Counselling Services. One potential explanation for clients not accessing other resources could be the perceived inaccessibility of the other, non-walk-in services that are offered by Counselling Services. Interviews with walk-in clients at the Eastside Family Centre found that clients chose to access the walk-in service and not more traditional services because the walk-in service was perceived to be "hassle-free, convenient, and especially appealing because of the ability to come in at a moment of need" (Miller, 2011, p. 186). Walk-in researchers elsewhere have also noted the walk-in model as being culturally syntonic for many clients; as put by Slive and Bobele (2014), "since everyone is familiar with walking in for a variety of services, choosing a walk-in counseling option can be a good fit for them as well" (p. 86).

Once the single-session service was implemented, there was no immediate buy-in from the clinical staff, even among the clinicians who volunteered to participate in the delivery of walk-in appointments. Clinicians were primarily worried about the potential for clients to attend walk-in appointments over and over again. While this can be disruptive to the service, the frequency that this occurs is relatively small (Slive & Bobele, 2011b). As clinicians became more familiar with the walk-in service, it became clearer that this was not the case. Results of appointment information analyses also demonstrate the low frequency at which walk-in clients return and that the few clients who do return do so only a small number of times.

Clinicians were also worried about the general effectiveness of the single-session model of therapy. While training was provided, most clinicians were unfamiliar with such a brief mode of therapy. To keep the team motivated, clinicians were sent summaries of the responses to the anonymous feedback forms each week. Again, with time, clinicians were able to see the fruit of their labours themselves. Apprehension regarding the effectiveness of WI SST is understandable, given the historically time-intensive nature of psychotherapy.

Even with the movement from more traditional time-unlimited therapies towards shorter-term therapies, the sheer brevity of single-session therapy may make it alienating for some (Bloom, 2001). However, single-session researchers point out that every appointment has the potential to be a single session (Slive & Bobele, 2011b). A large proportion of clients attend only one session, and while these were traditionally believed to be "therapeutic failures," clients who attended WI SST tend to not return because they were satisfied and believed the session to have been sufficient (O'Neill, 2017, Young et al., 2014). This also seemed to be the case for 'Counselling Services' WI SST service.

Qualitative interviews with clinicians demonstrated while there was concern around risk and counsellors did speak about the challenges involved in providing service in a new delivery mode (WI SST), they also thrived in the new service delivery model. While there are many potential risks associated with campus culture (e.g. risk of sexual assault and risk of substance/alcohol use), death from suicide is arguably the most feared by CMH (Higgins et al., 2016). As has been discussed, the UW model includes access to a "triage appointment", whose primary purpose is often to determine suicide risk. Some have argued that the nature of a triage-based assessment implies that regardless of the reason a student seeks services, the risk of suicide must be at the forefront of conversations (Sands, 2007) and increasingly, the responsibility to accurately predict the likelihood of suicide falls on the shoulders of clinicians (Stanford, 2010). This can often lead to a culture of increased anxiety about who is "responsible" should risk, in this case, student death by suicide, come to pass (Webb, 2006). Concerns about risk assessment and mitigation are commonly reported among SST clinicians (Slive & Bobele, 2019). While there is growing evidence to challenge the validity of risk assessments (Carter & Spittal, 2018), this does not appear to be a generally accepted view among policymakers. The ways that WI SST is either already managing risk or planning to manage risk is an area that warrants further exploration.

Some clinicians were motivated by wanting to provide timely, accessible services to students but also were motivated by the real-time change they saw with clients, "right there in the room." For some counsellors they were able to build on their skills and diversify their skill set, a change that was felt throughout their ongoing work. Other counsellors noted the profound personal changes in their stress levels at the end of the day, and a shift in their own sense of hope and possibility about a student's ability to change. The common factors research (Lambert & Bergin, 1992) identifies factors that lead to change in psychotherapy and include empathy, acceptance, therapist's belief in a client and hope. Many researchers in the field have postulated that the therapist's belief in the client's ability to move forward in a positive way, and by extension, the therapist's ability to increase hope within the therapeutic process, is one of the most important findings of the common factors research (Duncan & Miller, 2000). The desire for clients to experience increased hope figures prominently throughout the SST literature (O'Neill, 2017, Slive & Bobele, 2012), and it has been postulated that increasing hopeful thinking within SST has the potential to maximise the impact of SST (Courtnage, 2020).

A growing number of evaluations have been published supporting the effectiveness of the WI SST delivery model (Stalker et al., 2016). Clients not only appear highly satisfied with WI SST but also appear to view the single session as sufficient. Accessibility and effectiveness of WI SST are important for university students struggling with mental health concerns. Research in this area and the increasing prevalence of WI SST models of delivery are sending a message to the mental health community to not underestimate the profound change.

References

American College Health Association. (2019). American College Health Association-National College Health Assessment II: Canadian Consortium Executive Summary Spring 2019. Silver Spring, MD: American College Health Association.

Barwick, M., Urajnik, D., Sumner, L., Cohen, S., Reid, G., Engel, K., & Moore, J. E. (2013). Profiles and service utilization for children accessing a mental health walk-in clinic versus usual care. *Journal of Evidence-Based Social Work*, *10*(4), 338–352. https://doi.org/10.1080/15433714.2012.663676

Bloom, B. L. (2001). Focused single-session psychotherapy: A review of the clinical and research literature. *Brief Treatment and Crisis Intervention*, *1*(1), 75–86. https://doi.org/10.1093/brief-treatment/1.1.75

Bloom, K., & Tam, J. A. (2015). Walk-in services for child and family mental health. *Journal of Systemic Therapies,* *34*(1), 61–77. https:// doi.org/10.1521/jsyt.2015.34.1.61

Braun, V., & Clarke, V. (2012). *Thematic analysis.* American Psychological Association.

Cait, C. A., Skop, M., Booton, J., Stalker, C. A., Horton, S., & Riemer, M. (2017). Practice-based qualitative research: Participant experiences of walk-in counselling and traditional counselling. *Qualitative Social Work*, *16*(5), 612–630.

Cameron, C. (2007). Single session and walk-in psychotherapy: A descriptive account of the literature. *Counselling and Psychotherapy Research*, 7(4), 245–249. https://doi.org/10.1080/14733140701728403

Carter, G., & Spittal, M. J. (2018). Suicide risk assessment: Risk stratification is not accurate enough to be clinically useful and alternative approaches are needed. *Crisis*, 39(4), 229–234. https://doi.org/10.1027/0227-5910/a000558

Clements, R., McElheran, N., Hackney, L., & Park, H. (2011). The Eastside Family Centre: 20 years of single-session walk-in therapy. In Slive, A. & Bobele, M. (Eds.), *When one hour is all you have: Effective therapy for walk-in clients* (109–128). Zeig, Tucker & Theisen.

Cornish, P. (2020). *Stepped care 2.0: A paradigm shift in mental health* (p. 15). New York, NY: Springer International Publishing.

Cornish, P. A., Berry, G., Benton, S., Barros-Gomes, P., Johnson, D., Ginsburg, R., Whelan, B., Fawcett, E., & Romano, V. (2017). Meeting the mental health needs of today's college student: Reinventing services through stepped care 2.0. *Psychological Services*, 14(4), 428–442. https://doi.org/10.1037/ser0000158

Courtnage, A. (2020). Hoping for change: The role of hope in single-session therapy. *Journal of Systemic Therapies*, 39(1), 49–63.

De Somma, E., Jaworska, N., Heck, E., & MacQueen, G. M. (2017). Campus mental health policies across Canadian regions: Need for a national comprehensive strategy. *Canadian Psychology/Psychologie Canadienne*, 58(2), 161–167

Duncan, B. L., & Miller, S. D. (2000). The client's theory of change: Consulting the client in the integrative process. *Journal of Psychotherapy Integration*, 10, 169–187

Dunley, P., & Papadopoulos, A. (2019). Why is it so hard to get help? Barriers to help-seeking in postsecondary students struggling with mental health issues: A scoping review. *International Journal of Mental Health and Addiction*, 17, 699–715.

Ewen, V., Mushquash, A. R., Mushquash, C. J., Bailey, S. K., Haggarty, J. M., & Stones, M. J. (2018). Single-session therapy in outpatient mental health services: Examining the effect on mental health symptoms and functioning. *Social Work in Mental Health*, 16(5), 573–589.Gallagher, R. P. (2012). Thirty years of the national survey of counseling center directors: A personal account. *Journal of College Student Psychotherapy*, 26(3), 172–184. https://doi.org/10.1080/87568225.2012.685852

Harper-Jacques, S., & Leahy, M. (2011). From imagination to reality: Mental health walk-in at South Calgary Health Centre. In Slive, A. & Bobele, M. (Eds.), *When one hour is all you have: Effective therapy for walk-in clients* (167–184). Zeig, Tucker &Theisen.

Heck, E., Jaworska, N., DeSomma, E., Dhoopar, A. S., MacMaster, F. P., Dewey, D., & MacQueen, G. (2014). A Survey of mental health services at post-secondary institutions in Alberta. *The Canadian Journal of Psychiatry*, 59(5), 250–258. https://doi.org/10.1177/070674371405900504

Higgins, A., Doyle, L., Morrissey, J., Downes, C., Gill, A., & Bailey, S. (2016). Documentary analysis of risk-assessment and safety-planning policies and tools in a mental health context: Analysis of risk policies and tools. *International Journal of Mental Health Nursing*, 25(4), 385–395. https://doi.org/10.1111/inm.12186

Hymmen, P., Stalker, C. A., & Cait, C. (2013). The case for single-session therapy: Does the empirical evidence support the increased prevalence of this service delivery model? *Journal of Mental Health, 22*(1), 60–71. https://doi.org/10.3109/09638237.2012.670880

Jaworska, N., De Somma, E., Fonseka, B., Heck, E., & MacQueen, G. M. (2016). Mental health services for students at postsecondary institutions: A national survey. *The Canadian Journal of Psychiatry, 61*(12), 766–775.

Lambert, M. J., & Bergin, A. E. (1992). *Achievements and limitations of psychotherapy research.*American Psychological Association.

Linden, B. (2019). *Development and psychometric evaluation of the Post-Secondary Student Stressors Index (PSSI)*. Queen's University.

McElheran, N., Harper-Jaques, S., & Lawson, A. (2020). Introduction to the special section: Walk-in single-session and booked single-session therapy in Canada. *Journal of Systemic Therapies, 39*(3), 15–20. https://doi.org/10.1521/jsyt.2020.39.3.15

Mcelheran, N., Harper-Jaques, S., & Lawson, A. (2020). Introduction to the special section: Walk-in single-session and booked single-session therapy in Canada. *Journal of Systemic Therapies, 39*(3), 15–20.

Miller, J. K. (2011). Single-session intervention in the wake of hurricane Katrina: Strategies for disaster mental health counselling. In Slive, A. & Bobele, M. (Eds.), *When one hour is all you have: Effective therapy for walk-in clients* (185–202). Zeig, Tucker & Theisen.

Mojtabai, R., Stuart, E. A., Hwang, I., Susukida, R., Eaton, W. W., Sampson, N., & Kessler, R. C. (2015). Long-term effects of mental disorders on employment in the National Comorbidity Survey ten-year follow-up. *Social Psychiatry and Psychiatric Epidemiology, 50*(11), 1657–1668. https://doi.org/10.1007/s00127-015-1097-z

O'Neill, I. (2017). What's in a name? Clients' experiences of single session therapy. *Journal of Family Therapy, 39*(1), 63-79. https://doi.org/10.1111/1467-6427.12099

Robinson, A. M., Jubenville, T. M., Renny, K., & Cairns, S. L. (2016). Academic and mental health needs of students on a Canadian campus. *Canadian Journal of Counselling and Psychotherapy, 50*(2), 108–123.

Sands, N. (2007). Assessing the risk of suicide at triage. *Australasian Emergency Nursing Journal, 10*(4), 161–163.

Shefet, O. M. (2018). Ultra-brief, immediate, and resurgent: A college counseling paradigm realignment. *Journal of College Student Psychotherapy, 32*(4), 291–311. https://doi.org/10.1080/87568225.2017.1401790

Slive, A., & Bobele, M. (2011a). Walking in: An aspect of everyday living. In Slive, A. & Bobele, M. (Eds.), *When one hour is all you have: Effective therapy for walk-in clients* (pp. 11–22). Zeig, Tucker & Theisen.

Slive, A., & Bobele, M. (2011b). Making a difference in 50 minutes: A framework for walk-in counselling. In Slive, A. & Bobele, M. (Eds.), *When one hour is all you have: Effective therapy for walk-in clients* (37–64). Zeig, Tucker & Theisen.

Slive, A., & Bobele, M. (2012). Walk-in counselling services: Making the most of one hour. *Australian and New Zealand Journal of Family Therapy, 33*(1), 27–38. https://doi.org/10.1017/aft.2012.4

Slive, A., & Bobele, M. (2014). Walk-in single session therapy: Accessible mental health services. In Hoyt, M. F. & Talmon, M. (Eds.), *Capturing the moment: Single session therapy and walk-in services* (73–94). Crown House Publishing.

Slive, A., & Bobele, M. (2019). Ideas for addressing doubts about walk-in/single-session therapy. *Journal of Systemic Therapies, 38*, 17–30. https://doi.org/10.1521/Jsyt.2019.38.4.17

Stalker, C. A., Horton, S., & Cait, C.-A. (2012). Single-session therapy in a walk-in counseling clinic: A pilot study. *Journal of Systemic Therapies, 31*(1), 38–52. https://doi.org/10.1521/jsyt.2012.31.1.38

Stalker, C. A., Riemer, M., Cait, C.-A., Horton, S., Booton, J., Josling, L., Bedggood, J., & Zaczek, M. (2016). A comparison of walk-in counselling and the wait list model for delivering counselling services. *Journal of Mental Health, 25*(5), 403–409. https://doi.org/10.3109/09638237.2015.1101417

Stanford, S. (2010). "Speaking back" to fear: Responding to the moral dilemmas of risk in social work practice. *British Journal of Social Work, 40*(4), 1065–1080. https://doi.org/10.1093/bjsw/bcp156

Universities Canada. (2017). https://univcan.ca/universities/facts-and-stats/enrolment-by-university/. Universities Canada publishes enrollment headcounts

University of Waterloo. (2017). President's advisory committee on student mental health: Final report. Retrieved from: https://uwaterloo.ca/mental-health-wellness/sites/default/files/uploads/documents/mental_health_experts_panel_final_report.pdf

University of Waterloo. (2018b). About Waterloo: Waterloo facts. Retrieved from: https://uwaterloo.ca/about/facts

Vallianatos, H., Friese, K., Perez, J. M., Slessor, J., Thind, R., Dunn, J., Chisholm-Nelson, J., Joober, R., Boksa, P., Lal, S., Malla, A., Iyer, S. N., & Shah, J. L. (2019). ACCESS Open Minds at the University of Alberta: Transforming student mental health services in a large Canadian post-secondary educational institution. *Early Intervention in Psychiatry, 13*(S1), 56–64. https://doi.org/10.1111/eip.12819

Webb, S. A. (2006). *Social work in a risk society: Social and political perspectives.* Palgrave MacMillan.

Young, J., Rycroft, P., & Weir, S. (2014). Implementing single session therapy: Practical wisdoms from down under. In Hoyt, M. F. & Talmon, M. (Eds.), *Capturing the moment: Single session therapy and walk-in services* (121–140). Bancyfelin: Crown House Publishing.

Chapter 14

Looking Forward

Arnold Slive and Monte Bobele

This book presents the case for, and examples of, the introduction of open-access/single-session therapies (OA/SSTs) internationally. We are not proposing replacing current mental health delivery systems with open-access scheduling, nor are we proposing reducing or eliminating longer-term therapies. There is value in the appointment system for clients and therapists. Likewise, longer-term therapies are beneficial for some clients. For example, the options of brief and longer-term psychotherapies, where a client sees the same therapist over the entire course of therapy, remain essential options and may be the best fit for many people. As we illustrated in the first two chapters, the fact remains that researchers have established that when someone makes a first appointment for psychotherapy, the likelihood of their returning is about 50% or less; the modal number of sessions people attend mental health services is one, with positive reports of outcomes and satisfaction with the services they received during that one visit (Talmon, 1990).

Let us imagine, therefore, that OA/SSTs become offered as an option where mental health services are available. These locations could include community mental health centers, university counseling centers, private practices, psychiatric hospitals, and medical practices. Imagine creatively using OA/SST services in alternative locations such as libraries, churches, and employee assistance programs. In Chapter 1, we proposed the four benefits of OA/SST. Here, in our concluding chapter, we would like to speculate about what we might then begin to observe. We offer three more specific benefits to the adoption of OA/SSTs.

OA/SST Provides Early Intervention and Prevention

Perhaps, by reading the examples in this book, you may already be grasping the idea that in many, though not all, instances, a band-aid may be the best choice. In fact, we might begin to call what we do

DOI: 10.4324/9781003351375-14

"band-aid therapy." The objective in many SSTs is for clients to leave with a co-created idea of the next small step to take to address a pressing concern. When we began doing this work, a common skepticism about SST we heard from our professional colleagues was that SSTs were "just a band-aid." According to archaeologists, bandages have been around at least since the time the pyramids were built in Egypt. Recently, public health researchers have suggested that, if anything, we do not use bandages enough. They recommend that for many injuries, bandages could be used more frequently and for a longer duration. The reasons for the centuries-long utilization of this relatively low-tech invention are simple–bandages promote healing and prevent the spread of infection. In mental health terms, SSTs promote healing and well-being while preventing things from getting worse. And we all know that if a problematic situation is left unremedied, it can worsen and possibly become troublesome for other people in the client's family and work environment. SSTs may prevent things from getting worse, especially in the case of OA services. So, when we're asked if SSTs are a band-aid approach, we say, "Yes. And thank you for the compliment."

As Malcolm Gladwell put it in his book *The Tipping Point*:

> A critic looking at these tightly focused, targeted interventions might dismiss them as Band Aid solutions. But that phrase should not be considered a term of disparagement. The Band Aid is an inexpensive, convenient, and remarkably versatile solution to an astonishing array of problems. In their history, Band Aids have probably allowed millions of people to keep working or playing tennis or cooking or walking when they would otherwise have had to stop. The Band Aid solution is actually the best kind of solution because it involves solving a problem with the minimum amount of effort and time and cost. We have, of course, an instinctive disdain for this kind of solution because there is something in all of us that feels that true answers to problems have to be comprehensive, that there is virtue in the dogged and indiscriminate application of effort, that slow and steady should win the race. The problem, of course, is that the indiscriminate application of effort is something that is not always possible. There are times when we need a convenient shortcut, a way to make a lot out of a little, and that is what Tipping Points, in the end, are all about.
>
> (Gladwell, 2002, pp. 256–257)

As more services offer OA/SSTs as a mental health delivery option, we anticipate that the band-aid idea will be praised rather than disparaged.

OA/SST Reduces Costs While Improving Community Mental Health

In a pilot study, Stalker et al. (2012) found that in one community, the mere presence of a readily accessible OA/SST service reduced clients' initial distress, the agency's waitlist was virtually eliminated, and no-shows were reduced for scheduled psychotherapy. They also found that costly medical services such as hospitals were used less frequently and that OA/SST clients returned sooner to their daily activities and work. Thus, the presence of the OA/SST option could reduce the overall cost of service delivery systems (Lamsal et al., 2018).

Here are some possible examples of why that might be the case: (1) reduced no-shows mean less downtime for service providers; (2) an open-access service can reduce utilization of more expensive services such as emergency rooms; (3) the collaborative relationship that develops between clinician and client in an OA/SST session means that referrals for additional services are likely to be a good fit for clients; and (4) most OA/SST sessions are solution-oriented and focused on collaboratively developing steps for addressing the most pressing concern. That means the session highlights the client's strengths and resources; therefore, many clients will not see a need for further services, and one session is enough for now. In other words, sessions focus on solutions rather than problems and pathology. Long waiting lists are commonly the initial motivator for a mental health service to begin offering OA/SST (Young et al., 2008).

For example, we previously described how Arnie assisted a large city's child guidance center to start an OA/SST service. The agency's motivation was, indeed, their lengthy (both in terms of numbers of families waiting for services and the weeks- or sometimes months-long waits) waitlist. Waiting lists require costly administrative attention and distract from getting families the timely help they need. Families on a waiting list are often in severe distress that may only get worse as their problems are left unattended. As we suggested earlier, a psychological band-aid can go a long way toward preventing untreated issues from becoming worse. When an appointment finally becomes available at this agency, families may often no longer be interested or fail to show up for the first scheduled session (perhaps because they found more available services while they were waiting). These no-shows consumed valuable personnel time and contributed to additional costs (Slive & Bobele, 2011).

This agency started its OA/SSTs service by eliminating its waitlist altogether. Instead, when a family called for an appointment, the staff member offered one if one of their clinicians had an opening within two weeks. Otherwise, the staff member asked them to call back; they were no longer offered an option to be on a waitlist. However, they were offered an invitation to the OA/SST service. In any case, they were free to call back until the agency had an appointment available. In other words, families were offered the opportunity to receive quick help by walking in and retained the option to continue waiting for an appointment slot to become available. During their subsequent session, the clinician reminded them that they could return for another such session if needed while waiting for an appointment slot to become available. Depending on the situation, families and clinicians also discussed other service options at their agency or community. Most of the families found the OA/SST session helpful and left with a plan for the next step in addressing their concerns. Many clients no longer needed or sought additional appointments because their problems had received immediate attention.

As community members become aware of this easier accessibility to a caring conversation at times of distress, might that awareness be a form of community mental health intervention, whether a given person chooses to use the service or not? Stalker's research and others' (Lamsal et al., 2018) are beginning to suggest the answer is "Yes." As noted in Chapter 2, researchers have not been successful at identifying risk, nor have suicide prevention programs been as successful at reducing death by suicide as we would like. Would widespread availability of OA/SST reduce suicides? We have heard anecdotal stories from university counseling centers and some provincial community mental health centers in Canada that communities find the presence of a readily accessible, brief therapy center comforting whether they use it or not. One college student reportedly pointed out it was like the spare tire in their trunk. Knowing it would be there when they needed it gave them peace of mind.

Some agencies have made OA/SSTs the main entry point for services. No wait was necessary. That entry session would be conducted from a single-session mindset. In other words, it is not an intake interview but an opportunity to address the client's concern. In addition, the session was also understood as a possible pathway to other agency services. We believe this increases efficiency in mental health agencies. The opportunity to have a therapy session without the usual hurdles and waits means that many OA/SSTs clients arrive at a moment of readiness and high motivation. This is rewarding for clinicians. Oh, and there would be no no-shows!

An Open Door Is Easier to Enter

Easy access with fewer hurdles may lead to more people meeting with a mental health professional when in need. Would open access with no expectation of a commitment beyond one session be seen as inviting those skeptical about mental health services to try it out? Could this lead to a greater diversity of clients, including those from cultures where "talking therapy" is not a usual practice? Would those who are worried about discriminatory practices, such as members of the LGBTQ community, be more open to taking this risk? What about those considering suicide; this could increase the opportunity to be heard at a moment that could be crucial. So, wouldn't the open-access option be a well-received addition to mental health service delivery systems?

Expanding OA/SST Services

In Chapter 2, we described recently developed examples of increased availability of OA/SSTs. One was Wellness Together Canada, a nationwide immediate-access telephone therapy service made available to Canadian residents during the COVID-19 pandemic. In a time of crisis and with considerable support from the Canadian government, this service was up and running in an extraordinarily short time. Now that the pandemic has quieted down, it is no longer being funded. Its success can be seen by the concerns that have been expressed since its closure (e.g., https://www.casw-acts.ca/en/shutting-down-wellness-together-canada-bad-mental-health-substance-use-health-policy).

Currently, very few graduate programs offer SST training in their curricula. We expect that to change. Single-session therapists have adapted their psychotherapy models for use in SSTs. However, if they are not already, some graduate programs might become increasingly motivated to offer training in some strength-based and brief therapy approaches that fit remarkably well for SSTs. Examples of these counseling models might include solution-focused therapy, narrative therapy, or cognitive behavior therapy. We can also expect online training resources for single-session therapists to increase. One example is The Bouverie Center in Melbourne, Australia, which offers online training in SST available to mental health professionals worldwide (https://bouverie.trainingvc.com.au/login/index.php).

As training in OA/SSTs increases in academic settings, this could lead to increasing research into the efficacy of OA/SSTs, its impact on communities, and its contribution to the reduction of such issues as suicide/self-harm and family violence. Indeed, there has been an explosion of SST books and journal articles in the last ten years.

Some Final Thoughts

This book provides numerous examples demonstrating the benefits that a single therapy session can make in people's lives. These benefits can include the simple yet profound experience of being heard and understood. It can also mean the collaborative effort between the client and therapist to develop ideas for steps to take in addressing a concern. Single sessions can effectively address complex problems such as risk issues and severe trauma. The open-access form of single sessions also simplifies the process of entering a psychotherapy session by eliminating cumbersome intake processes and delays in being seen. It can be an easy entry point for gaining access to further services. The ease of access often means motivated clients, which is rewarding for therapists.

These pages have provided many examples of OA/SST services in different parts of the world. We have also described a wide variety of options for how and where those services can be delivered, such as traditional mental health service offices, churches, libraries, virtual formats, telephone, and texting.

We look forward to hearing from our readers about other new and creative OA/SST services as they are developed!

References

Gladwell, M. (2002). *The tipping point: How little things can make a big difference*. Back Bay Books.

Lamsal, R., Stalker, C. A., Cait, C.-A., Riemer, M., & Horton, S. (2018). Cost-effectiveness analysis of single-session walk-in counselling. *Journal of Mental Health, 27*(6), 560–566. https://doi.org/10.1080/09638237.2017.1340619

Slive, A. B., & Bobele, M. (Eds.). (2011). *When one hour is all you have: Effective therapy with walk-in clients*. Zeig, Tucker & Theisen.

Stalker, C. A., Horton, S., & Cait, C.-A. (2012). Single-session therapy in a walk-in counseling clinic: A pilot study. *Journal of Systemic Therapies, 31*(1), 38–52. https://doi.org/10.1521/jsyt.2012.31.1.38

Talmon, M. (1990). *Single-session therapy: Maximizing the effect of the first (and often only) therapeutic encounter*. Jossey-Bass Publishers.

Young, K., Dick, M., Herring, K., & Lee, J. (2008). From waiting lists to walk-in: Stories from a walk-in therapy clinic. *Journal of Systemic Therapies, 27*(4), 23–39.

Index

For Product Safety Concerns and Information please contact our EU
representative GPSR@taylorandfrancis.com
Taylor & Francis Verlag GmbH, Kaufingerstraße 24, 80331 München, Germany